THE 8 LOVE LINKS

Shahn Baker Sorekli & Helen Robertson

THE 8 LOVE LINKS

Relationships are complicated but they hold the potential for life's greatest joys

First published in 2024 by Shahn Baker Sorekli and Helen Robertson
© Shahn Baker Sorekli and Helen Robertson
The moral rights of the authors have been asserted.

A catalogue entry for this book is available from the National Library of Australia.

ISBN: 978-1-923225-24-4

Printed in Australia by Pegasus
Project management and text design by Publish Central
Cover design by Julia Kuris

Disclaimer

The material in this publication is of the nature of general comment only, and does not represent professional advice. It is not intended to provide specific guidance for particular circumstances and it should not be relied on as the basis for any decision to take action or not take action on any matter which it covers. Readers should obtain professional advice where appropriate, before making any such decision. To the maximum extent permitted by law, the authors and associated entities and publisher disclaim all responsibility and liability to any person, arising directly or indirectly from any person taking or not taking action based on the information in this publication.

Contents

Acknowledgements

We firstly want to thank the hundreds of clients we have been privileged to work with over the years. Our clients offer courage and vulnerability when engaging in the therapy process. Their trust in us does not go unnoticed and is deeply respected. Further, our clients have offered us the greatest learning through the sharing of their stories, insights, growth and change.

We also want to thank our first readers, who kindly agreed to take time out of their busy lives to read early drafts of this book and provide us with insightful feedback. Thank you to Kate, Brodie, Angela, Sarah-Jane and James. We are grateful for having such thoughtful and supportive friends.

To our children, Mikael and Tayla, who had to put up with many 'work discussions' around the dinner table, in the car and on walks. Thank you for allowing us to be distracted and preoccupied – and also bringing it to our awareness so we could switch off and reconnect.

And finally, to each other. We appreciate the love, support, kindness and commitment to resolving conflict in our relationship. We are also appreciative of and understand the need for work and play and the continued journey of learning.

Introduction

Have you ever been left feeling disappointed in your current or past relationships?

You are not alone. Many people, despite their best efforts and intentions, feel lonely, misunderstood or unfulfilled in long-term relationships. You might be stuck in a relationship rut or in negative relationship cycles. Either way, relationship stress and dissatisfaction can absorb your energy, leaving you feeling exhausted and hopeless.

In *The 8 Love Links*, we provide the antidote to your less-than-amazing relationship experiences. Whether your relationship has room for improvement or you want to take it to the highest level, this book is for you.

How this book can help you

The 8 Love Links is a step-by-step guide to unlocking the unrivalled and amazing benefits of a thriving and fulfilling long-term relationship. If your sole aim in your relationship is to reduce stress and conflict, then you are setting the bar way too low. You have an opportunity to realise your dream relationship and create a meaningful life.

We are not selling a fairytale here. All relationships exist with some tension and stress. However, imagine a life where you associate your relationship exclusively with words such as the following: strength, love, care, passion, a sanctuary, friendship, desire and fulfilment. When you exist within a thriving relationship, it becomes the springboard to all things positive in life, rather than a weight dragging you down.

Read this book now. Why? Because time is precious and change is possible. Processing the information we provide and implementing the processes we advise will take effort, and even some sweat and tears (but no blood, please). The effort is worth it. You will feel more positive and less lonely; more connected and less dissatisfied. This time and effort could also save you from the heartache and the financial loss of separation.

The 8 Love Links can help you if your relationship is in trouble. Untreated relationship issues can build up over time to create irreparable damage. However, because prevention is better than cure, *The 8 Love Links* is also for anyone who is in or wants to be in a relationship. It provides a boost to any relationship – sailing or stuck.

This means that no matter where you are in your relationship journey – from single to being in a long-term relationship – the time to take *The 8 Love Links* journey is now.

Why we wrote this book

We (Shahn and Helen) are both clinical psychologists and couples therapists – and we are also a married couple. Together, we founded a private practice in Sydney.

We came together after both having had previous long-term relationships. In other words, we had tried and failed in relationships before we met. This time, we wanted to create a relationship full of love, support and excitement. To do so, we have had to navigate the complexities of a blended family while juggling the demands of being therapists and business partners. We have conflict in our relationship. We are also committed to resolving and repairing tensions as soon as possible. We have a successful relationship not because we found the 'right partner' but because we keep turning up to '*be* the right partner' for each other.

As therapists, we have practised thousands of hours in the couples space. We have digested clinical experience and research so we can pass on the most helpful theories and strategies to improve your relationship.

We created *The 8 Love Links* because we felt increasingly dissatisfied with other approaches to couples therapy. Our clients kept telling us that their prior experience of couples work seemed to lack structure and practical skills. To this day, we encounter new couples who say their previous therapist 'just talked to them about problems' and they just felt they were going round in circles in the therapy room.

As a result, we started to formulate a more complete couples therapy program, drawing on theory and strategies from many different psychological theories. Over the years, the program started to yield amazing results in the therapy room. Our aim was to equip couples with the right skills and strategies so they had a road map for all areas in their relationship. We wanted to equip couples to move on from therapy and thrive in life.

In our private practice in Sydney, our calendars filled quickly. Feeling frustrated at not being able to help more couples, we started our mission to create Australia's first ever couples coaching app, My Love Your Love. We designed the app as a practical guide to help couples as they worked together to unlock the full potential of long-term relationships. Now we have written *The 8 Love Links* to provide the theory behind the app, and to help you – individually or as a couple – to dive much more deeply into your relationship. While My Love Your Love is a joint couples journey, you can take *The 8 Love Links* journey in your own time at any point in your relationship, or even if you are single. If you have a partner, we recommend sharing this book with them so you can discuss each of the love links as you learn about them together. However, don't wait if your partner is not yet ready to commit to self and relationship discovery and learning.

Relationships should add to your life, not cause you more stress. If being in a relationship is not better than your best single life, something needs to change. You should either break up, or create a relationship that is worthwhile.

The 8 Love Links teaches you everything you never learnt about relationships. It gives you a clear path to having the relationship you always dreamed of – one which offers you a partner, a friend, a lover and a safe haven from the perils of life.

While you can work your way through the book individually, navigating your way to a thriving relationship involves a commitment from both partners. You will discover theories and strategies for reducing conflict, creating deep connections and growth, and increasing validation, passion and excitement. This might seem like an impossible task. But it really isn't – and *The 8 Love Links* shows you how. By taking you on a journey of self and couple discovery, it will become the relationship handbook you always refer back to when your relationship requires help or a boost.

We are excited to take you on *The 8 Love Links* journey.

Why love links?

Each of the eight love links we outline in this book represents a fundamental pillar in long-term relationships. Relationships exist within nuanced cycles that are either negative or positive. In turn, these cycles create negative or positive feedback loops. The love links represent these cycles and feedback loops – they are interconnected and mutually influencing. Improving one link will have a positive impact on other love links. The opposite is also true – a fracture in one link will eventually bleed into other links, changing the overall tone of your relationship. *The 8 Love Links* is a holistic, multifactorial and practical guide to a thriving relationship.

In the following eight chapters, each love link is laid out in a specific order, and each is important. As you progress through the book, you will discover which of your love links are solid and which ones are weak. Read the book in its provided order. While you might think some links are more important than others (and so want to jump ahead), it's all the links together that create and hold a beautiful relationship.

Here's a bite-sized introduction to each of the love links to whet your appetite for discovery and growth:

1. *Me in We love link:* The first step to change is insight. You can't change what you cannot see. While some people are more self-aware than others, we all have behaviours and patterns that we are blind to. Coming to terms with and shining light on new insights into your personality isn't easy, and can invoke vulnerability. However, it is this discomfort that leads to change and increased self-esteem. This love link is all about developing your personal power through self-reflection and accountability.

2. *Couple's Base Camp love link:* This chapter focuses in on your attachment and relationship styles, and how they influence how secure you feel in your relationships – and how they can change over time depending on your relationship. Attachment styles have been widely spoken about in recent years and are commonly referenced on social media. If you haven't heard about them, don't worry – we provide a brief summary in this chapter. In general, couples who have a rocky foundation or a vague concept of boundaries in their relationship are more likely to experience personal and couple attachment distress. The Couple's Base Camp link is your guide to setting agreed underlying foundations and flexible principles for your relationship so you can have a greater sense of trust and safety to be your authentic self.

3. *Magic Moments love link:* Small moments are powerful and are occurring all the time between you and your partner. If the sum of your small moments is positive, you will have a good relationship. However, the opposite is also true. If your daily interactions are too negative or neutral, they will compound and lead to disconnection. In this chapter, we outline how to create a habit of small magic moments that can compound to bring more joy into your relationship.

4. *Feeling the Story love link:* Humans need to feel understood, seen and heard. They need validation. This is a basic human need. People tend to overestimate how good they are at listening and validating their partners, perhaps because they are good at this skill at work, or with other family members and friends. In this chapter, we dive into how to attune to and validate your partner while improving your emotional intelligence and ability to recognise, understand and navigate your own emotions.

5. *Conflict Compass love link:* We're sure it will not be news to you that one of the biggest reasons relationships fail is conflict. Conflict is complicated and we are not going to pretend otherwise. That's why this chapter is huge and you should take your time reading and digesting it. The good news is, however, that you can learn to navigate conflict. Conflict is inevitable and can be a positive tension point to ensure continued growth for both of you in your relationship. So strap yourself in, because you are about to learn mind-blowing insights and strategies that will change the way you look at yourself and your relationship forever. In this chapter, we share the secrets and strategies we have learnt over decades of clinical practice to help you break negative patterns and instil new healthy strategies to bring more harmony and less stress to your relationship.

6. *Deep Connections love link:* This love link explores the necessary bonds and couples growth that is required to build a lasting relationship across the lifespan. We are sure you have heard that it is important to have quality time with your partner. But how exactly do you do this? And what are the obstacles and patterns of behaviour that either block or promote deep connections? In this chapter, we provide pragmatic strategies to bring a closeness to your relationship. This can increase the value of your relationship, bringing security and companionship as you move through the journey of life and love together.

7. *Baggage Claim love link:* In this chapter, we help you go deep within yourself to understand your vulnerabilities. It might get uncomfortable, but it will be worth it. Each partner brings to the relationship their own vulnerabilities and insecurities. As these emerge within the relationship context, they cause tension and disconnection. The way forward for self-healing is together-healing. Through following the strategies in this chapter, you can learn insights into the vulnerabilities of you and your partner. You can also learn how to name these vulnerabilities and strategies to heal them together, fostering trust and care.

8. *Sex and Desire love link:* This chapter is an invitation to embark on a journey of self-discovery and mutual exploration as sexual partners. This eighth love link is about increasing sex and desire in your relationship. We outline ways to reignite the flames of desire and break unhelpful dynamics and myths that can stifle your sex life. We shine a light on your sexual connection and its evolution throughout your relationship. We explore the interplay of emotions and sexual intimacy, and examine how attraction, communication and relationship connection form a foundation for a fulfilling and lasting sexual connection.

Throughout the following chapters, we've provided examples from our own relationship and from our clients. (All names have been changed, and client examples combined and/or generalised to avoid any identifying elements.) To really help you work through the strategies provided and embed your learning and development, we've also included activities through each love link. Make sure you take the time to dive in to these activities and, if possible, complete them with your partner.

Working through *The 8 Love Links*, you will learn as much about yourself as you will about your relationship. This book can help you identify unhelpful relationship cycles and traps you may be in. It can teach you how to identify your problem areas and provide you with strategies to create positive relationship habits. Further, you will learn the secrets to strengthening each of the eight love links, bringing more validation, closer bonds, less conflict, and more excitement and passion to your relationship. So let's get started!

Link one
Me in We

In the summer of 2017, we (Helen and Shahn) married. We had arranged a permit from the council for the ceremony at a quiet little park on the water, and were both feeling pretty relaxed. The park we chose was not popular, nor did it have the best view, but it was lovely all the same and had sentimental value. The day gave us clear blue skies with a gentle breeze, and was warm enough to help you look forward to a cool drink, but not make you sweaty-hot. Both our families had travelled from out of town to attend. The scene was set.

As tradition suggests, we planned to arrive at the park separately – Shahn first, waiting with the guests, and Helen second, with her father via a staircase that scaled down a rock face to the park. We both felt some pre-ceremony anxiety, but more overwhelming was the feeling of gratitude. We were grateful for the relationship and life we had created, thankful for the weather gods who had granted us a stunning Sydney day, and glad to have our family around us.

As Shahn waited for Helen to arrive, he was approached by a cousin, a nice guy, but also someone who does not have much of a filter. Looking around, Shahn's cousin uttered, 'This wedding is a lot different from your first one. Let's hope it lasts this time.' Showing very poor timing, this was an inappropriate, off-putting and disappointing comment right at the wrong time. Thanks, cousin.

While the comment was horrendous, it did not rattle either of us that day. We were both in our 30s when we met and the reality was we both had experienced failed relationships. In fact, it was a good reminder on the first day of our marriage that, according to the statistics, our relationship had a high probability of not lasting.

However, we were confident we now held a secret weapon. When our previous relationships came to an end, like most people, we had narratives locked onto all the negative behaviours of our ex-partners. This is a common reaction, helping you to feel more comfortable and to make sense of the break-up. However, it is much more powerful to reflect on your own behaviours – the subtle but undeniable truths of your personality that contributed to and had a compounding effect on your previous or current relationship.

Prior to our wedding day, we had come to understand the importance and the minutiae of ownership and what we now call the 'Me in We' link. In fact, this understanding was necessary to be together. We had hit serious roadblocks in our relationship prior to our engagement. We had been stuck on them for months, with both of our minds set on our own needs and finding fault in the behaviours of each other rather than focusing on the less comfortable, more vulnerable self-reflection.

We have been together for over 11 years at the time of writing. We both now feel strong and secure in our relationship. Being conscious of the Me in We love link has allowed us to continue to grow as individuals and bond as a couple. Our understanding of relationship dynamics has been accumulated through life experiences, study, professional development and more than 20 years of clinical experience working with individuals and couples.

The abrupt comment by the insensitive cousin on our wedding day strengthened our resolve for continued self-reflection to ensure we would keep trying to be better partners to each other.

Focusing on the problems of your partner is normal, natural and easy. It's harder to see your own contribution, reactions and role in relationship problems. However, if you just focus on your partner's problems, you will continue to feel stuck and frustrated in life.

In this chapter, we outline how to bring positive change to your relationship through self-focus, reflection and behaviour change. We help you recognise your own unhelpful behaviours – what we call 'relationship-interfering behaviours' – as well as the strengths you bring to your relationship. In doing so, you can work through strategies to build your insight muscle, and discover ways to both work through unhelpful behaviours and utilise strengths in your relationship.

Understanding the Me in We love link

Many of your behaviours require deep reflection because you are blind to them. You respond to certain situations with unconscious patterns that have become ingrained without realisation.

The Me in We love link involves taking full responsibility for your part in your relationship. Every interaction between partners is a shared experience. You are the Yang to your partner's Yin (and vice versa). This is true for every positive, neutral and negative interaction. Even when your partner is in a negative state, you're still contributing to the experience of the relationship. The most powerful thing you can do in a relationship is look at your own contributions. This is difficult when you feel your partner is acting unfairly and/or has negative traits that impact the couple or family unit. Even so, you have some room for self-reflection, even if it is to confirm you are acting in line with your values and holding healthy boundaries.

You have a responsibility for self-reflection, insight, growth and change if you want your relationship to improve. The Me in We link is about moving away from focusing on your partner's change and bringing the focus to yourself. If you are the type of person who's always self-sacrificing, this is not about sacrificing more. Having unlimited patience or allowing yourself to be treated like a doormat won't be helpful. Taking a look at your own behaviours can also be about learning to set boundaries, asserting yourself more and getting some power back.

We have one important caveat here: if you're in an abusive relationship, you should exit that relationship as soon as possible with the right professional help. We do not advocate staying around and working on yourself in any relationship in which you feel you are suffering or in danger. While it's good to look at yourself, it's okay to have deal breakers. Leaving a relationship when you have a partner who doesn't respect you is always a good option. This love link is based on the assumption that you and your partner value your relationship and want it to thrive.

With the Me in We love link, we are asking you to look at your own behaviours – nuanced or obvious – that you can change to make your relationship better. As mentioned, we call these unhelpful behaviours 'relationship-interfering behaviours', and looking at such behaviours can give you multiple points to create change. This is powerful even when it is obvious that your partner has their own relationship-interfering behaviours. In this case, we're not asking you to ignore your partner's unhelpful behaviours. Rather, you can learn how to move out of conflict cycles and avoid getting tangled up in these relationship-interfering behaviours – your own, and your partner's. (We look at the different types of these behaviours in more detail later in the chapter.)

We don't want to dismiss the idea that you might be currently doing really well as a partner and as a couple. And to be clear, your emotions and your point of view are important and you have strengths we want you to utilise. However, as you move through life, your relationship health will fluctuate. So you will need to be open to self-reflection and commit to work on obvious behaviours – perhaps getting frustrated easily, for example, or having anger outbursts or struggling with patience.

Sometimes, however, what behaviours are contributing to relationship stress might be unclear. You might have to look at your relationship from another angle. As an example of this, let's consider Zara. Zara's husband has been out of work for a while, and it was starting to take a toll on their finances. Zara's husband kept saying he would look for work soon, but he spent his days playing video games, meeting up with friends and neglecting the household chores. Zara was picking up all the slack, and felt like a parent living with a teenager. However, she suffered from self-sacrificing guilt and did not raise these issues because she thought her husband would feel inadequate. Zara also told herself the narrative that she was being a patient and supportive partner because she wanted to avoid conflict. In this case, the relationship-interfering behaviour was something she was *not* doing – that is, Zara was failing to enforce boundaries or express her needs, and was over-functioning for an under-functioning partner.

Again, we are not saying Zara was the entire problem or even the cause of this dynamic. However, it takes two to tango. Accepting that you have a behaviour that needs to change is liberating and empowering, moving you from hopelessness and helplessness towards empowerment in every situation. We've never met a perfect partner. The people who think they're perfect partners and have nothing to change are part of the problem, and feel dissatisfied and frustrated with life.

As another example, here is a Me in We experience from Shahn.

'Cute and quirky' or 'intense'?

We have a joke in my family that all the men have a tendency to become obsessive once they decide they want something, and this can drive everyone around them crazy. My father has this tendency, my brother has it, my son has it and so do I. This can be great when the obsessiveness is focused on a goal. But it can be a bit much for other family members who are less invested.

This tendency has led to my brother travelling with his son to the outback to buy a particular car, my son picking up a pair of shoes three hours' drive away, my dad spending weeks or months researching the next TV he wants to buy, and me starting another hobby (motor biking, kickboxing or freediving, for example) and talking in an excited way about this new hobby to whoever would listen.

These stories were all considered cute and harmless, if not a bit quirky. However, one day Helen and I were having an argument about a renovation we were working on and I was eager to arrive at a decision to resolve it. She called me intense and the word cut through and landed somewhere deep. I had never considered myself to be intense before – at least not in the relationship. It was also contrary to what Helen usually said about me – that I was patient and a calming influence in her life. To be honest, the calm, patient influence was a narrative I was much more comfortable with.

However, when I thought about it and visualised myself as a third person watching the argument, I had to agree I was intense! Furthermore, with the behaviour named, I could identify a sense of urgency within myself that was not congruent to the situation. On reflection, I realised the sense of urgency was related to feeling overwhelmed with multiple responsibilities at the same time and having the desire to have one box ticked. This was an uncomfortable but valuable realisation. I had to admit to myself that I had likely behaved like this many times in the past. Once I could admit this to myself, I owned the behaviour and validated Helen's experience on the receiving end. This cut through the tension and we were able to reconnect and become a team again.

For me, this is an example of coming to a 'Me in We' awareness, and it helped me in many ways. For instance, whenever I feel a sense of urgency now, I ask myself whether it is reflective of the situation. This has allowed me to pause more in those moments and have conversations with openness and curiosity, letting go of the notion that I need a solution to feel more comfortable.

Helen also has a Me in We example.

The negative side of perfectionism

Shahn has always said he really respects my commitment to a cause and the discipline I possess. And I know I have a tendency to be a perfectionist about things I have passion for. When it has come to education, my career or even planning and engaging in a hobby or project, this tendency has served me well. However, through our relationship, I learned that this perfectionism had a negative side.

Whenever I felt like I was under-performing, this would lead to feelings of distress, anxiety or overwhelm – and my subsequent desire to feel back in control would then affect others. For example, if I had a hard day at work, I could come home easily frustrated by the state of the house or the amount of screen time the kids were having. I would insist we needed immediate change in these areas. No surprises, this would lead to arguments.

After one such argument, Shahn calmly told me that while he agreed the topics I was raising were important to discuss, he was left feeling ambushed and controlled. On reflection, I was able to realise that while I was looking for a sense of control and productivity to ease my anxiety, I was not collaborating with Shahn in the way we usually do when making decisions. This was a lightbulb 'Me in We' reflection.

Through continued self-reflection, I became aware of this tendency to want immediate change and instead started to talk about the vulnerability I had experienced that day. This has allowed me to be more open in the relationship and connect with Shahn. It has also contributed positively to my life generally.

The Me in We love link provides an opportunity for learning to help you take better care of yourself and your relationship. The two examples we've just provided are of subtle behaviours we were not initially aware of but were able to learn and grow from once they were in our awareness. Blind spots are normal, allowing you to adopt a position that makes you feel more comfortable. However, identifying your relationship-interfering behaviours is life-changing, and something you should start reflecting on now!

Change the 'me' to influence the 'we'

Receiving validation and care is a core need of all humans. If you don't feel validated or cared for by your partner, you will feel unsettled in the relationship. When this occurs, you are likely focused on this unsettled state and the desire for your partner to be different. The problem is your partner might not want to change just because you've asked them to. This is because they, like you, have ingrained patterns of responding, and might also be feeling hurt and invalidated. Unless you or your partner find intrinsic motivation to change, change is unlikely to occur. Even if they change a behaviour to appease a situation, chances are this change will be short-lived.

On this journey, you will need to go out of your comfort zone, face vulnerabilities and self-reflect in order to grow. The good news is there is no better feeling than honing in on areas you can improve and becoming more self-aware. This creates the most powerful tool you have for relationship change.

Think of your relationship as a Yin-Yang symbol. Both sides are necessary to create perfect balance and harmony. The forces on each side may be similar or different, but they're complementary. For example, one might be a little more logical and the other more emotional, but together you fit. Your relationship Yin and Yang exists in a state of constant flux and change. The elements are interdependent, meaning one cannot exist without the other. The forces on one side changing can affect the other in a positive or negative way. For example, if you become more loving, your partner may in turn become more loving and your Yin-Yang relationship strengthens.

If Yin and Yang symbolises a harmonious and balanced relationship, its opposite or undesirable state can be represented by a fractured Yin and Yang. A fractured Yin and Yang signifies a lack of balance, disharmony and a state of discord between partners. Imagine the symbol but instead of the two elements complementing each other in harmony, a break or separation exists between them. This break represents an undesirable disruption to the natural balance, leading to conflict, tension and an overall lack of unity.

The goal is to mend the fractured Yin-Yang symbol, striving to restore balance and unity in the relationship. This involves each side addressing the sources of the fracture. Of course, we want you to work together but the point here is that you always have a role in influencing the Yin and Yang of your relationship. You changing what's happening on your side will influence the other side – and that's one of the most important messages we want you to take from this chapter.

This is just the beginning of *The 8 Love Links* journey, but hopefully you're already starting to learn about yourself. Waiting for your partner to change means you have no power. You're simply *hoping* change will happen. With self-change, you can start making gains right now. In our clinical work, we are often asked, 'Is couples therapy going to work?' Our answer is, 'Our program will work 100 per cent of the time, as long as there's two invested parties wanting the relationship to work and willing to reflect on themselves and change.' We stand by that comment, and it is proven true every time.

Let's take a look at an example of this from Shahn.

Change must come from both sides

At our private practice in Sydney, I was seeing Gary and Zelda – a couple who experienced regular undesirable conflict. Zelda had an anger management problem, was obsessed with work and had little time for their relationship. Gary felt alone and unvalued in the relationship. Zelda couldn't deny what Gary was saying. She was, in fact, often angry and frustrated. Zelda said she was overwhelmed and couldn't stop thinking about work and deadlines. As the higher income earner of the couple, her inner perfectionist was getting all the air time, driven by financial goals that came at a cost to her energy and stress levels.

Zelda was not prioritising the relationship. However, that was just part of the picture. While both Gary and Zelda agreed that Zelda's anger and obsession with work was a big deal, I was starting to notice something else also going on. I felt pushed and controlled by Gary in session as he tried to instruct me to tell Zelda how she should change. He was blind to his behaviour because it was fuelled by strong emotion. This boundary violation with me mirrored how he approached the situation with Zelda in their relationship. His vulnerability of feeling undervalued meant Gary was persistently pursuing Zelda to change in a way that was unhelpful. According to Gary, however, he wasn't doing anything wrong and he just couldn't understand why Zelda would not change when he had asked her so many times.

I had to confront Gary and tell him that I, as a therapist, was feeling controlled by him in session. He wanted to direct the session and corner me into telling Zelda to change. This is an example of a subtle behaviour that is hard for the person to see because of the level of suffering they are experiencing in the relationship. Once I told Gary that I felt uncomfortable being directed by him, however, he was able to observe the dynamic. In a future session, he commented that he had found this confrontation very uncomfortable. However, with the power of insight the discomfort quickly turned to increased self-esteem because he was able to demonstrate flexibility and implement a more constructive response.

Until this realisation, every time he felt hurt or uncared for, he would pursue Zelda in a way that was unhelpful. Her defences would go up and it would lead to conflict in the relationship. He wasn't explaining how he was feeling; he was just pursuing her to change and her refusal left him feeling more hurt and invalidated. With his newly formed insights from the Me in We reflection, instead of pursuing Zelda he was able to communicate his feelings more calmly and put in place healthy boundaries. This was much more conducive to a positive response from Zelda.

Gary changing this behaviour allowed more room for Zelda to step up and be more accountable as a tension in the dynamic was removed.

This aspect of the Me in We love link can seem unfair. After all, you are the responsible partner who has decided to read this book. To a point, you changing first might be a bit unfair. Some partners are the bigger problem in the relationship and, if they changed, things might be a whole lot better or even great. Don't worry – we are big on boundaries and having your emotions and needs heard and validated. We'll get there in chapter 4, when looking at the Feeling the Story love link, and chapter 5, covering the Conflict Compass love link.

As mentioned, we know when both partners are willing to change, you'll get the best outcomes. Even if you are the 'better' partner, it will feel good to take some responsibility. Also, it feels great to live in a more open and curious way. You'll be winning, because you'll feel better within yourself.

So stay open to your contribution to the relationship system. Let go of the 'they do this, so it is only fair that I do that' mentality. See the interactions with your partner through the Yin-Yang analogy. It's half you, and half them. Is your Yin-Yang intact or is it fractured?

 **TIME FOR ACTION**

Divide a piece of paper into two columns. Write a list of all the problem behaviours your partner does in one column. In the other column, write down how you react to these behaviours. What do your reactions tell you about yourself? For example, do you become reactive with anger and frustration? Or do you over-function for your partner, always picking up the slack for what they're not doing? Or maybe you react in an open, healthy way – if so, great! Complete this activity with vulnerability, curiosity and openness, and also ask your partner to list the things they find difficult about you.

If you (or they) are not ready for this discussion, do the exercise in reverse. That is, make a list of unhelpful behaviours you might do and in the other column how your partner responds. This gives you a 360-degree view of the relationship.

Remember – you don't have to bring your partner into your journey if they can't be open, caring and sensitive. Self-reflection, at this stage, is more important. If negative conflict exists in your relationship, you might worry about your partner shaming you if you present them with vulnerabilities about yourself. If that does happen while you talk to them, stay open, ask your partner to be gentle, and own what you can. But if they continue to be unsupportive, stop sharing with them for now.

This process might also seem a bit negative. Don't worry – we'll get to strengths later in this chapter. And the rest of *The 8 Love Links* emphasises bringing positivity into your relationship.

Identifying relationship-interfering behaviours

In order to reflect on our own contribution to conflict, identifying any relationship-interfering behaviours is helpful. You need to be open and curious about these behaviours, understanding that insight is the first step to change.

In this process, you may identify relationship-interfering behaviours that are more obvious but still uncomfortable to admit – for example, any anger, from frustration to rage, being critical and mean to your partner or being passive-aggressive. However, sometimes behaviours are less obvious and harder to identify. These include submission or compliance behaviours, entitled behaviours, over-functioning behaviours, pursuing behaviours and avoidant behaviours.

In this section, we explain some of the less obvious behaviours in more detail. You may identify with some of these behaviours or see them in your partner. For now, we just want you to focus on self-reflection and recognising patterns of behaviour. As you progress through the book, you will learn much more about relationship-interfering behaviours and how to change them.

Submission or compliance

If you find yourself surrendering your needs and submitting to what your partner wants all the time, you're in a submission and compliance dynamic. You may feel you're making the relationship run smoother because you are avoiding feelings of guilt or potential conflict. However, this behaviour is contributing to a negative relationship cycle.

Relying on submission and compliance to defuse conflict or avoid guilt means you are not being authentic. Your genuine needs, wants and interests are not shared and not prioritised. This can lead to resentment within you and an imbalance in the relationship. It can even result in your partner respecting you less and your value in the relationship being reduced.

Entitlement

It's not just people with narcissistic personality disorder who are entitled. Each individual is at the centre of their universe and, therefore, capable of entitlement. Often people are quite blind to it. Entitlement might be as simple as feeling you deserve something and getting fiery when you don't receive it.

When present, this relationship-interfering behaviour means you are not willing to put yourself in an empathetic position to understand your partner's needs. Instead, you pursue your own needs with little compassion for them. Reflecting and identifying entitlement requires deep commitment. If you do not realise you are being entitled, you will likely remain stubborn in your pursuit with little awareness of the impact you are having on others and on your own reputation.

Over-functioning

Many partners feel like a parent in their relationship, dealing with under-functioning partners who constantly let them down. Labelling their over-functioning as a problem seems unfair, because they're picking up all the slack and doing all the heavy lifting in the relationship. However, let's say you are taking care of 75 per cent of all relationship requirements. That only leaves 25 per cent of space for your partner to function. There is no room for them to step up.

Continuing to over-function enables their under-functioning and causes you a lot of pain and stress because the dynamic does not change. If you do not learn to step back, lower your standards and put in healthy boundaries, you will always feel like the parent in the relationship and that's not fair to you.

Pursuing behaviours

Pursuing behaviours refers to behaviours that are intense, insistent and persistent. This could be repeatedly bringing up an issue in the relationship that needs resolving, insisting on an immediate behaviour change from your partner, or passionately expressing opinions or desires.

Pursuing behaviours are commonly driven by feelings of anxiety, overwhelm and insecurity, making people feel required to address issues in the relationship. Such behaviours, however, can come across as controlling and bossy. Unsurprisingly, these pursuing behaviours can lead partners to feel controlled and pestered, resulting in avoidance and distancing.

Avoidant behaviours

If you dodge the difficult conversations and issues, you are engaging in avoidant behaviours. Avoidance leads to communication procrastination and white lies. Internally, the behaviour is driven by the desire to avoid conflict or friction, and so feels rational or justifiable. However, when you avoid a problem or issue in the relationship, it inevitably surfaces and you end up dealing with the problem at hand plus the fallout from the avoidance. This means double the problem and double the stress.

Stepping back to develop self-insight

Some relationship-interfering behaviours trump others. For example, aggression and intimidation is much worse than submission. But that's not the point. The point is all relationship-interfering behaviours are maladaptive and counterproductive to good solutions or connections. Over time, they can have dire consequences on your relationship because they bring more negative associations and stress. And, as uncomfortable as it might be to admit, each partner is always playing a role in the relationship system. Your partner might be mean or entitled and you might be thinking, *Why should I have to change?* We're not suggesting your partner's behaviour isn't bad or worse than yours. It might be, but if you get stuck on that, you relinquish any power to change. Learning, identifying and taking responsibility for your own behaviours provides opportunities to break conflict cycles.

Here is an example of this from Helen.

Acknowledging the impact of your behaviours

Sandra and John presented to my practice in Sydney for couples therapy. While they were both increasingly dissatisfied in the relationship, Sandra had initiated therapy, reporting that she felt John was resentful toward her all the time.

Sandra and John are both professionals working in the corporate sector. Sandra enjoyed 'couple time' by staying up late and watching TV, while John preferred to be in bed by 9 pm for an early start the next day. However, John was in a pattern of complying with what Sandra wanted because he felt she would be disappointed and grumpy if he refused to stay up.

During therapy, Sandra stated that she would press a little bit for them to stay up but John never said no so she thought he was okay with it. In this example, John felt Sandra was the problem. He was frustrated at feeling tired all day and he blamed Sandra. Until he attended couples therapy, he was blind to his own compliance.

Sandra was shocked to hear John disliked staying up that much, and was sad to hear John felt he could not raise issues in their relationship. This theme ran deep throughout their relationship. In order to break this relationship-interfering behaviour, John had to be more assertive in stating his wishes and position. Sandra supported this effort by being open to his needs and willing to compromise.

You may believe your relationship-interfering behaviour is healthy. This is quite common, and can be confusing. For example, in our couples therapy sessions we often hear 'being angry is healthy' or 'I shouldn't have to change; my anger is healthy'. To clarify, anger can be a healthy emotion. It is signalling an unmet need or vulnerability. And everyone gets angry in relationships. Despite all our knowledge and clinical experience, occasionally we get angry at each other. It's normal in relationships for anger to come out, but when anger is directed at each other it is aggression, and it only harms the relationship.

How you deal with anger is important. For example, if you take some time out to journal about your anger, go to the gym or run until you feel calmer, then you are defusing your angry mind state. If you can then talk to your partner in a calm way about your feelings of anger, you are expressing your anger in a healthy way. To clarify, if you feel angry and express the feeling of anger in a healthy way, you are doing great. However, directing (through shouting, or being critical, aggressive, hostile or intimidating) anger at your partner is always unhelpful and will lead to a negative reaction.

Reflecting on your own relationship-interfering behaviour – and the effect of this behaviour – can be easier when looking at another relationship. Think about your parents' relationship when you were a child, for example. How did your parents react in times of conflict? Who yelled, who withdrew and who over-functioned? Did they swap around in their relationship-interfering behaviours? Now, think about their behaviours toward each other. Which parent was more self-focused and which was more self-sacrificing? Or were they egalitarian and equal? Did one do more heavy lifting in the relationship while the other seemed to take advantage? Was one or both more obsessive and uptight or were they lax? Once you've identified some of the different behaviours in your parents' relationship, you can think a little bit more about your relationship.

Another helpful way to develop self-insight is to use the 'three Os' intervention, as coined by Dr Dan Siegel in *Mindsight*. Dr Siegel is a clinical professor at the UCLA School of Medicine and a bestselling author of books focusing on the brain, mindfulness, parenting and emotional awareness. Dr Siegel talks about the three Os as an intervention to help you develop insight into your own reactions and behaviours. This is a great exercise to do if you have had a conflict, feel overwhelmed with emotion or find yourself feeling detached.

Here's how the three Os come together:

1. *The first O is 'observation':* Take a step back to reflect. Think about where you're feeling emotions in your body and how intense these feelings are. Name the different parts of your body where you feel strong emotion. Come up with words to describe your emotions. For example, 'I am feeling frustration in my chest and it feels heavy.' Observe what's going on in your mind. What thoughts are racing? Are you ruminating or obsessing? Or are you feeling numb? By the end of this observation step, you want to have a good sense of how you are feeling in your mind and body.

2. *The second O is 'objectivity':* Pretend somebody else is viewing the scene. They don't know your history or the context of the situation. What are they seeing? Objectivity gives you opportunities to take a look at yourself through the lens of others. This is a powerful tool for insight when done with commitment.

3. *The final O is 'openness':* This is about being open to what is activating you right now and also how it might be linked to particular vulnerabilities from your past. For example, 'I am feeling abandoned by my partner because they made plans on the weekend without discussing it with me. However, I also know that some of this abandonment pain I'm feeling today stems from the loss of my father at a young age.' This level of insight might seem a bit difficult for now. But your insight will progress more as you read through the eight love links. Specifically, you will learn more about your vulnerabilities and activations in chapter 5, where we cover the Conflict Compass love link, and chapter 7, which outlines the Baggage Claim love link.

 **TIME FOR ACTION**

Make a list of any relationship-interfering behaviours you identify with – both the obvious and the less obvious ones. Ask your partner to do the same for themselves. Then, in the spirit of openness and curiosity, ask for their input. Maybe they can tell you something about yourself that you have not discovered. Then ask them if they would be happy to hear feedback from you. Remember, the point of this activity is to raise awareness, not to blame or jump to solutions.

If you struggle to have this discussion with your partner, it is reflective of how open you are in the relationship. If it is hard, that's okay. It's more common than uncommon. Talking about your relationship takes vulnerability and bravery. Being vulnerable is a strength because it's hard to do. We encourage you to be brave, because these difficult conversations are the door to connection and love.

Understanding the strengths you bring to your relationship

Time now to focus on something more positive – your strengths. Each partner brings strengths to a relationship. Identify, utilise and encourage them. Your strengths are the unique assets you bring to your relationship that contribute to the wellbeing and tenacity of the relationship. When you identify your strengths, you can advocate to have more room for them in the relationship.

Relationships need to feel equal, and this feeling of equity is more important than the exact distribution of responsibilities. For example, perhaps your partner is a natural negotiator in circumstances where you feel anxious. However, you might be better at analysing and planning. It makes sense that you both celebrate these strengths. Thank each other for them and work as a team.

Some strengths – and the way they interact – might be nuanced or subtle. For example, you might bring a sense of calm and stability to the relationship. Your partner might not bring the opposite to this strength and, instead, might have other unrelated strengths such as the strength of playfulness. Some strengths might be much simpler and practical. For example, you don't mind doing the shopping, while your partner is a better chef and they prefer cooking.

When you discover your strengths and those of your partner, you can play off these strengths and work together as a team. You can move away from 'it's not fair, because I do this and you don't do that' to 'you do that better and I do this better, so let's divide and conquer'. Dr Wayne Hammond is a leading expert on the concepts of resilience, strengths-based practice and positive psychology. Dr Hammond's strength-based approach focuses on the positives of individuals to facilitate change. When looking at these principles and factoring them into partner relationships, these are the main points to take home:

- Everyone is unique and has strengths.
- When you highlight each other's strengths, you tend to move towards these behaviours.
- Gratitude and supportive language promotes growth.
- Supporting each other will lead to a deeper, more meaningful relationship.
- You need to be collaborative and celebrate each other's differences and strengths to thrive together.

You bring many positive qualities and attributes to your partnership. Bringing a focus to each other's strengths helps you 'double down' on teamwork.

Research from Dr Todd Kashdan and colleagues into the impact of perceptions of partner strengths on wellbeing (outlined in their article

'Personality strengths in romantic relationships: Measuring perceptions of benefits and costs and their impact on personal and relational well-being') also supports the essential role of strengths and the benefits of acknowledging these in your relationship. The results of this study show that your perception of your partner's strengths plays a significant role in your own and your partner's wellbeing. The study demonstrated that adopting a positive and appreciative attitude towards your partner's strengths can enhance the quality of your relationship.

Shahn explains this further.

Playing to our strengths

We (Shahn and Helen) both have different strengths and we play to them in our relationship. We do lots together. We have many projects and we're always working together and playing together. Helen says I'm not limited by perceived constraints and I'm always coming up with good 'out of the box' ideas. Helen, on the other hand, is great at fleshing things out and fine-tuning. She's great at focusing on details.

This works well in our relationship because we're in business together on multiple fronts. While I'm great at coming up with the ideas, Helen can harness these ideas, and focus on them to bring out more details and the plans needed to achieve them. We're aware of each other's strengths and encourage them – and love each other for them.

You might be thinking, *I don't feel like I have any strengths*. Sometimes, when you're feeling down, focusing on your strengths can be hard. Think about a time in your life when you had a win. Now think about the strengths you hold that contributed to that win. Your win doesn't have to be in academics, career or sport. It could be a win in listening or helping somebody out.

Ask your partner what your strengths are. If for some reason you don't feel comfortable asking your partner, that's fine. Go to a friend or a family member. Hearing what other people think of you can be empowering.

On the other hand, you might be able to see your strengths, but aren't sure what your partner brings. If that's how you feel, then things aren't going so well in your relationship. Maybe the dynamics in your relationship are so fractured that things are in a constant conflict cycle. Think back to a time when your relationship was going well or when you first met your partner. Their strengths were likely more obvious then. If it is still difficult, take a third-person view on your relationship and pretend or actually ask an outsider what they would think your partner's strengths are. Bringing them to light might help soften the conflict.

Focusing on strengths in the middle of serious relationship issues can be difficult, and can feel overwhelming. However, when we work with couples, we see how it can also feel stressful to exclusively focus on the problems in the relationship. It's best to work on problems and strengths concurrently. You can't just try to untangle negatives; you also have to start creating positive experiences. Focusing on strengths is one way to bring positivity back to your relationship. (We provide other positive strategies in chapter 3, Magic Moments, and chapter 6, Deep Connections.)

It is important to note that you should never have to be a slave to your strengths. You're allowed to stop wanting to shine in these areas. If you are an organiser and you get tired of organising, you're allowed to put your hand up and say, 'Hey, just because I'm good at this, doesn't mean I need to carry the load on it.' Similarly, it's not okay to pass the buck because one partner is better at something. Just because you're better at organising things does not mean that you should be stuck organising all the date nights, for example, or all the holidays. If you enjoy doing it and you want to do it the majority of the time, go for it. But if you don't, then you're not practising a strength – because strengths are things you enjoy doing or get a positive feeling from. These can change over time.

You might also be stuck focusing on the negatives within yourself. In the spirit of the Me in We, try to connect to your behaviours that are positive. We are sure you bring or can bring plenty of positives to the relationship, so stay open.

Articulating your and your partner's strengths can be hard, so we've provided a handy list in the table overleaf.

 **TIME FOR ACTION**

Do you think about and acknowledge to yourself the positive strengths you bring to the relationship? What are your strengths? What do you think your partner's strengths might be? Using the table just provided, write your name next to any strengths you identify with, and acknowledge them. Write your partner's name next to any strengths they embody. (Use the highlight and notes functions if using the ebook.)

Now go to your partner and have a chat about what you have identified on the list. Talking about strengths can be a fun and exciting way to bring some positivity back to your relationship. Discuss how you can achieve more together by utilising each other's strengths.

Sometimes, celebrating your strengths can feel embarrassing or self-centred. However, you have the right to feel good about your strengths. Practise celebrating them by discussing them with your partner and friends. Go to your partner and tell them what you think their strengths are. Positive action often leads to a positive reaction in your partner, and can be a nice circuit breaker during any tension.

Strengths you or your partner might embody

<table>
<tr><td>

- ☐ Adaptability
- ☐ Adventurous spirit
- ☐ Appreciation for long-time goal alignment
- ☐ Artistic expression
- ☐ Assertiveness
- ☐ Attention to detail
- ☐ Calmness under pressure
- ☐ Caring nature
- ☐ Celebration of milestones
- ☐ Commitment to personal development
- ☐ Communication skills
- ☐ Conflict de-escalation
- ☐ Conflict prevention
- ☐ Conflict resolution skills
- ☐ Consistency
- ☐ Constructive feedback
- ☐ Creativity
- ☐ Crisis management
- ☐ Culinary skills
- ☐ Cultural sensitivity
- ☐ Curiosity
- ☐ Determination
- ☐ Diplomacy
- ☐ Emotional intelligence
- ☐ Empathy
- ☐ Encouragement
- ☐ Environmental responsibility
- ☐ Financial planning
- ☐ Financial responsibility
- ☐ Financial transparency
- ☐ Flexibility

</td><td>

- ☐ Forgiveness
- ☐ Gardening skills
- ☐ Generational insight
- ☐ Generosity
- ☐ Graciousness
- ☐ Gratitude
- ☐ Grit
- ☐ Healthy boundaries
- ☐ Healthy lifestyle choices
- ☐ Honesty
- ☐ Hospitality
- ☐ Independence
- ☐ Initiative
- ☐ Integrity
- ☐ Interest in learning together
- ☐ Interest in shared hobbies
- ☐ Intuition
- ☐ Kindness
- ☐ Leadership skills
- ☐ Loyalty
- ☐ Maturity
- ☐ Mind–body connection
- ☐ Mindfulness
- ☐ Mindfulness of language
- ☐ Moderation
- ☐ Networking skills
- ☐ Nurturing instinct
- ☐ Open communication about needs
- ☐ Open-mindedness
- ☐ Optimism
- ☐ Parenting skills
- ☐ Patience

</td></tr>
</table>

☐ Philanthropy	☐ Sensitivity
☐ Physical fitness	☐ Sensuality
☐ Problem anticipation	☐ Social intelligence
☐ Problem-solving collaboratively	☐ Spirit of adventure
☐ Problem-solving skills	☐ Spirituality
☐ Resilience	☐ Spontaneity
☐ Resilient optimism	☐ Supportiveness
☐ Resourcefulness	☐ Tactfulness
☐ Respect	☐ Teamwork
☐ Respect for independence	☐ Tech boundaries
☐ Responsibility	☐ Tech-savvy
☐ Sacrifice	☐ Time management
☐ Self-awareness	☐ Tolerance
☐ Self-improvement	☐ Tolerance for uncertainty
☐ Selflessness	☐ Trustworthiness
☐ Self-reflection	☐ Understanding
☐ Sense of humour	☐ Willingness to seek help

Summing up

You can't make the world around you change by asking it to. But if you change yourself, everything around you will shift. This is exciting and empowering. The Me in We love link implies that you can continue to discover many things about yourself through life. Reflecting on yourself might make you feel vulnerable. But getting to this point of vulnerability and self-reflection is a strength, and will be a valuable skill in your relationship with your partner and with yourself.

You present both relationship-interfering and strength-based behaviours in your relationship, and you need to bring both to the forefront. Self-reflection brings power for change. This is not about nullifying your partner's negative behaviour or brushing over past hurts. This is about you. *The 8 Love Links* journey is about growth and insight. Your job now is to stay open. You can't expect to learn it all after one chapter, after all.

If you feel you can't empower change in your life, it's time to let go of that fallacy. Once you start changing and growing, the world around you has to react to that change and things in your life will start to shift. It's not magic, it's just social science. Being vulnerable is about true strength. To confront yourself is much stronger and respectable than pretending that you are without flaws. Make it a habit to reflect on your interpersonal relationships. Use the strategies provided in this chapter to self-reflect whenever you feel tension or conflict in your relationship.

This chapter has been all about the Me in We. Now, it's time to bring the focus back to the 'we' and learn how to press the reset button on your relationship so you can set up a base to take your relationship to the highest level.

Link two

Couple's Base Camp

Before you scale the heights of possibility in your relationship, you need to set up some guiding principles and boundaries to keep your relationship stable and secure. We call this your 'couple's base camp'. When you set up your couple's base camp with care and attention, you can explore the world both individually and together with a sense of security.

The couple's base camp is made up of two elements:

1. relationship commandments
2. couple domains (including relationship boundaries).

The **relationship commandments** set the tone of your relationship. They are specific statements of how you, as a couple, will be with one another in your relationship. Relationship commandments are similar to wedding vows or a blueprint for building a house, providing a foundation to your relationship. They are statements in the present tense that can be acted upon in any given moment. For example, 'We speak up when something doesn't feel right and communicate it openly', 'We express affection regularly through words and actions' and 'We make our relationship a priority and protect it from external influences that could harm it'. Again, these are specific to you and your relationship, and we provide a list of specific relationship commandments to explore and choose from later in this chapter.

Couple domains are the common themes you must navigate together, or risk your relationship running into trouble. We have identified 11 couple domains: autonomy and togetherness; finances; domestic duties; others nearby the camp (such as in-laws, extended family, friends and exes); sexual connection; spirituality and religion; the vices; privacy; children and parenting; adventure and travel; and health and lifestyle. Your background, family of origin and cultural context influences your approach to these domains.

In each domain, you must establish mutually agreed upon **relationship boundaries** to protect the integrity of your relationship. Boundaries define acceptable behaviours, responsibilities and expectations within the relationship. They work to protect your and your partner's physical, emotional and mental wellbeing. The boundaries in each domain uphold the relationship commandments. Navigating the couple domains, and the boundaries within, can be challenging. Although you love one another, you may feel in opposition in different domains.

Relationship commandments and couple domains are inextricably linked. While relationship commandments set the tone and spirit of your relationship, couple domains set specific agreed rules around particular topics. You need both to have a cohesive relationship. If you live by the commandments, you will have a fantastic relationship. But life is complex, and the integrity of the commandments is always vulnerable. Clear boundaries within the specific domains help maintain the relationship commandments.

Let's see this in action. Meet Jill and Andrew, a married couple who attended our psychology practice in Sydney for couples therapy. Jill and Andrew have an agreed relationship commandment around teamwork: 'We collaborate on decisions as a team, considering each other's perspectives and preferences.' For Jill and Andrew, this teamwork commandment can be applied to the couple domain of finances. They will make financial decisions together and consider one another's views around finances.

Yet, Jill noticed Andrew making unilateral decisions around their finances. In the face of impending interest rate rises, Andrew decided to move their mortgage from a variable to a fixed rate without consulting Jill. By doing so, Andrew undermined the teamwork commandment in the domain of finances. This breach affected the stability and harmony of their relationship. They found themselves in conflict. Andrew felt frustrated and misunderstood. Jill felt unseen and disappointed.

Our concept of the Couple's Base Camp love link – and the commandments and domains that create it – is the foundation to a satisfying relationship. By focusing on your base camp, you will feel more secure while also having more freedom. You will be happier in your relationship and as an individual. Without a considered base camp, you'll undermine your relationship, making it difficult to relate to one another. A secure base within the relationship provides a safe place from which to navigate differences.

In this chapter, we outline how you and your partner can be united by creating your couple's base camp. You can choose your relationship commandments to guide your relationship. Then you can explore each of the couple domains. Finally, you can discover strategies to tackle the common problems that threaten a sturdy base camp.

Partner attachment as base camp

You've probably heard of attachment styles and attachment theories. These days, these concepts are widely spoken about and commonly referenced on social media and anything related to dating or relationships. However, they were developed back in the 1950s and 1960s.

Attachment theory was outlined by psychologist and psychiatrist John Bowlby and further developed by psychologist Mary Ainsworth. The theory refers to the ways people learn to connect and relate to others, based on their early experiences with their own caregivers. These attachment styles typically fall into the following categories: secure, anxious, avoidant and disorganised. As Ainsworth (and colleagues) outlined, these attachment styles describe your level of comfort with intimacy, and your ability to seek and provide support in relationships. Secure attachments provide a foundation for healthy relationships and emotional wellbeing. The other three attachment styles are defined as insecure, and these styles lead to difficulties in forming and maintaining relationships.

Let's not get caught up in which attachment style you or your partner may or may not have, and instead focus on the main message from attachment theory, which is helpful. You bring to your relationship your own attachment history, and this affects how you will connect with your partner. Without a secure attachment with your partner, you will feel insecure, lacking trust and commitment, with an excessive focus on yourself or your partner. You may feel constrained by your relationship or preoccupied with it.

Our concept of creating a couple's base camp is part of establishing a secure attachment with your partner. Just as children use a secure attachment with their caregivers as a base from which to explore the world, adults in relationships rely on their partner to be a secure base from which to navigate life's challenges and explore personal growth. The base camp serves as a source of comfort, support and safety, allowing partners to venture out into the world with confidence, knowing they have a stable foundation to return to.

A secure partner attachment refers to a healthy and stable emotional bond between you and your partner. Both of you feel comfortable and safe expressing your needs, emotions and vulnerabilities to each other. You trust your partner to be responsive, supportive and available during times of both joy and distress. You have the freedom to explore and play – both together and on your own – without feeling guilty or abandoned.

The good news is attachment styles can change over time. You can strengthen, or move to, a secure attachment style if you have a healthy stable relationship. Similarly, you can grow a secure partner attachment. The couple's base camp is the foundation for your secure partner attachment. Everything else we teach you in this book fosters and enhances this secure attachment.

 **TIME FOR ACTION**

Take some time now to reflect on your partner attachment. Find a quiet place and answer the following questions about your relationship. Spend about 10 minutes doing this.

1. Do you feel supported by your partner most of the time?
2. Do you feel free to express your own opinions without fear of judgement in your relationship?
3. Would you describe you and your partner as being a team?
4. Is there trust and security in your relationship?
5. Are you growing and evolving as an individual and also as a couple?
6. As a couple, do you work well together through the daily routine?
7. Do you have a strong sense you and your partner can be flexible and adjust when unexpected things pop up?

If you have answered yes to most of these questions, you are doing well and have a solid couple's base camp. If you have several no's, it's time to take a closer look at your base camp. Try to stay curious with these reflections. And don't worry – no matter what you discover, you will be guided through this chapter and book on how to create and maintain a robust couple's base camp.

As you reflect, you may come to realise your base camp hasn't even been set up or is in a bit of a mess. That's okay. In the following sections, we help you create and organise your secure base camp. Right now, we simply invite you to commit to this idea of the couple's base camp. You will allow your base camp's principles to lead you toward what you need in your relationship – security, safety and freedom. This commitment is not just to your partner or the relationship but also to yourself. Reflecting on your base camp and your role in it, and inviting your partner into the discussion is empowering.

Defining your relationship commandments

Your relationship is a dynamic wilderness expedition. With your partner, you embark on a journey together. Your relationship commandments serve as your North Star, guiding you through the terrain of love and companionship.

With these commandments as your guide, your couple's base camp then becomes an impenetrable stronghold, shielded from external threats and internal discord. Each of you has the freedom to explore, knowing that camp is but a heartbeat away.

Here are the main elements of your couple's base camp:

- At the perimeter of your couple's base camp stands the sturdy *camp fence*. This creates a fortress of trust reinforced by reliability, commitment and healthy boundaries.

- Within this safe haven, the *campfire* flickers with the warmth of care and validation, offering solace and reassurance amid life's storms.

- The *camp tent*, your cosy sanctuary, beckons as your retreat from the outside world. This is a sacred space for you and your partner where togetherness thrives.

- As you navigate the wilderness of partnership, your *camping tools* become your allies, emblematic of teamwork and mutual support.

Together, you wield the hammer of cooperation and the saw of compromise, building a life of joint benefit and shared victories.

- Consulting the *map*, you chart a course towards common goals while honouring individual aspirations and passions. You navigate the ever-changing landscape of dreams and desires with openness and adaptability.

- And when communication falters or distance threatens to separate you, reach for the *walkie-talkies*. These are symbols of re-connection and understanding. With gentle words and listening ears, you can bridge any gap, and reaffirm your bond with every thoughtful and sensitive exchange.

Our campsite metaphor represents the different parts of your relationship, each requiring a relationship commandment. With these commandments in place for each part of the camp, you are protecting your relationship from attacks from the outside or any breach of containment lines. Each camp member can safely leave and re-enter the couple's base camp when needed.

As mentioned, these relationship commandments are not dissimilar to wedding vows or a blueprint for building a house. They're statements in the present tense that can be acted upon in any given moment.

Here are some relationship commandments you may choose to adopt:

- *Building trust (camp fence):*
  - We trust in one another and are trustworthy.
  - We practise forgiveness and let go of grudges.
  - We keep promises and commitments to one another.
  - We are honest even when it's difficult or uncomfortable.
  - We avoid deception by never lying, cheating or hiding information.
  - We speak up when something doesn't feel right and communicate it openly.

- We take responsibility for breaking trust.
- We will work together if trust is broken and commit to rebuilding trust through transparency and consistency.
- We will be aware of jealousy and insecurity and instead commit to respectful open communication.
- We will share vulnerabilities and be respectful of each other's vulnerabilities.

- *Care and validation (campfire):*
  - We come from a place of love and care always.
  - We commit to taking care of each other when in distress.
  - We welcome and accept our differences (in preferences, opinions, personality).
  - We are kind and caring to one another.
  - We prioritise intimacy and emotional connection.
  - We listen to one another with full attention and without judgement.
  - We express affection regularly through words and actions.
  - We acknowledge each other's emotions even when we don't fully understand them.
  - We offer support through encouragement and assistance during both good and challenging times.
  - We show appreciation and gratitude for each other's presence and the positive things we bring to one another.
  - We celebrate each other's achievements, no matter how big or small.
  - We offer comfort when we are going through a tough time.
  - We apologise and forgive each other when a mistake is made.

- *Togetherness to the exclusion of all others (tent):*
  - We prioritise our relationship above all else and all others.
  - We are each other's biggest cheerleaders, providing emotional support and encouragement to one another.

- We try to be fully present and engaged with one another, minimising distractions from phones, work or other commitments.
- We make our relationship a priority and protect it from external influences that could harm it.
- We establish clear boundaries with friends, family and others about what is and isn't acceptable when it comes to our relationship.
- We go to one another to manage our disagreements and conflicts rather than involving friends or family members.

- *Teamwork (tools):*
  - We take influence from one another.
  - We listen and respect one another.
  - We collaborate on decisions as a team, considering each other's perspectives and preferences.
  - We share responsibilities equitably based on each other's abilities and schedules.
  - We face challenges and conflicts as a team.
  - We acknowledge and celebrate each other's achievements and successes.
  - We respect, acknowledge and appreciate each other's contributions and unique skills that we each bring to the relationship.
  - We express gratitude for each other's contributions to the relationship and acknowledge our efforts.
  - We address any obstacles or setbacks as a team, finding solutions together.

- *Joint and individual goals and values (map):*
  - We are free to be ourselves within the relationship.
  - We support each other's personal growth.
  - We make time for quality moments together.
  - We support each other's individual identities and interests.

- We respect each other's differences in perspectives and feelings.
- We prioritise our own and each other's self-care.
- We work together to define shared goals and aspirations for our relationship.
- We support each other's dreams – both personally and professionally.
- We allow each other time and space for individual pursuits and personal growth.
- We create shared experiences and adventures that we both can look forward to and cherish.
- We discuss and identify the values that we both hold dear.
- We collaboratively establish short-term and long-term goals that align with our shared values and aspirations.
- We encourage and support each other's personal goals and dreams, even if they differ from our joint goals.
- We periodically review and adjust our goals to ensure they remain relevant and attainable.
- We develop a shared vision for our future, encompassing various aspects of our life, including career, family and lifestyle.
- We work together to create a road map and action plan for achieving our joint goals.
- We hold each other accountable for taking steps toward our goals and supporting each other in the process.
- We maintain flexibility with our goals as circumstances change or as we both grow and evolve.
- We recognise that achieving long-term goals may take time and effort, and are patient with each other's progress.
- We continuously reinforce our shared values through our actions and decisions in our daily lives.
- We support and encourage each other to nurture our individual friendships.
- We encourage healthy interactions with each other's families.

- *Coming back together and communicating (walkie talkies):*
  - We communicate openly, honestly and without judgement.
  - We value our relationship above the need to be right.
  - We resolve conflict with empathy and compromise.
  - We understand that we each may need different amounts of time to process our feelings before returning to the issue.
  - We make the effort to initiate contact and express our desire to resolve conflict and reconnect.
  - We listen attentively to each other without interrupting, showing empathy and understanding.
  - We try to avoid blame and criticism when discussing challenging topics.
  - We seek common ground when we can by looking for points of agreement or compromise to build a bridge toward resolution.
  - We apologise sincerely if we are in the wrong and are willing to forgive if we receive a sincere apology.
  - We pay attention to our body language and tone of voice when discussing challenging topics.
  - We encourage each other to share our feelings and perspectives.
  - We seek solutions that work for both of us.

Without these relationship commandments, your relationship doesn't have a stable footing. You have no agreed upon way of being in your relationship, and so have no guidance when you need it. When things get tough, you will resort to old patterns of behaving and responding that undermine your couple bond. This will result in you feeling lost, confused and without a sense of stability.

Many couples assume they have relationship commandments in place but have never discussed or agreed on them. Without this you may be living in a relationship with conflicting rules and expectations, which can cause conflict or hurt.

If a relationship commandment falls down or if it's never established, it can lead to a crisis in the relationship. Let's take a look at Shahn's experience with a client.

Building – and tending to – your campfire

A long-term client, Melanie, came into therapy one day to declare she no longer felt love towards her partner, Jacob. She went on to explain she had been feeling down after resigning from her job. Melanie had certain expectations surrounding the campfire commandment that her partner Jacob did not share.

The campfire represents care and validation, comfort and warmth. During this difficult time, Melanie was expecting extra care, support and comfort from Jacob. When he failed to build this campfire with her, Melanie felt alone and detached.

The problem was they had different expectations around how much support they should give one another in a crisis. Once they realised this, they were able to work together to establish what satisfactory partner support would look like. How would their campfire be? How big and how roaring? How could Melanie also access other supports outside of the relationship? This work brought them back together again.

You might be wondering how on earth anyone remembers to use their commandments. Things you remember are things you rehearse and think about. Being clear about your relationship commandments and coming back to them regularly will mean they become embedded in your consciousness.

Our clients often question if the relationship commandments are really necessary. Some state they just want to get on better with their partner, and that the relationship commandments are too simplistic or wishy-washy. We don't expect your relationship to magically improve once you've selected your relationship commandments. The rest of this book provides you with the skills to improve your relationship. But setting up and committing to your relationship commandments means you have a North Star for your relationship. They're reminders of how you and your partner will come together over and over again. The relationship commandments are a choice you make together. And with choice comes motivation and accountability.

 **TIME FOR ACTION**

Using the list provided in this section, spend some time choosing the relevant commandments for your relationship. Invite your partner to do the same. As you do this exercise, you may find that you and your partner prioritise different relationship commandments. This can be challenging. Don't worry about this for now. Highlight the ones you agree on and mark the ones you disagree on to revisit later. You will learn how to address such inevitable differences within this book, and especially in chapter 5, where we cover the Conflict Compass love link.

Exploring the couple domains

Imagine embarking on a journey to trek a towering mountain. To reach the summit successfully, each part of the journey requires careful consideration and planning. Preparation is key. Your physical fitness and health must be assessed. The ever-changing seasons and weather conditions must be considered. You must equip yourself with the necessary tools and gear for a successful climb, such as a sturdy pair of hiking boots and a reliable map. Having a well-defined route and emergency plans in place helps ensures safety and preparedness during the trek. Finally, navigating local regulations and obtaining permits for your mountain expedition is essential.

Trekking a mountain takes much planning and organisation for it to be successful. The same goes for your relationship and your couple domains.

By approaching couple domains with intentionality and mutual respect, couples can conquer the peaks and valleys of life together. Without this careful consideration and planning, your couple's base camp will be at risk.

Our concept of 'couple domains' refers to certain themes and topics all couples need to navigate in their relationship at some point or another. Your background, family of origin and cultural context has influenced your approach to these domains. Without planning and attention around these domains, you risk stumbling into power struggles and conflicts with your partner.

We have identified 11 key couple domains you need to attend to in your relationship. In some, you and your partner may be cohesive, and in others, you may struggle. That's okay. In the following sections, each couple domain is explored to demonstrate the varied influences each of us have in our assumptions and attitudes within the domains. Such attitudes are automatic, and you will often feel justified or correct in your position within these domains. It's important not to criticise each other for your attitudes and assumptions. Rather, the goal is to make these invisible influences visible – so you and your partner can choose a path together that is respectful of both of you. The aim here isn't just to find a compromise. Rather, it is about carving out a new space you both choose to inhabit. Exploring your influences and biases, and then making deliberate choices within each domain based on your values, ensures you are no longer simply defined by your historical influence.

The following sections outline the key domains that need to be considered and discussed when setting up your couple's base camp.

Autonomy and togetherness

This domain encapsulates the balance between individual independence and the collective bond within your relationship. In your approach to relationships, you will sit somewhere on the spectrum from independence/autonomy through interdependent/mutuality to dependence/co-dependency. Let us explain what these mean:

- *Independence/autonomy* in a relationship context refers to each partner maintaining a sense of self-identity, personal space and individual decision-making. You are individuals first, and a couple second. An individual's needs are prioritised over the needs of the couple. Having the expectation you can behave in an autonomous way within the relationship creates issues when a partner's behaviour leaves the other feeling dismissed, overlooked or unimportant.

- *Interdependent/mutuality* refers to the idea that the couple bond is prioritised while maintaining respect for the inherent differences of each partner. Both partners rely on each other for support, respect each other's differences, and work collaboratively towards shared goals.

- *Dependence/co-dependency* refers to a dynamic where one or both partners rely excessively on the other for emotional validation, self-worth and fulfilment. Partners in a co-dependent relationship live through or for each other. Their own needs and desires are often sacrificed, which can lead to feelings of resentment, imbalance and emotional distress.

Your experience growing up in your family of origin affects your comfort level with more or less personal space and self-reliance within relationships. The dynamics of your parents' relationship served as a model for understanding intimate connections, and your relationship with each parent established a framework for the expected level of togetherness and reliance on others.

Similarly, cultural attitudes toward individualism and collectivism can shape the degree to which autonomy or togetherness is valued within a relationship. In simplistic terms, cultures prioritising individualism tend towards a strong emphasis on personal freedoms, independence and self-expression. In such contexts, individuals may prioritise their own needs and desires over collective concerns, valuing autonomy and personal agency within relationships. Conversely, cultures that prioritise collectivism have a greater emphasis on familial or communal ties, where the wellbeing of the family or community is prioritised over individual interests. Your cultural context is likely not to be as simplistic as this.

The idea here is to get you thinking about how your family and cultural context has influenced your automatic approach and preferences around autonomy and togetherness.

Finances

The couple domain of finances encompasses your implicit attitudes and approaches towards money, spending, financial priorities, debt, financial risk-taking and investment.

Growing up within your family of origin, you likely absorbed some of your family values and attitudes towards money – either directly taking on such values or responding in opposition to them. For example, if your family emphasised frugality and saving, prioritising security and stability above all else, you are more likely to approach your own money in a similar way. You might find yourself pushing for saving rather than spending. Alternatively, if your family was very disorganised with money, resulting in stress within the family, you may find yourself now being very frugal and also prioritising stability, as a way to protect yourself from the hardships you endured in childhood. These very different childhood experiences can result in similar behaviours around finances as adults.

There is no 'cookie cutter' response to familial experiences with money. Rather, when it comes to money in your relationship, you are likely responding in some way to your early exposure to attitudes and behaviours around finances.

Similarly, different cultures may place varying degrees of importance on aspects such as saving for the future, supporting extended family or conspicuous consumption. These cultural values can significantly impact your financial priorities later in life. For example, if you grew up in a culture where familial bonds were highly valued with a strong expectation of supporting extended family members, you may find yourself allocating a significant portion of your income to providing financial assistance or resources to relatives in need.

When reflecting on the couple domain of finances, think about how your family of origin approached debt, prioritised saving and investment, and emphasised security and stability. Consider the potential influence this has had on your current approach to finances. Also reflect on your wider cultural context and its influence on your attitudes and behaviours around finances.

Domestic duties

The couple domain of domestic duties includes the daily tasks and chores essential to maintaining a shared living space. This domain includes the distribution of domestic responsibilities, standards around cleanliness and order, and expectations of one another to complete such tasks. Whether it's the uneven distribution of chores, differing standards or the lack of initiation in responsibilities, this domain can be a great source of discontent in relationships. Traditional gender roles, expectations regarding division of labour and attitudes towards household responsibilities all play a significant role in influencing your approach to sharing domestic duties. Your background, family of origin and cultural context shape not only your approach to household chores, but also your perception of fairness and equity in sharing responsibilities.

Reflect on your upbringing, family of origin and wider cultural context when it comes to the distribution of labour within the home. How have these influenced your approach to domestic responsibilities in your current relationship? This might include the roles each family member held. Did you see a shared commitment to maintaining the household or were responsibilities more segregated? Were children part of this or was it maintained predominantly by one family member or both parents? To what extent were cleanliness, tidiness and organisation prioritised in your family? What were the cultural messages you received around the roles and the importance of domestic responsibilities?

Remember – your family or culture having certain attitudes and assumptions towards domestic responsibilities doesn't mean your relationship must mirror this today. If you fail to unpack your assumptions and biases within this domain, you will continue to stumble, clashing with your partner – who similarly is clamouring around on automatic biases and assumptions.

Others nearby the camp

This domain encompasses the interactions with individuals who exist beyond your partner attachment. This includes parents, siblings, extended family, friends and ex-partners. Your background, family of origin and cultural context will significantly shape how you approach the dynamics and boundaries with such relationships.

Cultural and family norms may dictate expectations for the level of involvement of extended family in your partnership. The significance of friendships within your family unit may shape the importance of maintaining connections with friends outside of your relationship. Expectations around how to handle exes, including how much contact, may differ and be influenced by your experience in past relationships and also your family of origin.

For example, in some cultures and families, it's expected for extended family members to have significant involvement in your partner relationship. This sets up an expectation of the involvement of extended family in decision-making and daily interactions within your partner relationship. Conversely, if you experienced a family and culture in which individual autonomy is highly valued, you might feel more comfortable with firm boundaries with extended family members, limiting their involvement in your partner relationship.

Understanding these familial and cultural influences is essential for you and your partner to navigate such relationships outside of your relationship.

Sexual connection

The domain of sexual connection traverses the landscape of intimacy, monogamy, sexual behaviours, pleasure, modesty and generally the role of sex within your relationship. Your background, family of origin and cultural context profoundly shape your attitudes and expectations regarding your sexual connection with your partner.

Families vary in attitudes towards sex and the values surrounding sex and intimacy. This includes beliefs around premarital sex, contraception, monogamy, sexual orientation, openness in discussing sex and the imparting of moral messages about sex in general or certain sexual behaviours. Similarly, cultural norms and religious beliefs can dictate expectations surrounding sexual behaviours, modesty and the role of sex within relationships.

You may have experienced sexual abuse or trauma, either in your family, community or as an adult. These experiences can have profound impacts on your attitudes towards sex and intimacy.

Establishing boundaries within the couple domain of sexual connection involves defining what you both are comfortable with, ensuring a consensual and supportive environment.

Spirituality and religion

The domain of spirituality and religion encompasses personal and subjective experiences, beliefs, practices and values connected to the divine or something greater than oneself. Upbringing, family traditions and cultural norms all contribute to the formation of beliefs and practices you hold about religion and spirituality that you bring into your relationship. Whether your family of origin adhered to a specific religious faith or practised a secular approach, this upbringing lays the foundation for your spiritual outlook. In some cultures, religion is deeply intertwined with daily life, while others may have a more secular or diverse approach.

Like all the domains, there is no predictable outcome from your cultural or family background in the realm of religion and spirituality. Rather there are influences. Your background could be influencing you to adopt similar approaches from your family and culture or, alternatively, to move away from them. For example, if you grew up in a family with strong religious traditions, such as attending church services regularly or observing specific religious holidays, you may bring these practices and beliefs into your relationship. However, someone with a similar experience may move away from such traditions, appreciating other approaches, and shedding their familial or cultural religious views.

Conversations about spirituality and religion must involve a shared exploration of beliefs, promoting respect for one another. Boundaries will need to be set around expectations of one another when it comes to decision-making in this domain.

The vices

The realm of vices encompasses behaviours that are potentially contentious within the relationship dynamic. This includes, but is not limited to, illicit drug use, alcohol abuse, partying, porn, gambling and gaming. Conversations about vices involve negotiating a balance between individual freedoms, personal preferences and shared expectations for your lifestyle.

Cultural attitudes and familial experiences with any of these vices will inherently influence your approach to them. Cultural and familial attitudes vary widely, so it's necessary to unpack your particular experiences to understand your attitudes and approaches to the vices.

Observing the behaviours and attitudes of family members, including parents, siblings or extended family, can serve as powerful role models that influence your relationship with the vices. For example, growing up in a family with a history of drug abuse or addiction may lead someone to adopt a strict stance against any form of drug use, viewing it as potentially harmful or dangerous. This can lead to conflicts if the other partner has not had such negative experiences with drugs and alcohol or has more permissive attitudes towards recreational drug use.

Cultural expectations of the level of appropriateness of any one of the vices can influence your approach to them today. For example, growing up in a culture that normalises alcohol consumption and, in particular, binge-drinking behaviour may result in you having a higher tolerance of alcohol use in your relationship. Whereas someone not exposed to or buffered from those cultural norms may expect less alcohol consumption.

Open communication about individual experiences, family background and cultural influences fosters a better understanding of each partner's perspective. Respecting and acknowledging these differences contribute to a healthier and more informed approach to managing vices within the context of your relationship.

Privacy

This particular domain involves the boundaries and expectations surrounding personal space, individual autonomy, self-disclosure and the right to retain certain aspects of one's inner world, such as thoughts, feelings and fantasies. This domain covers privacy within your relationship and also privacy of your relationship in the context of others.

In this domain, you must consider factors such as expectations and comfort levels in sharing personal details and experiences with your partner. Your family background and cultural context influence how you approach privacy within your relationship. Some families may be more private about personal matters, choosing not to discuss personal struggles and experiences, influencing your comfort level with sharing details of your life with your partner. Cultural attitudes towards privacy can also vary. Some cultures may encourage open sharing of personal information, while others may emphasise maintaining a degree of privacy. If one partner comes from a family or culture where personal matters are kept private and discussions about emotions or personal struggles are uncommon, they may feel hesitant to share intimate details with their partner. This can lead to conflicts or misunderstandings about communication and emotional support within the relationship.

Also within the domain of privacy, you need to consider your expectations and level of ease in communicating personal details with others outside the relationship, such as family and friends. Your family background and cultural context will likely influence how you approach this. Families differ in their attitudes toward sharing personal information with others outside the partnership. Some families involve themselves in each other's lives, sharing personal details with a multitude of family members, whereas others prioritise strict bounds of privacy, where personal information is expected not to be shared outside the partnership.

Setting appropriate boundaries that define what is considered acceptable and what is not okay regarding personal space, communication with external parties and the sharing of personal information is imperative in this domain.

Children and parenting

Whether or not to have children, parenting styles, disciplinary approaches and the division of child-rearing responsibilities are all part of the domain of children and parenting.

First and foremost, your level of interest in having children must be explored with your partner. Family and cultural expectations to have children can be dominant, so it's important you reflect on these, along with your own preferences.

If you and your partner wish to have children, it's helpful to consider factors such as family and cultural expectations regarding the role of extended family, the balance between work and family life, and the impact of personal experiences in shaping parenting approaches. The parenting style you experienced during childhood can significantly influence your own approach to raising children. You may automatically return to the only parenting style you know, or perhaps you are motivated to parent in a different way. Your experience of the level of involvement and influence of extended family members raising you may impact your expectations regarding the role of grandparents, aunts, uncles and other relatives in the upbringing of children. Cultural norms may dictate certain parenting styles considered appropriate or effective, as well as the level of involvement in child rearing of extended family. This, in turn, will necessitate how to approach well-meaning relatives who offer unsolicited advice or try to assert authority over parenting decisions.

Gender roles in parenting are also impacted by your background, culture and family of origin. Gender roles in parenting include expectations about who is responsible for certain tasks and caregiving responsibilities.

By exploring the domain of children and parenting, you and your partner can establish a collaborative framework that respects both of your backgrounds while fostering a strong and unified parenting foundation within the relationship.

Adventure and travel

The domain of adventure and travel includes travel preferences, level of risk tolerance, and the allocation of time and resources for adventurous pursuits. Again, your background and culture influences your approach.

You may come from a family or culture that prioritises and encourages travel as a means of broadening one's horizons through new experiences. Travel may have been viewed as a worthy investment and means of leisure. Alternatively, your family may have placed less emphasis on adventure and travel, and more on stability and familiarity. What is considered enjoyable regarding leisure and travel may vary greatly.

Understanding these influences can help you navigate the adventure and travel domain.

Health and lifestyle

The health and lifestyle domain encompasses the collective wellbeing, habits and choices that shape the overall health and quality of life for both you and your partner.

You must consider factors such as dietary preferences, exercise routines, work–life balance and attitudes toward mental health – all of which can be influenced by family values and cultural norms. The dietary practices and eating habits witnessed during childhood, including the types of food consumed, meal structures and attitudes toward nutrition, can influence your approach to food and dietary choices. The level of emphasis placed on physical activity within the family, whether through organised sports, outdoor activities or exercise routines, can influence your attitudes toward and engagement in physical fitness. Familial and cultural stigma or acceptance regarding mental health issues can influence your openness to discussing and addressing mental health concerns. The work–life balance observed within the family can influence your approach to managing stress and leisure time, and the importance you place on personal wellbeing outside of professional responsibilities.

By acknowledging and understanding these influences, you and your partner can work together to create healthier habits and support each other's wellbeing.

Setting boundaries within each domain

Most couples struggle with at least some of these couple domains. Similar to preparing for a mountain trek, if you don't plan your approach, your relationship could be in danger – leaving you feeling alone, misunderstood, at odds with your partner or even disliking them. Any one of these domains has the potential to ruin your relationship.

By unpacking the couple domains, you will learn about yourself and your partner. This will bring you closer together and also increase your self-knowledge. If you don't examine your own influences, you won't understand why you approach things differently to your partner, leaving you ignorant and feeling frustrated, confused and disconnected from them. But if you do, you'll achieve self-awareness and insight. This will give you more choices and more flexibility, which will make you more settled and peaceful.

Exploring these domains means setting appropriate and considered boundaries within them. Boundaries allow couples to be more authentic in their relationship while experiencing love and care. If you feel stuck in how to find common ground with your partner in any of these domains, don't worry. We teach you a specific skill, the 'two truths' approach, in chapter 5, which will help you to make difficult decisions together, thereby setting boundaries.

In our couples therapy, we have seen these domains be sources of conflict for couples. When we help couples unpack each domain by looking at their own position and background influences, they grow stronger and closer. They're able to resolve disputes and have more empathy, with the benefit of feeling more understood and loved.

Shireen and Martin, a couple Helen saw for couples therapy, demonstrate this.

Conflict in the finances domain

Shireen and Martin had ongoing fights and tension around money – to the point where they were considering breaking up. Shireen would spend money both on herself and her family of origin without informing Martin. This frustrated him. Martin himself focused on saving and building wealth. Both of them believed they were right in their positions. In therapy, I wanted to look at the meaning beneath the topic of finances and what influenced both of their positions.

It became clear Shireen had been brought up to be responsible for her single mother. She was the eldest child of three and was close to her mother. Being a single mother, Shireen's mother struggled financially when the kids were small. When Shireen was old enough, she sought part-time work to help her mother. She had strong beliefs that money was to be used to support family, and was a way to express love and care. Shireen felt immense guilt when she resisted spending money on her family.

Martin, on the other hand, grew up believing financial growth was the cornerstone to stability and security. He had a hard-working immigrant father who worked to support his family and build his wealth. Money was for increasing financial security for the future and setting up the family for future success. It was not for spending. Martin would become anxious when money disappeared out of their joint bank account.

By reflecting on their past and influences, Martin and Shireen were able to have a renewed empathy for one another. Neither was right or wrong. By understanding this, they were able to find a space where both histories could be honoured but, more importantly, a new approach to finances within their new family – their couple's base camp – could be formed. This resulted in reduced conflict around money and the couple went on to commit further to their relationship by becoming engaged.

You may be thinking, *What if my partner and I are in opposition to one another in any of these couple domains? How will we ever resolve such major issues?* It's not uncommon to be at odds in opinion around these domains. That's why we've included them. This first step is bringing awareness to what influences your opinions and positions. Right now, it is more important to focus on the meaning behind the opposing position rather than coming up with a solution. This builds understanding and empathy both for yourself and for your partner. Rather than it being a debate, these couple domains can be a discussion and result in greater understanding of one another. And don't worry – by the end of *The 8 Love Links* journey, you will have all the skills and strategies you need to navigate any differences in your couple's base camp.

TIME FOR ACTION

Read through the different domains again. Reflect on your position and opinions in each of these domains, and how you might have been influenced by your family and culture. Ask yourself, 'Would my partner have a different opinion or stance to me? Why might that be?' Be kind and curious with yourself and your partner as you do this reflective exercise. If you have a different position to your partner in any of these domains, do not fear. We will guide you on how to sit with conflicting opinions and also how to come to agreements with one another later in this book. To self-reflect and admit you are a product of your history, background, family and culture can be difficult, and can feel uncomfortable and destabilising. This is a normal human experience. Yet persistence will lead to growth.

Embracing opposites: Stability and flexibility

Marie had been married to James for many years. They'd built a strong bond over the years, often participating in joint activities such as going to the gym together. However, as time passed, Marie found herself reassessing her interests and preferences. Despite their shared history at the gym, Marie began to realise that the routine no longer sparked joy for her.

Approaching James with sensitivity and honesty, Marie initiated a conversation about her evolving feelings towards their joint activity. She expressed her desire to explore new avenues of exercise, such as playing team sports.

Marie demonstrated authenticity by openly sharing her shifting preferences honestly. She acknowledged James's attachment to the gym while emphasising her need for a change. Importantly, she reassured him of her continued support for his gym endeavours, underscoring her respect for his individual interests.

James, displaying flexibility and understanding, listened to Marie's perspective. Rather than resisting or dismissing her desires, he embraced her need for change and supported her decision to pursue a different form of physical activity. Marie quit the gym and joined a netball team.

In this exchange, Marie's authenticity fostered open communication and mutual respect within their relationship. James's flexibility and support not only validated Marie's autonomy but also strengthened their bond by demonstrating a willingness to embrace change together. Marie and James were flexible within the couple domain of health and lifestyle. Their relationship commandments around communication and joint and individual goals and values remained intact as they spoke respectfully to one another and supported their separate goals around fitness.

If Marie had chosen to keep her evolving feelings about the gym to herself, continuing with the activity as originally agreed upon, she would likely end up feeling resentful and angry. With Marie's discontentment simmering beneath the surface, tension could have seeped into her interactions with James. He would remain oblivious to the cause of the growing discord between them.

You are more likely to achieve stability in your relationship when you subscribe to the relationship commandments and explore and set boundaries within each of the couple domains. However, this agreement also requires flexibility.

The relationship commandments of your couple's base camp will remain the same over time. However, the couple domains will need to be reviewed and altered as the relationship evolves through different life stages. This is an integral part of maintaining positive relationship health. Individuals change over time. It's inevitable and welcomed.

By remaining constant, the relationship commandments provide you with security and clarity. You can relax knowing you both have stable guidelines on how to be in your relationship. Having flexibility around couple domains is essential. If you don't have flexibility and continue to rigidly stick to your commitments, it can lead to resentment and a sense of being constrained.

You might be wondering, 'What if my partner changes their position in one of the domains in a way I just cannot get on board with?' For example, perhaps your partner develops a drinking problem and you can't compromise on that. If you cannot find common ground and your partner will not respond to compromise or appropriate boundaries within a domain, it may be a sign your relationship is not going to work and you may be better off without it. But before you strike off your partner, keep reading. We provide much more information on solving complex problems and setting appropriate limits around unwanted behaviours in chapter 5. For now, focus on how your current base camp is functioning and identifying areas that need maintenance or repair.

 **TIME FOR ACTION**

Go through the list of couple domains and identify three domains you are doing well in. Then select three domains you need to work on in your relationship. For the three domains you're doing well in, congratulations! Reflect on which relationship commandments are embodied in these domains. Make it clear. For the three domains which need work, choose one relationship commandment for each domain. Try to embody the commandment to bring positive movement and goodwill in your chosen domain. Try it out with your partner.

Navigating relationship traps: Base camp hazards

Some common relationship traps can weaken your couple's base camp. Being aware and responsive to these maladaptive relationship dynamics will protect your base camp.

The relationship traps that can weaken the base camp are as follows:

1. *The self–other imbalance:* One partner is too compliant and puts their own needs and wishes aside too often. Alternatively, one partner is too entitled and focused on their own needs and wishes to the exclusion of their partner's. Either way, there is a risk the relationship commandments are no longer working to protect both partners. An example of the self–other imbalance is Chang and Jane. When Chang and Jane first came to our practice, there was a stark power imbalance in their relationship. Jane had a strong personality and she made the decisions in the relationship. Chang, who was capable but less assertive, surrendered more and more as Jane took control over the decision-making. Jane felt good holding the power in the relationship and she often made wise decisions. As the years went by, Chang became increasingly uncertain and found it hard to make any decision. He felt he had lost himself and started to resent Jane, experiencing her as overbearing and controlling. Jane, on the other hand, had lost

respect for Chang. She resented the fact she didn't have an equal partner who she could rely on to take control when needed. Chang and Jane illustrate how the self–other imbalance can lead to a breakdown in the relationship connection.

2. *The drift:* There is too much self-exploration by one or both partners and not enough base camp maintenance. When this happens, one or both partners are focused on their individual growth and not on their partner's growth or the growth of the couple. Jenny and Arjun, for example, came to therapy reporting they felt little warmth or affection for one another. Jenny was busy taking care of the kids and trying to be the kind of mother she'd dreamed of. She was re-establishing her career in a part-time job and also following her passion for tennis. Arjun was busy working, often interstate for a few nights a week. He was progressing in his career, which made him feel good and confident. In his spare time, he was attending soccer training and playing on the weekends with his friends. Although both Jenny and Arjun were chasing their dreams, there was little base camp maintenance. There was no connection or any alone time together. This left them feeling like acquaintances within their relationship. Jenny and Arjun demonstrate that when partners become too focused on their own dreams and goals and don't remember to carve out time to pursue joint aspirations and endeavours, they grow apart and put the relationship at risk.

3. *The third party:* People, activities or vices outside of the couple's base camp are prioritised over the other partner. In couples therapy, Richard and Sonya reported having a good relationship. But something was getting them stuck. Richard enjoyed attending his after-work drinks every Friday night. Sonya encouraged this as they both supported each other to stay connected with their own friends. An issue arose with this situation, however, after they

had their first child. Richard increasingly came home later and drunker on Friday nights. Sonya increasingly became frustrated with Richard when he could not get up early on Saturday mornings for family time. Shared plans and responsibilities Richard had committed to were put into jeopardy due to his hangover. He would often be too unwell to attend the plans or keep his commitments. Occasionally, he would push through but was grumpy and negative. Sonya reacted with frustration and tended to speak shortly to him or ignore him altogether. This put strain on the relationship and often led to conflict. In this scenario, the third party is the excessive alcohol consumption by Richard. Richard was prioritising drinking over his relationship with Sonya. Previously alcohol was not a problem for them. However, their circumstances had changed and now it was a point of tension. Without attention to the evolving nature of their relationship, this third object was causing conflict and disconnection. A third object (or person) can form a wedge between you and your partner. Even in a good relationship, the third party can destabilise the relationship.

These relationship traps are problems when they repeatedly turn up in the relationship dynamic and go unaddressed. Being alert to these relationship traps and addressing them as they arise is essential. If these relationship traps go unchecked and unmanaged, they can destroy your relationship.

You might have spotted a relationship trap in your relationship and are wondering what to do now. If so, that's great. Insight is the first step to change. Learning to talk about these matters in an open and supportive way fosters positive change. We will teach you everything you need to know about navigating these relationship traps in chapters 4, 5 and 6.

 **TIME FOR ACTION**

For now, if you think you are in a relationship trap, take the following steps:

1. Identify which trap you are in – the self–other imbalance, the drift or the third party.

2. Write down the situation that is occurring and how it is affecting you. How does it make you feel and how does it impact your quality of life?

3. Identify the relevant couple domains that are being impacted.

4. Identify which relationship commandments are being breached.

5. Reflect on yourself and your partner and think about the relevant boundaries that may have been stretched or broken.

Considering the preceding five steps, make time to discuss this with your partner. You will need to address resetting some of the boundaries within that domain. If your partner is not interested in discussing this with you or the behaviour does not change, you might have to start setting some boundaries on the specific behaviour. We show you how to do this in chapter 5, where we cover the Conflict Compass love link.

Maybe you don't feel safe expressing your feelings and concerns. Maybe you are concerned about your partner's reaction if you bring up one of these relationship traps. You might be fearful they'll become defensive, critical or rejecting. This is tough. However, success comes from having the insight and being brave to speak up. Success is not measured by your partner's reaction. You have control over your behaviour, not your partner's reaction. Focus on that. We cover these types of discussions and conflict resolution in much more detail in chapter 5.

Summing up

Through this chapter, you've discovered the value in creating a secure partner attachment. This partner attachment, your couple's base camp, sets your relationship up for success. The key ingredients of your base camp are your relationship commandments, and your capacity to navigate the couple domains. Your relationship commandments will guide your relationship in a happier and healthier direction, and traversing the couple domains will bring empathy and understanding of one another, to fortify your relationship.

We've also highlighted that relationship commandments remain stable over time. This allows you to relax, knowing your relationship is on course. Flexibility within the couple domains means you can grow as individuals and together as a couple without being stifled. We've also explored the common relationship traps that can threaten your couple bond. Awareness of these will give you more agency to address them when needed.

Stop trying to climb Mount Everest without setting up your base camp first. Take the time now to plan. Start thinking about how you want the tone of your relationship to be. How do you and your partner want to approach different domains in your relationship?

With this understanding of the importance of setting the intention for your relationship using relationship commandments and couple domains, it is now time to start creating magic moments together.

Link three

Magic Moments

Sometimes you only need to be on social media for a few seconds before you're bombarded with images of relationship grand gestures – the stunning view from the fancy hotel, the anniversary shot at the exotic location or the new car with the ribbon around it. The message is clear: 'Our relationship is amazing because of these grand gestures'. Grand gestures, such as an exotic holiday, a public declaration, a special gift or an amazing date, can be a good tonic for your relationship. However, the good feeling can be short-lasting and superficial.

As an example of this, consider this client anecdote from Shahn.

Big gestures end up empty

I had a young couple come to me in conflict. Paul and Mei were in their 20s and Mei was frustrated. She felt like there wasn't enough romance in their relationship. She wanted to feel special through big moments.

Paul did his best to try to create these moments for Mei. They attended all of the trendy night spots in Sydney. He arranged surprise picnics at beautiful locations and even declared his love online on multiple occasions. While some of these grand gestures brought a sense of enjoyment, soon after they both felt dissatisfied and uneasy.

Rather than these grand gestures, the small interactions are what add up to make the biggest impact on your relationship. A warm smile, a touch, doing something nice for your partner, and being open, curious, respectful and caring each day facilitate more connection than grand gestures. A small act could be as simple as holding hands, having a hug, sharing good humour, making a cup of tea for your partner or having a present conversation. These small moments communicate love, value and care, and dictate the feeling of your relationship. They are the glue that culminates and brings value to your relationship bond. This is why we call this link the Magic Moments love link. The wonderful thing about magic moments is you have an opportunity to create them on a daily basis.

Small moments are powerful and are occurring all the time between you and your partner. If the sum of your small moments is positive, you will have a good relationship. However, the opposite is also true. If your daily interactions are too negative or neutral, they will compound and lead to disconnection. If you ignore the small moments, you are putting your relationship at risk.

A relationship is like a mosaic. A mosaic is an image made up of small tiles or coloured stones to produce something beautiful or something messy. The whole image can be stunning and cohesive or it can be a jumbled mess. The entire image can't exist without the small tiles and each tile is a joining block to the entire piece. Although the tiles are small, each tile has an influence.

Your relationship mosaic maintains you in a negative or a positive and stable space. For example, if your relationship is filled with little tiles of mistrust and conflict, you will have a volatile relationship. Adding a couple of positive tiles to this mosaic won't bring stability – no matter their size. You need many secure and positive interactions over time to build trust.

The opposite is true if your relationship is filled with positive feelings, acts of care, validation, fun times and humour. If you throw a couple of undesirable tiles into this mosaic, the general positive tone of the relationship will hold. Staying in the beautiful pattern is easier because adding negative tiles is going against the grain of the relationship.

The accumulation of small moments shapes the feel and direction of your relationship. So if your small moments are generally magical, you will have a healthy relationship 'holding pattern'. This holding pattern will be protective because returning to a positive space after conflict will feel natural. Small moments can keep you stagnant, in a conflict state, or flourishing, in a positive state. When you think of your relationship like a mosaic, holding you in a positive pattern, you will value each small interaction more.

In this chapter, we outline why the small moments can be magic for your relationship. You will see why magic moments are easier in the honeymoon phase and how to generate them afterwards to make them a habit. We show you how a commitment to magic moments can lead to a more mindful existence, with benefits extending beyond your relationship. And we highlight how small magic moments are contagious, protective of your relationship and good for your self-esteem.

Why the small magic moments matter most

While grand gestures are nice, they won't compensate for a lack of regular small positive interactions. Grand gestures are akin to doing a big clean up in your home when you leave it a mess every other day of the year. Yes, you feel great afterwards. But if you have not developed the positive habits to keep your home tidy, it will soon be messy again. The small magic moments are points of connection that are joyful, thoughtful, present, caring, helpful, affectionate or flirtatious. Grand gestures are big plans, such as holidays, elaborate gifts or amazing date nights that can't easily be replicated. They can be an amazing experience, but they're just not enough to dictate the nature of the relationship.

With a little thought and commitment, small magic moments can be done on a daily basis. Some examples are holding hands, making your partner a cup of coffee, getting off the couch to greet them at the door, looking them in the eye, giving them a touch or a hug, sharing a smile, giving them a flirtatious look or compliment, doing a chore for them, and asking how their day was and giving your full attention to the answer. Grand gestures need to be the icing on the cake – they're a celebration, not a bandaid.

Small moments of intimacy are the building blocks to your relationship for the following reasons:

- *Small interactions build intimacy:* The little things you do for one another every day build a deep sense of intimacy and bond between you and your partner. These gestures communicate that you value your partner and prioritise their happiness.

- *Small interactions show effort:* Relationships take effort, and small interactions demonstrate effort. If you listen, offer a hug when needed, or drive your partner to an appointment without being asked, you demonstrate you care about your partner and are willing to put in the work to support them. These efforts communicate 'I value you' and, in turn, lead to feeling valued.

- *Small interactions create positive associations:* Positive associations are the mental connections you make between an experience and a feeling. Small, positive interactions with your partner create large positive associations for your relationship. Over time, these positive associations can sustain a relationship through tough times. The value of the relationship becomes larger than any difficult time you might have to endure.

- *Small interactions can form habits:* Any relationship will have moments of conflict or misunderstanding. However, if you have a habit of small, positive interactions, they will offset negative moments, making your relationship more secure. When you develop a habit of showing affection, expressing gratitude or offering support, these small acts become automatic, creating a strong foundation for the relationship. Establishing these small habits in the relationship leads to faster conflict resolution. Sitting with unresolved conflict becomes uncomfortable, and you have a natural tendency to want to realign with one another.

Avoiding disaster and becoming a master

Renowned psychologist and researcher Dr John Gottman, co-founder of the Gottman Institute, has spent four decades researching successful relationships. His 'love lab' studies revealed two distinct groups of couples – 'masters' and 'disasters'. Masters had lower physiological arousal, meaning they were physically calmer and less reactive. This created a safer space for masters to foster trust and intimacy, leading to lasting connections. Disasters, on the other hand, were reactive and experienced quicker relationship deterioration. Putting it simply, masters were couples who had regular magic moments. Disasters were couples who neglected to prioritise the small moments in the relationship. Gottman's exploration extended to 'bid interactions', where partners make requests for connection. Disasters often neglect bids for connection, leading to divorce or unhappiness. Masters, on the other hand, turn toward each other during these moments, offering and responding to bids for connection, nurturing emotional connection and sustained relationships.

Gottman asserts gratitude is crucial to these small moments and these connections, identifying it as a muscle requiring exercise. The habit of appreciating and expressing gratitude is what distinguishes masters from disasters. Disasters focus on criticism and contempt, and these continued and accumulated small moments are the primary factors tearing couples apart. Even in conflicts, masters expressed anger in a kind manner, addressing issues without hostility and allowing couples to navigate conflict.

Gottman's research emphasises that when kindness and generosity is expressed often, it is returned with increased sharing of joys and constructive responses in the relationship. The accumulation of these moments fosters stability and healthy connections. In times of stress, practising kindness becomes a vital tool in preventing the erosion of the relationship. The opposite is true when neglect and resentment are at the forefront.

Small magic moments breed more magic moments

The small moments are the glue to your relationship. Your interactions add up, and they either keep you safe or take a toll on your relationship.

We often ask our couples, 'How much better or worse do you think your life would be if you were single right now?' The answer to this confronting question either reveals gratitude for the relationship or highlights the chronic stressed state of the relationship. The presence or absence of small magic moments makes the difference! Your life quality should be better with your partner. If it's not, it is a strong indicator your relationship needs to change.

You might be thinking, *I'll be nice and generous when they are nice and generous to me*. It is important to note you are having interactions, regardless of whether or not you're being nice to each other. Even if you're not talking, you're still communicating something. You can change your side of the Yin-Yang relationship anytime you want to influence it. If you and your partner keep delivering negativity or passivity, your relationship Yin and Yang will remain fractured. You can't negative your way into a positive relationship. If you move toward positive action and your partner stays negative, their behaviour becomes more obvious, creating more room for accountability on their part.

This is a powerful concept to remember. When you have two partners acting in a negative way, you are justifying the unhelpful behaviours. This makes it okay to continue. If you move toward magic moments, sooner or later your partner's negative behaviours will become more obvious. They have less room to hide and will have to take a look at their own behaviour.

Magic moments need to be consistent. Even if you're in conflict, magic moments still matter. And while every effort is commendable, magic moments can be undone if they come with expectations or strings attached.

Some exceptions exist to this rule. For example, you or your partner need time and space to process conflict. In this case, one of you is distancing or getting more frustrated when attempting to connect via small magic moments. Taking some time and space when there is tension is fine. Some people need distance to reflect and process conflict. If you find yourself pursuing your partner and getting a negative reaction, you (or they) need to take a step back. We will talk about this dynamic in more detail and give you effective strategies on how to navigate this in chapter 5.

With that said, you can still do a nice gesture for them when you are ready to connect again. Such acts can be a circuit breaker to conflict. Use your judgement. If you or your partner isn't ready to connect, it is okay to wait for the right time.

By now, you're starting to understand the relationship you're looking for is in the small magic moments. Small magic moments will breed more magic moments.

 **TIME FOR ACTION**

Write a list of the interactions you might have with your partner on any given day. Put a tick next to the interactions that are already magic. Remember, the small magic moments are points of connection. They can be joyous, thoughtful, present, caring, helpful, playful, affectionate or flirtatious. What feelings do you get when you connect in this way? How does it affect your mood, your relationship and other interactions?

Now look at the interactions that are not ticked. What is blocking these moments from being magic? Are you on your phone or multi-tasking while talking to your partner? Are you caught up in your own mind or worry list? How can you introduce magic moments into these other interactions? What new interactions or actions could you create to bring more magic moments in your relationship?

Acting opposite to find the magic

If you don't feel in the mood, creating small magic moments can seem too hard. 'Acting opposite' can be a helpful strategy in this situation. For example, say you've had an argument with your partner, and you feel like ignoring them or staying angry. Acting opposite would involve taking a deep breath, approaching your partner, giving them a hug and saying you value the relationship. Another example may be you've come home from work feeling tired and stressed, and just want to zone out in front of the TV. Acting opposite would be asking your partner if they're up for going for a walk and debriefing your days together.

You may think this intervention sounds lame or would be too hard to do. However, acting opposite is a tried and tested skill from dialectical behaviour therapy (DBT), a therapy for people with borderline personality disorder (BPD). People with BPD feel emotions at a much higher intensity than the general population and can struggle with emotion regulation. We have both led DBT groups and have seen acting opposite to be a powerful tool for emotion regulation and interpersonal relationships. If people who literally experience emotions at a higher intensity can do it, then so can you! We have also both used acting opposite in our relationship plenty of times and experienced the tension-cutting benefits. Forcing yourself into a certain behaviour and trusting a positive feeling or mind state will follow can also rapidly change your mind state. This might feel like 'fake it 'til you make it', but we don't see it that way. It is more like connecting to a healthier version of yourself that's hard to access in that moment.

The more kindness and gratitude you have, the stronger your relationship will be. The less time spent in conflict, the less damage you are doing to your relationship. Don't worry – we outline how both you and your partner can feel validated in your relationship in a structured way in chapter 4 when we explore the Feeling the Story love link. And we explore how to manage conflict in great detail in chapter 5.

When in a conflict state, doing nice things for your partner can feel like you're letting them off the hook or sweeping issues under the carpet. We do not want you to ignore or avoid concerns. Instead, tell your partner the conflict is important and set up a time to discuss it. However, also inform them you'd like to connect in a positive way in the meantime. By doing this, you are communicating, 'I have confidence our relationship will overcome all difficulties'. Refusing to reconnect is communicating, 'Our relationship is on hold unless we work this out!' Magic moments can bring walls down. Remember – your relationship is bigger than the conflict!

Making magic moments a habit in your relationship

Christina worked in the banking sector and was highly successful. She was charismatic, attractive and wealthy, and described an amazing lifestyle with a good balance of work, travel and health. Christina came to therapy stating her relationship was on the rocks and she felt like she was going around in circles and living on repeat. Christina, now in her late-30s, stated she wanted to have a long-term partner and even consider children if the relationship was right. Christina said she had experienced the feeling of love in many past relationships. However, anywhere from three to 12 months in, she'd feel like the attraction waned. She didn't feel the connection or sparks anymore. She would start to seriously doubt the relationship and eventually end it. All of her relationships had followed this same trend since she was a teenager.

For Christina, the loss of sparks and chemistry confirmed the person was not right for her. The relationship wasn't 'the one'. Her partners would start to feel her withdrawal and this would cause them anxiety and subsequent problematic behaviours such as overly pursuing her. She would then feel smothered, value them less and see their behaviours as further confirmation the relationship was not right. This pattern had endured. Through therapy, Christina came to realise she stopped committing to the relationship when the 'honeymoon phase' ended. She was able to see her withdrawal came before the problematic behaviours of her partners. This was a confronting and difficult insight. She experienced regret and remorse for the pain she had caused and even reached out to apologise to some past partners. She was also able to turn her current relationship around and commit to forming deeper bonds. (You can also learn how to form deep connections in chapter 6.)

During the honeymoon phase, you don't have to think about generating magic moments. They come with ease. The sparks fly and you can't wait to see, touch and connect with your new partner. However, after a while, spontaneous self-generating magic moments decline. Couples get familiar, comfortable and the magic moments stop flowing.

Putting in the work after the honeymoon phase

If you believe the myths around romantic love, you believe you should feel loved up, spontaneous and have a desired connection with your partner without too much effort. These feelings should continue if you're with the right person. But the reality is different. When connection, novelty and spontaneity turn to familiar and mundane, it becomes harder to generate the magic. And you can drift apart if you don't take responsibility and put the energy in to generate magic moments.

In the beginning, the intense and exciting pull toward one another is seamless and magnetic. These are moments to be savoured because many people don't ever recapture the feeling of the honeymoon phase. This newly forming connection is a privileged journey for those who are single and moving into a bonded relationship, and is often described as a 'love drug' between two people.

From a psychological perspective, the honeymoon phase occurs for a variety of reasons, with several strong undercurrents at play. One of the most important is related to the vulnerability and excitement of attachment insecurity. In the dating period, you have no agreed or felt sense of a secure attachment bond. This means you are in a vulnerable and insecure position. The 'what if they don't like me?' creates an insatiable desire for confirmation to satisfy this insecurity. If you have ever experienced a food fast, you will understand how food deprivation can lead to food delight. The simplicity of good bread, butter and jam becomes a scintillating gastronomic experience. This is similar to the loved up feeling in the honeymoon phase. The insecurity, the unknown and the vulnerability heighten the experience of every bonding moment. The simplicity of a touch, a look, a gesture and holding hands brings with it sparks, electricity and heartbeats as you move toward feeling accepted and attached to your partner.

Why does the honeymoon phase come to an end? And why is it so important to create magic moments when it does? After the honeymoon phase, you feel more attachment security and less vulnerability, which means fewer sparks. At this point, magic moments commonly fade. However, the phase after the honeymoon is important because it is where relationship habits are formed. Couples who continue to be kind and nice to each other set the stage for their relationship. If negative habits occur along with a lack of kindness and joy, it can set the relationship up for future conflict, drift or even a negative association. The good news is you can turn your relationship around at any time. However, to do so, magic moments need to become a habit – and, as with any habit, they require intentional effort and consistency. Only then do they come more naturally and do you see the pay-off. These small efforts scream, 'I love you; you are important to me' and set the foundation for your relationship.

You must make a commitment and choose to invest in your relationship. By doing so, you can achieve a thriving relationship and a higher quality of life. A never-ending, exciting, self-generating love doesn't exist. Instead, you have to *create* a thriving relationship that generates enduring and deeper love – by choosing to focus on your partner and your relationship, time and time again. If you're stuck on the idea that true love lasts forever without effort, you're putting your relationship at risk. Worse still, you might find yourself on a never-ending quest across multiple relationships, waiting for a true love that never lasts and, instead, leads to inevitable disappointment.

Remember – magic moments come naturally in the honeymoon phase but then it is up to you and your partner to set the pattern for your life together. If the honeymoon phase is long behind you, you may have some catching up to do. That's okay, because change is possible at any point as long as you have two committed people.

Escaping the grip of unwanted habits

In our practice in Sydney's Inner West, couples often come to therapy when their relationship is in real trouble. They are stuck in a pattern of negative interactions. While we can make inroads in our therapy sessions, outside of the sessions, couples often continue on with their habits. This is because forming new habits is difficult and defaulting back to ingrained ones is easy. (This is one of the main motivations for our couples app, My Love Your Love. We wanted couples to have a tool they could access in real time to prompt them to use and maintain new habits and strategies.)

Don't underestimate the grip of unwanted habits. Think about a time you decided to do something new – perhaps it was committing to more reading, going to the gym, walking more or reaching out to family on a more regular basis. Often, once the motivation declines, so does your effort. It's natural. Your unconscious brain isn't wise. It just defaults back to prior learning even if it is less helpful.

As another way of thinking about this, imagine you're at point A and you want to get to point B – but between point A and point B is a large overgrown grassy field. The grass mostly extends above your head, but you spot a clear pathway through so you walk down it. It feels quite comfortable and it is the only clear way through. However, when you come out of the grass field, you realise you're far from point B. The path hasn't taken you where you wanted to go. The next day, you return to the same field and you take the same path, because it is the path of least resistance. Forging your way through uncharted territory just seems too difficult.

If you're creating a new habit, you need to walk through the tall, overgrown grass. It's uncomfortable and it's difficult, but when you pop out at point B, you'll get loads of positive reinforcement. Your brain will flood you with dopamine, giving you the message that this was a good outcome. If you return to the field the day after, you will see a slight bend in the grass showing you your new path. But it will remain an uncomfortable walk for some time. The other pathway is like a super highway compared to your newly formed track. It will continue to be attractive and feel more natural.

Walking through the grass is a metaphor for going for a walk or having dinner with your partner without distraction instead of flopping down in front of the TV. Or, it is putting your hand up and owning an unhelpful behaviour. It could be stepping in for a hug or giving a genuine smile after a conflict. Taking the old clear pathway is having a glass of wine, 'doom scrolling', watching Netflix and avoiding connection, or being passive and/or aggressive.

As you walk down the new pathway through the tall grass, the slight bend in the grass gives way to a new path – narrow at first, uncomfortable, the grass still brushing against your body, but a path nonetheless. Each day you take this path, it becomes more defined beneath your feet. The pathway becomes visible, more reinforced, and feels more natural. You'll still see the old path. However, the grass will start to grow over it. Eventually, the old pathway will be overgrown and less desirable. Your new behaviour of magic moments becomes natural and takes far less effort. You have now broken the need for motivation. The new path becomes the easiest way.

If you're looking for some extra help in this habit formation, we've included love-generating challenges on our My Love Your Love app. You and your partner are prompted to perform challenges to create playful and thoughtful interactions. Each partner is unaware of the other's challenges but they can keep an eye on each other's score. This healthy competition is intentional, designed to facilitate regular completion of challenges so couples can build a habit of magic moments. Don't make the common mistake of just focusing on problems in your relationship. We always ask couples to start generating positive change while working on difficult aspects of the relationship. Couples who take this concurrent process feel better sooner and value each other much more.

We want you to focus on creating positivity on a regular basis in your relationship. Thinking you might do it one day won't help! You need to make a commitment and a plan if you want to have more magic moments in your relationship.

Remember – even if things are not going well, you can start to influence the overall tone of your relationship by creating magic moments.

Persisting through the hard bits

You might think, *We have so many problems in our relationship and my partner doesn't understand me. I can't see how this is going to work.* We understand. When things are not going well, creating magic moments can feel impossible. We cover tackling relationship problems in much more detail in chapter 5 (the Conflict Compass love link) and chapter 7 (Baggage Claim love link). Chapter 5 is by far our longest chapter because we have so much to share with you. You can discover how to navigate conflict throughout your lifespan, and how to recognise and change relationship dynamics. But for now, it is worth trying to break the tension. Remember the mosaic analogy from earlier in this chapter – the sum of continued small negative interactions is contributing to your overall relationship health.

Conflict is tough! It feels terrible and can take over your entire existence. You often start judging your entire relationship based on the associated feelings, and can easily lose sight of positive associations. Magic moments can be the circuit breakers that bring back more positive information about the relationship.

You may find yourself in a position where your problems seem too great to try magic moments. If this occurs, take some time out to meditate on positive aspects of your relationship. Remind yourself the relationship is bigger than the conflict and then act opposite.

If you're doing magic moments and getting none in return from your partner, continuing will be a struggle. Just remember – you may not always get an immediate positive reaction. Try to let go of wanting an immediate return. The accumulation of magic moments has a big influence. Again, you keeping on top of your positive behaviours brings the spotlight onto your partner's unhelpful interactions, and they are more likely to be accountable.

Rather than using your partner's reaction as your measure of success, instead focus on personal values that align with magic moments. For example, if you would like to work on the values of patience, compassion, kindness, generosity and creating joy, each time you commit to a magic moment, you're succeeding, with or without a good reaction from your partner. This can be motivating, and lead to you feeling better sooner.

You might think magic moments should come easily if your relationship is good. Habits, good or bad, come naturally. We always say, 'Grab the concept that magic moments should come naturally and throw it out the window.' If the habit comes naturally for you, fantastic. If not, that's okay too. Magic moments can feel like they're going against the grain until they don't. They're hard before they're easy.

The magic is in the moment

Have you ever had a tech-free weekend with your partner?

A couple of years ago, we found ourselves under lots of stress with work, family commitments and the creation of our My Love Your Love app. It was ironic – we were working on an app all about bringing couples together, yet we found ourselves distracted, distant and easily frustrated with each other. We decided our relationship needed immediate priority. We booked a weekend away without the kids in the Blue Mountains (about an hour and a half outside of Sydney). We committed to a tech-free weekend and bunkered down in a beautiful cabin in the middle of winter.

Turning off our phones and our computers slowed the world down, and meant the small moments were easier to commit to. We were forced out of the easy distractions into more meaningful connections. We cooked dinner together, played board games, enjoyed the fireplace and went for walks. Simple things, but also the best life has to offer. Doing things such as tech-free weekends or even tech-free hours can facilitate magic moments and help you reset. After our trip, we committed to regular walks without devices to ensure we had a space to connect when times were busy.

You need to create space and remove obstacles to be more present with each other. It's unfair to say it's always easy to create magic moments in a world so busy and stimulating. At times, you must consider obstacles you can remove.

Forget future happiness

Many relationships fall victim to the 'arrival fallacy' – a term coined by well-known psychologist and bestselling author Dr Tal Ben-Shahar.

The arrival fallacy is the assumption that when you reach a goal or get over a hurdle in the future, your life will be better with lasting happiness. The arrival fallacy is dangerous and can put your relationship at risk as you focus on this future goal or hurdle, rather than the present.

The arrival fallacy, for example, may make you say something like the following:

- 'It's just a stressful period; we will have time to focus on our relationship later.'
- 'I am sure my partner will change once we are married.'
- 'Our life will be better when the mortgage is paid down.'
- 'We're just busy right now and it won't always be this way.'
- 'Things will be okay once we can afford the vacation.'
- 'I'm sure the relationship will be back on track when I get a new job.'
- 'Things will be better once the kids are older.'

Believing in the arrival fallacy gives you permission to procrastinate on improving your relationship. However, you can only change your relationship in the present. All positive feelings and connections associated with milestones are temporary. Celebrate and savour these moments but do not rely on them as the fix for your relationship. Holding on for these moments is dangerous because your relationship might not last the distance or it could fall apart shortly after. You likely know this from your own experience. When you've achieved important goals or gotten over those hurdles in the past, how long has the happiness lasted for? Moments, hours, days? If you're lucky, a couple of weeks. In our psychology practice and in our personal lives, we have seen neglected relationships fall apart around important milestones. I am sure you have too.

Here are some examples we see time and time again:

- The couple who are miserable in their relationship but cling to an upcoming holiday as the circuit breaker. They have a better time away and feel somewhat connected. They return home and before a week is out they feel miserable again.

- The couple who renovate or build their home only to separate soon after completion.

- The couple who separate soon after children are born.

- The couple who separate not long after their marriage.

We could go on with examples but we are sure these stories will sound familiar to you.

The best judge of your relationship health and the biggest predictor of where it will be in the future is where your relationship is right now! It's not where it has been or where you think it might be in the future. For a snapshot assessment, reflect on how your relationship has been trending over the past month. This is a good predictor of where your relationship is heading. If you'd like to take this analysis a little further, our My Love Your Love app includes a relationship health graph to help you track your satisfaction over time. While we are delighted to say the graph trends positively when people use the app, this is not the point. The point of the graph is to keep the relationship authentic and honest. You can reflect on how you feel about the relationship. If the relationship starts to tip, both parties can then address issues and invest in their relationship to get it trending back in the right direction.

Focusing on the moment

While relationships fluctuate and evolve over time, you can only experience relationship contentment and joy in the present moment. The best times you've had in your life have also been the times where you have been present in the moment. No-one had the best time in their life stuck in their thoughts. Sure, you can enjoy a daydream but it is not the same as tasting the richness of life in the moment. Getting stuck in your mind can also lead to worry, distraction and depression. Living a more mindfulness-based existence cultivates more contentment and joy. This is true in relationships also. When you pay attention to and prioritise the small magic moments, you encourage a more mindful existence with your partner. This is because magic moments are intentional, present and connecting.

Mindfulness-based living in relationships is when individuals strive to bring their complete attention and presence to interactions with their partner. This is where connections, care, love and joy exist. While mindfulness-based living doesn't mean you will be without negative emotions, it does mean you are more likely to be open and communicative. Being present with your partner is the window to a fulfilling relationship.

How present are you and your partner with each other? Perhaps you try, but you notice they're half there or they're multitasking (or vice versa). Importantly, magic moments are not magic unless you are trying to be present. You can't experience joy while multitasking. If you're half there, you've lost half the magic.

It's easier to experience mindfulness when you have more play and love in your life. If you're present and more mindful with your partner, more joy will come into your life. You will have more connection, validation, flirtation and even desire. This safeguards your relationship during more difficult times.

Don't wait for a mythical milestone in life to somehow arrive at never-ending positivity. It simply doesn't just happen – you have to choose it over and over.

If you are mindful in your relationship, you will take these positive feelings into other domains of your life. For example, if you feel more joy, openness, patience and curiosity in your relationship, imagine how this will affect the way you engage with other family members, friends or work colleagues.

Magic moments help you develop a deep connection by facilitating authentic and present-minded moments and interactions. Being attentive and responsive to each other's needs creates a safe space for vulnerability and emotional intimacy. If you feel overwhelmed and stuck in your head, you will find it more difficult to regulate your emotions. You might not even be aware of your emotions. Practising mindfulness will lead to improved understanding of your emotions. It will also improve your ability to attune to your partner's feelings. This places you in a position to be able to offer care and validation, or to cut through conflict easier.

Turning off distractions and being present

Living in the moment all the time is impossible. Your brain is an incredible machine that helps you innovate, think, reflect and plan. You also live in a stimulating world and it's easy to be distracted by entertainment, technology, devices, worries and the busyness of work and life. Creating magic moments is bringing your awareness to your own distractions and being present with your partner for the small moments.

Being present might look like this. You come home from work and you put your phone and computer away. You turn off other distractions. You become aware of your own ruminations and commit to putting them aside. You connect with your partner in a genuine, open, curious and present-minded manner with intention. This connection might be a hug or a conversation while cooking dinner or giving them a little gift. Perhaps you're just asking them how their day was or you're trying to be tender.

The important message is this: life is right here. It's not in some future magical fantasy land. If you get stuck on the arrival fallacy in your relationship, you'll just be holding onto something false – a better existence in the future that never comes. If you want a better future relationship, you need to focus on your relationship today. It has to be done now. Day by day, this is where you live. Doing this now means the sweet moments you are looking forward to in the future will be icing on the cake.

Perhaps you've told yourself something like the following:

- 'I can't get out of autopilot.'
- 'I can't get away from my phone.'
- 'I'm stuck at work.'
- 'Streaming is how we wind down and relax.'

We get it. Life's stressful and you want to zone out. However, all these things are taking up valuable parts of your life. Do you really value where your time is going? Are these distractions more valuable than your relationship? You need to kickstart some new habits to make a space with less distraction. Planning activities is part of carving out space for magic moments – for example, doing a dance class together, going on a hike with your partner, scheduling a no-tech meal together or taking up tennis together.

When you are interacting with your partner are you on your phone? Are you thinking about work? Are you multitasking? Make an effort to be more mindful every day in all your interactions. Magic moments on autopilot won't have the same effect. If you're making a cup of tea and flicking through your emails while asking your partner how their day was, you can't experience the magic. Stop multitasking your relationship. If you are in the middle of something important, tell your partner you can't give them your full attention and you need a few minutes. Stop having half a conversation and either connect 100 per cent or create time to do so.

Some personal habits can also help with mindfulness. For example, you might take up meditation, yoga or even gardening. These habits will help slow your mind down. A slower mind is more present. Connection is easier. More energy and intention is possible.

If you find yourself inundated with worry, stress and tasks, mindfully connecting can be difficult. If you are having a hard time being present, rather than trying to force it, let your partner know. Ask them if you can have a conversation about your worry, if they can give you a place to vent. This can be a mindful interaction. Or if you need personal time for self-care, set up a time to reconnect.

Magic moments are contagious

Meet Tom and Deepa, who were seen by Helen at our practice in Sydney. Tom and Deepa had been locked in disconnection and conflict for a long time. Helen asked them to commit to doing one magic moment each for homework, despite their conflict state. They both agreed to the task with limited enthusiasm. Yet when they returned to therapy the next week they couldn't believe the snowball effect it had had. Even the attraction they felt for each other had moved to a place they hadn't experienced for a long time.

Magic moments became contagious. Tom and Deepa were locked in a major conflict. When they committed to doing and receiving a magic moment from each other, they had a positive experience – and this feeling felt more desirable than continuing the conflict. This feeling snowballed, leading them to a much better place where they were then able to negotiate the conflict in a much more respectful and validating way.

Are you wondering what they did? Well, it was nothing out of this world. The day after therapy Deepa offered Tom a heartfelt hug, which he accepted. Tom felt so moved, he then arranged for one of Deepa's favourite activities – a day out at a beach where he arranged everything needed for the day. Deepa, surprised and excited by Tom's organisation and thoughtfulness, was warm and affectionate to him that day and the following days to come. Tom enjoyed this affection and returned in kind.

When your relationship is thriving, you won't care who started the momentum. You'll feel proud and happy in your relationship. So don't wait for your partner to commence magic moments. Do them ASAP and keep doing them. If you can kickstart a positive cycle or break a conflict cycle, then you're winning. Kindness and magic moments are contagious.

Commit to making magic moments and accept it will take many small moments to create a beautiful mosaic. As Dr John Gottman's research indicates, the aim is to have two people who turn towards one another with love and kindness. This ensures the underlying tone of your relationship is positive and warm. The process is a commitment to creating a little bit of love every day.

As well as boosting your relationship, creating magic moments will also increase your self-esteem. Being kind reinforces positive beliefs about yourself and cultivates your ability for empathy and compassion. The focus on your partner's experience will improve your emotional intelligence. You'll become more aware of your own emotions and more attuned to your partner. When your partner starts returning magic moments, life just gets better.

Your life won't be better in the future if you are not working on it now. A life worth living is one filled with magic moments. Take the lead and reap the benefits. Don't wait around for your partner to start, as you could be waiting a long time.

Perhaps you're thinking, *Why should I start the magic moments? It's always me doing everything.* If so, we've got a question for you: Are you planning on breaking up with your partner? If the answer is yes, then sure, don't waste your time with magic moments. However, if the answer is no, then don't waste another minute in this mindset. You will only bring more tension to the relationship by being wilful. No matter what is occurring, you are capable of creating change through positive behaviour. You can take satisfaction in adhering to the standards you aspire to cultivate and uphold. For example, living in accordance with the values of kindness and joy! The one exception here is if you're prone to self-sacrifice. In this situation, you need to be careful.

Magic moments are about living within our values – they're not about surrendering your needs or self-sacrificing for the sake of your partner. It's not about pleasing a partner to avoid guilt, anxiety or conflict.

If you're prone to self-sacrificing, ask yourself, 'Why am I doing this action? Is it to create an authentic magic moment?' If it is, wonderful. Go for it. If it's to avoid guilt, anxiety, fear or conflict, press the pause button. Maybe there's another behaviour you should be doing here. We address this in chapters 5 and 7.

 **TIME FOR ACTION**

Remembering it takes time to build a habit, make a list of 10 magic moment exercises you can do over the next 14 days. If you're struggling to come up with any yourself, we've provided here some example challenges. These are examples only, so please also come up with some that are relevant to you.

Consider adopting some of the following magic moments:

- Call or text your partner and tell them you love them.
- Ask your partner if you can give them a hug.
- The next time your partner comes home, greet them with a kiss, hug and a smile.
- Offer to make your partner a cup of tea.
- Suggest a no-tech walk together.
- Arrange a date night with an emphasis on being present.
- Tell your partner you are sorry for a past hurt you may have caused.
- Give your partner a short massage.
- Cook a meal for you and your partner and eat it without devices.
- Arrange a road trip together.
- Suggest going to the gym or on a hike together.
- Suggest watching a movie or series together. Make some popcorn and snuggle.

- Arrange care for your pets or children and go to a museum.
- Walk your partner to the door and kiss them goodbye.
- Ask your partner how their day was and offer unwavering support.
- Create time for your partner's hobby.
- Look your partner in the eye and express gratitude for something they do.
- Look for opportunities to thank your partner for anything they do that benefits the relationship or family.
- Surprise your partner with a small gift.
- Send your partner a flirty text.

If you want to create change, you have to make time. All the excuses in the world will not help your relationship. This is akin to complaining you have no time to exercise and hoping your health improves. The relationship you have now is the best predictor of the relationship you have in your future. If your time is filled with things less valuable than your relationship, you can expect a relationship that has less value. Being wilful can get in the way. Wilfulness maintains the status quo of the relationship. We explore this concept further in the next chapter.

Summing up

Through this chapter, you've learned the small moments are what matters most in your relationship because relationships are like a mosaic. The many small tiles, like magic moments, converge together to create a beautiful image or a chaotic mess.

Grand gestures are the icing on the cake, but they're not enough to maintain or sustain the relationship. Without the cake, all you're left with is a short-lived sugar rush.

Magic moments come naturally in the honeymoon phase and then require effort and consistency. Your small moments are driven by habits and can be magic or negative. This affects the likelihood of you and your partner staying together or parting ways.

The arrival fallacy is dangerous because it helps you justify procrastination and not working on your relationship. The Magic Moments love link helps you embrace a mindfulness-based existence.

Doing magic moments for your partner will leave you feeling good. Love is felt when given and not just when received, and magic moments create many benefits to your self-esteem and emotional intelligence. Practise patience and goodwill by committing to magic moments. Don't wait for your partner to change. Only after a few months of enacting magic moments on a regular basis should you judge the impact of them on your relationship.

It is okay to set the bar low. Start by committing to three magic moments a week. Put a reminder in your calendar. If you want to do more than three, go for it. If you're short on ideas, download the My Love Your Love app. You'll receive new challenges every couple of days and, after a few weeks, you'll find your groove.

Now you know small magic moments matter most, leading to more joy in your relationship. In the next chapter, we cover the art and importance of empathic listening, outlining how you and your partner can empathically validate each other. Our experience shows even couples who have great emotional intelligence struggle to validate each other. You can discover why this happens and how to step out of the point-scoring contest that always leads to two losers. By learning the Feeling the Story love link, you will solve more than 50 per cent of your problems without ever needing a solution.

Link four
Feeling the Story

If you've ever been to couples therapy, you were likely taught a listening exercise. Perhaps it was the speaker–listener technique, active listening or empathic listening. Couples therapy offers plenty of listening exercises because listening is essential for good communication. It allows for understanding and empathy. Without listening, communication falls down.

Our concept of 'feeling the story' is similar but different to other listening exercises. The Feeling the Story love link gets to the essence of this fundamental relationship concept and tool. There is a storyteller (speaker) and a listener. On a simple level, feeling the story demonstrates the two important components to the concept – the story and the feelings of the storyteller. The listener must pay attention to both of these. They will 'feel the story' of the storyteller. In any interaction with your partner, two stories are always at play. Your story is your experience, and is exclusive to you. Your story is a narrative, not a fact-reporting mission. As the speaker in an interaction, you are communicating your story. As the listener in an interaction with your partner, you won't just listen to your partner's story, but you will also feel it, sense it, understand it, empathise with it and, finally, report it back. This makes our feeling the story concept go beyond simple communication to be an exercise of attunement, validation and connection.

In this chapter, we explain the necessity of attunement and validation. We demonstrate how feeling the story can help resolve and stave off many future conflicts, without focusing on solutions. We outline the importance of keeping an open mind and committing to this exercise with what we call willingness. This helps maximise the benefits of feeling the story. Finally, we teach you, step by step, our simple yet powerful skill – which will change your relationship forever.

Understanding attunement and validation

Humans need to feel understood, seen and heard. On a basic level, they need attunement and validation. We are not the only ones who believe this. Many psychological theories champion this concept – in particular, schema therapy and attachment theory.

Schema therapy is a type of therapy that helps people change unhelpful patterns of thinking and behaviour developed in childhood for healthier and more positive ways of living. Developed by Jeffrey Young, schema therapy posits that individuals have core emotional needs, including the need for empathy, understanding and validation. Schema therapy emphasises that when these needs are not met during childhood, individuals can develop maladaptive 'schemas' or deeply ingrained beliefs about themselves and others, as well as coping strategies that can lead to emotional distress and psychological issues. Schema therapy underscores the importance of fulfilling basic human needs in order to promote emotional wellbeing and mental health.

Another psychological theory, attachment theory, supports our premise that to feel understood, seen and heard is a basic human need. As covered in chapter 2, attachment theory explores how early relationships with caregivers influence an individual's emotional bonds and interpersonal connections throughout their life. Attachment theory posits that humans have an innate and fundamental need for emotional bonds and secure attachments with others. Feeling understood, seen and heard by attachment figures, typically caregivers, is a critical component of these secure attachments. When caregivers respond sensitively to a child's needs, it fosters a sense of being valued, which forms the foundation for healthy emotional development. This theory highlights that the need to feel understood, seen and heard is essential for the establishment of secure and emotionally fulfilling relationships. This, in turn, contributes to overall wellbeing and mental health throughout your life.

Your relationship is no exception – and the two key processes you need to understand here are attunement and validation.

Attuning to your partner

Attunement is the ability to connect with and understand another person's emotions, thoughts and needs. Attuning to your partner's experience involves being sensitive and responsive to their cues, both verbal and non-verbal, and adjusting your actions and responses accordingly to create a deeper and more meaningful connection. You need to prioritise this in your relationship.

You might be thinking, *Why do I need to attune to my partner's illogical feelings?* Because emotional reactions hold meaning. Emotions that seem out of place or illogical in certain situations all hold meaning, even if that meaning is hidden. Attuning to this emotion holds the key to resolving issues within your relationship. If you (or your partner) become defensive because 'your emotion is illogical', the opportunity to resolve the emotion/issue is lost.

As an example of this, let's consider Juan, a 35-year-old pilot, and his wife, Julie, who works in finance. When this couple came to therapy, Juan stated that he and Julie had a great relationship except for when he was leaving the home to fly. Juan's schedule meant that he was often home for a week and then away for five days. Juan reported that in the mornings before he left for work, Julie would start at him about chores and his lack of responsibility. This angered Juan and meant he was always going off to work in a bad mood. Juan stated that Julie's emotional response was crazy and made no sense. And perhaps, in the context of the situation, it didn't. Julie knew he was a pilot and his work routine had been stable for several years.

When we worked together to understand Julie's emotions, however, we became aware of the story behind the emotion. Julie had been feeling more vulnerable since the death of her mother, with whom she had been very close. She felt more alone with Juan away and had been struggling to express this. This revelation meant that Juan was less defensive to Julie's 'illogical emotions'. If they arose, he was able to offer care and comfort because he was aware of the meaning behind them. Needless to say, Julie was able to better understand her own emotions because they were not ignored. Julie stopped getting angry when Juan left and instead was able to ask for care when she needed it.

Even if emotions seem illogical, they hold a significant meaning and are worthy of exploration. In the spirit of the eight love links, both partners should be open to this for themselves and each other.

Adding in validation

Validation refers to the act of acknowledging, accepting and affirming the thoughts, feelings and experiences of your partner. You're not necessarily liking or approving of such experiences. Validation involves actively listening, showing empathy and demonstrating understanding without judgement or criticism. Validation communicates that you respect and care about your partner's emotional state. Their feelings are important and legitimate, even if you can't see the logic in them or share those feelings.

People need validation to move on from past hurts. It is inevitable that you and your partner will be hurt in your relationship.

Attunement and validation allows you to process these hurts and offer a way to reconnect back to one another.

Prioritising both attunement and validation can enhance your emotional wellbeing, strengthen communication, promote trust and intimacy and contribute to your overall relationship satisfaction. They are the fundamental building blocks of nurturing and maintaining healthy, fulfilling relationships.

Reducing your focus on solutions

We believe validation and attunement are more powerful than solutions. Jumping to solutions is common during tension in your relationship, or even when your partner is expressing their feelings. Perhaps your partner does the same. Likely, you don't want your partner to feel bad anymore. You see their suffering and you want to take it away by offering a solution. Your aim is often unconsciously to remove your discomfort of seeing them in distress.

If you have been the person suffering and being offered solutions, however, you will likely know it isn't always helpful – because solutions do not validate suffering. Instead, being offered solutions can make you feel worse. They can leave you feeling invisible, dismissed, unheard or misunderstood. Solutions can come across as judgmental, implying your feelings are wrong or you need to fix your emotions. Solutions are also the easy part. While they can be helpful, they need to be invited or have the right timing. Once you feel understood and validated, you will find you either do not need to hear a solution or are ready to discuss options.

In this chapter, we outline how to attune to and validate your partner using the Feeling the Story love link. Feeling the story involves not only hearing the words your partner is saying, but also trying to understand their emotions, perspective and underlying needs. Feeling the story is hard. It requires vulnerability for both the storyteller and the listener. As the storyteller, you need to acknowledge your own feelings. You have to take ownership of those feelings. As the listener, you are required to put your own story and feelings aside, which is challenging. You can't truly hear your partner if you are holding tightly to your own story.

Learning how to validate and attune to your partner can help improve your emotional intelligence – that is, your ability to recognise, understand, manage and effectively navigate your own emotions and those of others. Emotional intelligence enhances interpersonal relationships, communication and self-awareness. It also contributes to better decision-making and overall wellbeing.

Here is an example of how powerful feeling the story can be, demonstrated by Helen in a session with Fiona and Jeff.

Feeling the story for past hurts

In therapy, Fiona and Jeff reported they felt very stressed and disconnected in their relationship. As therapy went on, it became evident that Fiona was struggling with her mother-in-law. She described being made to feel childish by her mother-in-law whenever she raised any objections with her. She also felt unsupported by Jeff and that Jeff was not standing up for her.

An unprocessed historical hurt kept coming up in session for Fiona, which led to heated conflict. Two years prior, Fiona and Jeff had planned a quiet weekend away in the Blue Mountains. They were both excited about the trip and saw this as providing much-needed time to unwind and reconnect.

Jeff's mother found out about their trip via Jeff's sister – and then invited herself along, telling Jeff how lonely she had been since the death of her husband three years earlier. Jeff felt guilty and without consulting Fiona, complied with his mother, allowing her to join the couple.

As you can imagine, Fiona was furious. She felt her mother-in-law had hijacked their much-needed weekend away and Jeff had let it happen. Jeff and Fiona argued about this before the weekend away and it continued to come up in conversation for the next two years.

Fiona just couldn't let it go, and kept hounding Jeff for answers. 'Why would you invite your mother along?' 'Did you want her there?' 'Did you not think of me?' 'Why would you choose her over me?'

There was a sense that if she could just get the right answers, her frustration and hurt would dissolve. Jeff was prone to feeling guilty and became frustrated and avoidant when Fiona pressed him with questions. He would try to change the subject. When that didn't work, he would plead for her to get over it. And, eventually, he just sat there in silence while Fiona questioned him. He didn't know what to say. Nothing he said or didn't say seemed to satisfy Fiona.

More questions and answers were not the solution. The real issue was that Fiona never felt attuned to and validated. She never felt understood and, therefore, the hurt was never processed. Although she was chasing answers, she was actually seeking validation. This topic had become a wedge in their relationship. The path to reconciliation was Fiona being understood and validated.

In therapy, I taught Fiona and Jeff feeling the story and, with my assistance, they practised the exercise in session. I also set them homework to do feeling the story repeatedly on this same incident. Jeff worked hard at feeling Fiona's story over and over again. He finally knew what he needed to say. Once her story was retold in his words and he could identify her feelings in a heartfelt manner, they were able to move forward. With practice, Jeff nailed the attunement.

Suddenly the weight of the topic was able to lift. The need for answers to Fiona's questions disappeared. They stopped squabbling about what had happened or should have happened. Having felt understood, Fiona felt more secure in the relationship because she believed Jeff understood her experience and could be trusted in the future.

I could have easily focused therapy on Jeff having more boundaries with his mother, and on Fiona being more mindful and less critical of Jeff. And that wouldn't have been a terrible approach. But it wouldn't have got to the core of what this couple really needed – connection via attunement and validation. They needed this before boundaries could be set or other solutions sought.

The point of Fiona and Jeff's story is that past hurts will keep coming up if they're left unresolved. These past hurts must be attended to with attunement and validation. To move forward, you don't need more solutions, you need attunement and validation. Sometimes, depending on the size of the wound, this might need to happen multiple times.

The power of listening and being heard

As couples therapists, we see partners locked in conflict regularly. Even so, they will often claim to be great listeners of their partners, telling us something along the lines of, 'But I do listen to them; that's not the problem'. These same people think feeling the story is a big waste of time, yet they remain locked in battles with their partner. These couples are missing the vital ingredients of attunement and validation.

These are everyday people, just like you and us. Some may not be terrible at listening and validating. But when it comes to conflict, and particularly with their partner, they are not good at it. And we hate to break it to you, but most people aren't. Most couples are so focused on their own story and experience and ensuring that gets put into the conversation that they don't have the space to invest in listening and understanding their partner's experience. We've seen very little exception to this.

When we facilitate the feeling the story skill in couples therapy, we see partners soften right before our eyes. Afterwards, they report feeling understood and more connected with one another. We see couples start feeling the story from opposite ends of the couch, with their faces and bodies turned away from one another. After the exercise, these same couples will be turned toward each other, and holding hands or sharing a hug. This is beautiful to watch and is what makes us love our job.

As psychologists, we understand that it is easy to understand feeling the story but harder to put it into practice. It can be uncomfortable and difficult to execute. However, we also know it is a fundamental skill in couples therapy that needs to be acquired. It never gets skipped – sometimes to the frustration of our couples. Typically, the harder it is for couples to accept that feeling the story is important, the more they are not validating each other in their relationship. And despite the fact that we are armed with this knowledge, we will admit we are not the best at implementing it all the time in our own relationship. When in conflict, we also struggle with empathic attunement. In our relationship, we've found ourselves at loggerheads – unable to move forward until one of us takes the brave step and suggests, 'Hey, maybe we should use feeling the story here'. Once we come together and do feeling the story, everything changes for the better. It takes effort. It's hard. But it works. So it's worth the investment.

When you learn to give love and care through feeling the story, you can resolve many of your conflicts. Conflicts go unresolved because you and your partner feel misunderstood by one another – not because a solution needs to be reached. When you don't feel understood, you won't be able to move on from conflict cycles, and so conflict continues. Instead of processing and reconciliation, you'll use dysfunctional methods to move on. You might shove the issue under the carpet or pretend it never happened. You might emotionally detach from your hurt because every time you bring it up you feel like you're not understood. You may deny your own responsibility in the issue and keep pushing it away. All of these options breed resentment and disconnection in your relationship.

Understanding yourself to meet your needs

If you are not good at this particular skill of empathetic attunement, you were likely never taught how to do it or your needs for validation and attunement weren't met. To empathically feel the story and experience of your partner, you are required to put aside your own needs and emotions temporarily. This allows you to focus on understanding the experience of your partner. If you grew up in an environment where your emotional needs for validation and attunement were not consistently met, you may be constantly still trying to get these needs met. Consequently, shifting your focus to understand your partner's perspective and needs can be challenging.

Schema therapy and attachment theory help us to understand this. As introduced earlier in this chapter, schema therapy explains if your early childhood needs for validation are not met, you will develop maladaptive and ingrained emotional and cognitive patterns. These unhelpful patterns influence the way you see the world, other people and yourself. This, in turn, affects your capacity to form healthy relationships. This can result in self-esteem issues around how you value and feel about yourself, and can also lead to a persistent desire for external validation. You might seek out validation because you have a hole for attunement that was never filled.

Attachment theory suggests if your early childhood need for validation isn't met, you will develop insecure attachment styles such as anxious or avoidant attachment styles. This can lead to difficulties in forming close relationships because your anxiety or avoidance overrides a healthy connection. You may also have a persistent fear of rejection or abandonment that interferes with genuine relationships.

Yearning for validation and emotional security may guide your choices and behaviours in adult relationships, and can result in negative relationship dynamics. You may find yourself in a codependent relationship in which you are overly reliant on one another for a sense of identity, self-worth and emotional wellbeing. The constant need for validation and emotional security can lead to heightened levels of insecurity, which can manifest as jealousy, possessiveness and a fear of abandonment – all of which can strain the relationship. You may stay in unhealthy relationships simply to avoid being alone or to maintain a sense of security, resulting in you tolerating mistreatment or neglect.

Clearly, this need for validation and attunement has a huge impact on how you function and feel secure in your adult life and in your adult relationships. Feeling the story is your key to getting that need met in a healthy way. Later in this chapter, we give you a breakdown of how to do feeling the story in an easy to understand and stepped approach. Hang in there.

Validation breeds validation

Not feeling understood by your partner is the biggest cause of feeling dissatisfied in relationships, leading to loneliness and disconnection. No matter what the issue is or what you are arguing about in your relationship, if you feel like your partner understands and can attune to your point of view and feelings, you will feel better and more connected.

What you are arguing about is not the problem. You may think the content of the conflict is what matters most and if you could just unpack the content, everything would be better. But the real problem is a lack of understanding of each other. This is a massive shift. Attunement and validation are the ingredients that defuse arguments and challenge disconnection.

You might be thinking, *How can I empathically listen to my partner if they aren't understanding me?* If you have unmet needs for validation and attunement from your childhood, you may struggle to focus on your partner. Your unmet needs for attunement and validation may be gaping holes that make it hard to see anyone else's pain. This is tough. But the good news is you can learn to empathically listen, no matter how much you missed in childhood. Feeling the story is a skill that can be taught and learned. And by learning to do this, you increase the likelihood of your partner meeting your needs for attunement and validation. Why? Remember – validation breeds validation. That's the whole point of why your childhood matters. If you were validated as a child, you'll find it easier to validate others. If you validate and attune to your partner, it will meet their need for understanding and attunement and so they will be better equipped to do the same for you. This is a win–win.

We will give you a step-by-step guide to feeling the story later in this chapter but, before we do, keep in mind that feeling the story needs to go both ways. If you or your partner is being aggressive, domineering, shut off or submissive, you won't be able to complete the exercise of feeling the story. You won't be able to feel their story and they won't be able to feel your story, because emotions and mind states are getting in the way. If this is the case, you will need to take a different approach.

Take these steps to acknowledge the barrier and set a boundary:

1. *Acknowledge the behaviour that is getting in the way of you or your partner feeling the story:* For example, 'I'm noticing you seem cut off right now.'

2. *Express your desire to understand them:* For example, 'I can imagine there's something going on for you deep down and I'd like to understand.'

3. *Set a limit:* For example, 'I am unable to understand what's going on for you while you are so cut off from me.'

4. *Invite connection later:* For example, 'When you're ready to be open and vulnerable with me, I'd like to understand what's going on for you.'

We discuss boundary setting in more detail in chapter 5.

 **TIME FOR ACTION**

Over the coming days, reflect on how well you listen. Make a mental note or a literal one in your phone every time you stop listening. This might be wanting to jump in with a solution, or getting your next point lined up while the other person is still speaking. Reflect on how well others attune to you. When you are talking about an experience, do others jump in with solutions or their own experiences without understanding yours first? Do they talk over you or argue with what you are saying?

This is an observational exercise and you don't have to change anything here. Try to stay open and non-judgemental when doing this exercise. All humans are pretty terrible at listening, especially when things are running hot or tension exists in the interaction. It's not that you don't care. You are just not practised at it.

Stubbornness is a big barrier to feeling the story. If you don't feel validated and understood, you won't want to give that to your partner. Your own hurts might have piled up and you've lost all empathy for your partner. That's understandable. And you are not alone. Keep reading. It is challenging to put your own story and experience to one side to understand your partner. But the cost is too great if you don't try.

Willingness is the key

Imagine you are attending a party. Before you even arrive, you are tired and grumpy. You'd struggled to sleep the night before due to the neighbour's dog's relentless barking. This was followed by a frustrating day at work, in which it felt like you couldn't get anything ticked off your never-ending to-do list. As you trudge into the vibrant, pulsating atmosphere of the party, the dull throb in your temples seems to match the bass reverberating through the room. The flickering fairy lights mock your weary eyes. You press on. You'd promised your friend that you'd attend their event.

Dragging your feet across the floor, you exchange half-hearted pleasantries with friends, your words a feeble attempt to mask your underlying exhaustion. The vibrant hues of the room seem to mock your lacklustre mood, and you find yourself daydreaming about the warmth of your living room and the comforting glow of the TV.

As you navigate through the sea of animated faces, you can't help but yearn for the familiar embrace of your couch and the enticing allure of pyjamas and a cosy blanket.

It's clear you are not enjoying the party and would prefer to be elsewhere. But is the party the problem here?

No. The problem is you're not fully participating in the party. You've chosen to turn up to the party, but you are there only in the physical form.

While you might have a good reason not to participate in the party, you still can't blame the party for your unhappiness. Rather, it is the attitude you bring to the party that makes it a great party or not. The party itself isn't the problem. Likewise, the party itself isn't the solution either.

This is the same for feeling the story. You might have a good reason for not participating fully in feeling the story. But unless you embody an attitude of willingness to engage in the exercise, it will not work. You will be simply ticking boxes. Being willing is necessary to give and receive validation.

Willingness versus wilfulness

Willingness refers to a state of being open, cooperative and ready to do something with a positive and cooperative attitude. It implies a readiness to accept and work towards a goal or a task.

On the other hand, wilfulness denotes a stubborn or obstinate determination to pursue your own desires or wishes, without regard for the consequences to self or others. Being wilful is rejecting, rather than accepting, the moment. Wilfulness is resisting the consideration of alternatives or cooperating with others.

Your level of willingness versus wilfulness predicts the current state and future of your relationship. High levels of willingness means you will be better able to work as a team and come back together, even after disagreements. Increased willingness results in higher levels of empathy for one another. The more wilful you are, on the other hand, the more stuck on your own opinions, positions, desires and needs you will be. The greater your wilfulness, the more conflict, misunderstanding and anger in your relationship.

Therefore, higher levels of willingness in your relationship mean you will have a more positive view of one another, and a sense of teamwork and connection. Likewise, high wilfulness in your relationship will result in more conflict and disconnection.

Some of the positive rewards you can experience by being willing in your relationship include:

- *Improved communication:* Willingness fosters open and honest communication, making it easier to discuss issues and resolve conflicts effectively. You'll have more emotional connection and increased emotional intimacy and trust. You and your partner will feel heard and supported when both are willing to understand each other's perspectives.

- *Increased flexibility and adaptability:* Willingness to compromise and adapt promotes relationship flexibility, reducing rigidity and enhancing the ability to navigate changes and challenges together.

- *Increased conflict resolution:* Willingness to work through disagreements constructively can lead to quicker and more peaceful conflict resolution, preventing longstanding grudges.

- *Mutual growth:* Both you and your partner can learn and grow together when you are willing to support each other's personal development and aspirations.

- *Strengthened bonds:* Overall, willingness contributes to a stronger bond, greater satisfaction, and a more harmonious and fulfilling relationship.

Helen's following example from couples therapy demonstrates the essential role of willingness versus wilfulness in the success of feeling the story.

Willingness to participate is required

I was seeing Matt and Evelyn, a particularly challenging couple. (A reminder that all names have been changed for this book.) They had been together for many years with both claiming many hurts and emotional wounds suffered at the hands of each other. As with all my couples, I taught Matt and Evelyn feeling the story; however, it quickly became evident that something was amiss.

Evelyn would robotically repeat Matt's story and feelings with a blank look on her face. She followed the steps of feeling the story but she did not embody the spirit of the exercise – to willingly participate. This implies openness, kindness and curiosity. Remember – the listener must *feel* their partner's story. This means they must try to see and understand the experience from their partner's perspective. This builds empathy.

Unfortunately, in that moment Evelyn held tightly her own perspective and wounds, while only partially participating in the exercise. As a result, Matt did not feel validated and understood. And Evelyn was unable to experience compassion and understanding towards Matt and his experience.

This example demonstrates that feeling the story does not work unless you embody the concept of willingness. Validation and attunement cannot exist without willingness. Feeling the story wasn't the problem for this couple. It was that willingness was missing from the exercise on Evelyn's part.

Many of our clients tell us, 'I'm willing, but my partner isn't, so it's not going to work'. They are right. If your partner is being wilful, feeling the story is not going to work. But don't give up. Firstly, try to talk to them about their wilfulness. Validate how hard it is to be willing when hurt and upset. Invest in some magic moments (refer to the previous chapter) first to soften the mood and demonstrate your willingness to engage in a positive way in your relationship.

 **TIME FOR ACTION**

Try this experiential exercise to identify your own willingness or wilfulness:

1. Find a quiet spot and close your eyes.

2. Take a few breaths.

3. Bring to mind a current conflict or disagreement with your partner. It doesn't need to be big.

4. Tune into your body and notice any sensations or tension. Check out your jaw, shoulders, chest, stomach and hands. Be curious, but don't judge any of these sensations.

5. In your mind's eye, imagine drawing a circle around where this tension – this wilfulness – sits in your body.

6. Focus on the resistance you are feeling and ask yourself, 'How open am I right now to hear my partner's perspective without judgement or criticism?'

7. Then ask yourself, 'How open am I to listen to my partner's perspective without interrupting or becoming defensive?'

8. Take a few deep breaths and imagine the breath travelling through the circle of wilful sensation in your body. On the out breath, imagine you are exhaling the wilfulness.

9. Give this wilfulness a colour, breathe into it and make room for it.

10. On the out breath, see if you can soften the edges of the circle and the tension in your body.

11. Spend a few moments here, breathing in and making room for wilfulness, but also letting it go a little. Notice what that's like.

Willingness requires acceptance and vulnerability

In the Feeling the Story love link, willingness is required by both the storyteller and the listener. Conversely, wilfulness from either party will derail feeling the story. It may seem obvious that the listener must be willing. They are the one attuning to your story and feelings. But the storyteller also needs to be willing. When your partner is feeling your story, you must be open to accepting their validation and attunement. Accepting your partner's validation is an act of love, just as validating your partner's experience is.

By accepting your partner's validation you may feel like you are giving something up, or letting your partner off the hook. Notice this but try to let go and be open to their care. The only thing you are giving up is wilfulness. You can wilfully refuse your partner's attempts to be kind and attune to you. But this doesn't get you or your relationship anywhere. Unfortunately, the case of Evelyn and Matt demonstrates this. Evelyn's persistent wilfulness, even in the face of attempts to understand and validate her experience, coupled with boundaries around her disruptive behaviour, meant that Helen had to end therapy with this couple. This is an example of the essential role willingness plays both in feeling the story, couples therapy and your relationship as a whole.

Willingness also requires vulnerability. Being willing might mean you have to own mistakes or be open to your partner's perspective. This can be uncomfortable and invite feelings of shame. Your ego and pride can also get in the way of being willing. You may have a desire to be right or maintain your pride no matter what. This can hinder your willingness to see your partner's viewpoint, understand their feelings or accept their validation.

Self-reflection during this process is key. Examine what might be behind your struggle with willingness. Identify any past experiences or personal beliefs that might be influencing your willingness or wilfulness.

Remember the importance of the relationship as a whole. Prioritise its wellbeing over winning an argument. A strong, healthy partnership requires compromise and a willingness to work together.

Feeling the story step-by-step

We have created a two-step process to empathically attune to your partner during the Feeling the Story love link. Feeling the story is a crucial skill that forms a solid base for all communication in your relationship. It is the first step to increasing your own emotional intelligence and connection with others more generally.

The aim of feeling the story is to genuinely understand your partner's experience and emotions – and for your partner to understand yours. This practice can lead to increased feelings of validation and connection for both of you.

The focus here is on understanding and empathy, not conflict resolution. You also need to embrace the concept that emotions don't have to be logical to be valid and real.

Feeling the story in two basic steps

Feeling the story involves two basic steps, and both you and your partner must complete these two steps. So you must feel your partner's story and then they must feel your story. To do this, you and your partner need to agree on an issue to practise feeling the story on. Each of you will tell your own story about this issue.

Here are the two steps for the listener:

1. *Listen to the story and then retell it:* You need to listen to your partner's narrative with total attention and without interrupting. Your task is to then retell the story you have heard with as much detail as possible. Imagine yourself as a reporter verifying the story of an eyewitness. Avoid offering opinions, solutions, counterarguments or disagreements because these can undermine validation. Work on accepting your partner's story as it may be different from yours. Being right doesn't resolve relationship issues. When feeding back the story to your partner, you could start with something like, 'I can hear that ...' or 'You were ...' or

'So what you experienced was ...' Check if you have captured their entire story with something like, 'Please let me know if I have missed any part of your story.' Your partner can clarify any parts of the story you have missed, and you then need to tell that part of the story back to them.

2. *Uncover the feelings:* Identify the feelings your partner may have been experiencing, and then feed these feelings back to your partner. Not everyone expresses their feelings when telling their side of the story, so you may have to guess how your partner is feeling. It's okay if you don't get their feelings correct. It is more important you try. When feeding back your partner's feelings, you could start with something like, 'It sounds like you were feeling ...', 'You were feeling ...', 'I'm guessing you were feeling ...' or 'I'm thinking you were feeling ...' Don't forget to check in with your partner if your feedback is correct, using something like, 'Please let me know if that's not correct or I've missed some feelings.' Your partner can clarify any feelings you might have missed. Again, you then need to feed those particular feelings back to them.

Even if you don't believe or understand your partner's feelings, your job is to hear them without criticism, judgement or argument. Feelings are real and they matter, even if they're not fully understood or agreed on. Be open to correction and feedback from your partner for both the story and the feelings part of this exercise.

Feelings can be hard to identify – for both the storyteller and the listener. The table opposite provides a list of common feelings, and the layered feelings within them, that you and your partner can keep in mind when feeling the story.

Inevitably, some of the story you feed back won't be quite accurate. This is normal. Your partner can restate that particular part of their story, and you then need to feed that part back to them again. You will need to restate the story or feelings as many times as necessary to accurately represent your partner's experience.

Common feelings

Angry	Sad	Disconnected	Hurt	Fear
Agitated	Dejected	Aloof	Attacked	Abandoned
Annoyed	Dismayed	Detached	Criticised	Afraid
Bitter	Down	Distant	Crushed	Anxious
Enraged	Forlorn	Empty	Disappointed	Apprehensive
Furious	Hopeless	Indifferent	Discouraged	Insecure
Grumpy	Lonely	Invisible	Disrespected	Nervous
Hateful	Low	Isolated	Helpless	Panicked
Hostile	Miserable	Shut-down	Inadequate	Scared
Impatient	Negative	Unseen	Inferior	Terrified
Indignant	Overwhelmed	Unvalued	Let down	Threatened
Irritated		Withdrawn	Offended	Worried
Outraged			Rejected	
Resentful			Uncared for	
Scornful			Unimportant	
Stubborn				

Embarrassed/ shame	Guilt	Unsettled	Happy	Interested
Ashamed	Guilty	Apprehensive	Cheerful	Curious
Humiliated	Regretful	Confused	Elated	Engrossed
Mortified	Remorseful	Grouchy	Euphoric	Fascinated
Ostracised	Sorry	Perplexed	Gleeful	Focused
Put down		Pessimistic	Joyful	Intrigued
Self-conscious		Sceptical	Playful	
Undermined		Tormented		
Weak		Uncertain		
Worthless		Unsure		

Open	Peaceful	Shocked	Disgusted	Suspicious
Compassionate	Accepting	Alarmed	Appalled	Cautious
Connected	At ease	Shaken	Repulsed	Distrustful
Empathic	Calm	Stunned		Jealous
Free	Content			Paranoid
Receptive	Relaxed			
Welcoming	Serene			

General rules for feeling the story

Here are some general rules to consider when feeling the story:

- Listen.
- Do not offer opinions or solutions.
- Do not offer counterarguments.
- Do not criticise.
- Do not judge.
- Do not disagree.
- Give up the need to be right.
- Do not question the facts.
- Let the other person speak.
- Do not interrupt or speak over your partner.
- Accept feelings are valid because they're feelings.
- Manage distractions when feeling the story – put phones away, turn off the TV, and find a place where you can hear.

When you are the storyteller (speaker), you also have a few things to keep in mind. When you are telling your version of events, focus on expressing yourself using 'I' statements. Try to stick to what you see as the facts and your feelings around those. Resist accusatory statements and focus more on how your partner's behaviours left you feeling. Be open to accepting your partner's attempts at validation and attunement. This might be new for your partner, so it's important to be open, willing and encouraging.

Feeling the story must be completed by both partners. If you are finding that you are always feeling your partner's story but they aren't returning it (or vice versa), then you have a problem. This means that your relationship is out of balance. Feeling the story isn't about tit for tat, but empathy has to go both ways. Otherwise, you will find yourself in a relationship trap or conflict dance that will cause problems in your relationship. (We cover this in more detail in the next chapter.)

But even on a simple level, it's obvious that if only one partner is providing empathy and understanding in the relationship, the other one will eventually grow resentful and feel hurt at never being seen in the partnership.

Feeling the story is hard. You probably haven't been taught how to empathically attune and respond to others. So be kind and patient as you learn this skill. It will have a profoundly positive impact on your personal and professional life. The ability to empathically attune will promote better understanding, stronger relationships and improved problem solving.

Accepting the power of feeling the story

To understand why the Feeling the Story love link is so powerful, let's break it up into its two components – feelings and stories.

Repeating one's story back to them has a validating and de-escalating potential. This was demonstrated in a 2012 study by Maria Seehausen and colleagues. They explored the impact of empathic paraphrasing (recounting a story with validation) as a means of regulating negative emotions during social conflicts. They found when interviewers paraphrased participants' descriptions of conflicts, participants reported feeling less negative and their voices exhibited reduced intensity. Physiological measurements indicated increased autonomic arousal during paraphrasing, while simultaneously influencing their emotional state towards feeling better. This suggests an external emotion regulation technique may help transform and resolve social conflicts by enhancing emotional processing.

While the validation of emotions is associated with reductions in negative emotions, invalidation is associated with escalation of negative emotions. This has been studied time and time again, and particularly by Marsha Linehan in her work within dialectical behaviour therapy (DBT). Marsha Linehan is an American psychologist and the creator of this widely used therapeutic approach for individuals with borderline personality disorder. Her studies show when emotions are validated, distress is reduced, and when emotions are invalidated, distress or negative emotions increase.

These studies help explain that the Feeling the Story love link is so powerful because it asks you to pay attention and attune to both story and feelings. By doing this, the storyteller will eventually feel more at ease and experience more positive feelings and be less drawn to conflict.

A common dispute of feeling the story is this exercise is too simple and contrived and so it won't work. Feeling the story is a simple exercise but it's not easy. You will struggle with feeling the story in the beginning because it is difficult to remember someone else's stories and feelings and accurately reflect them back. Your full attention and a decent memory are needed to sit, focus, listen and then feed the story and feelings back.

Initially feeling the story will also feel a little strange and perhaps even forced. You probably aren't used to feeding back to your partner their experience. But the more you practise, the easier it will be and the less clunky it will feel. Persist, because the rewards are huge.

In our clinical practice with couples, we teach feeling the story to every couple who comes through the door. It is the essential underlying skill needed for all strategies to come.

Another concern we hear is, 'If we do feeling the story on every bump in our relationship, we will take forever to get anywhere. Should we really use it every time?' You do need to use it during every conflict and, yes, it will take forever in the beginning. We even encourage using feeling the story on non-conflictual topics when you're communicating with your partner about your own experiences (not relationship focused). This could be when your partner comes home, for example, and starts venting about their work. It's got nothing to do with the relationship perhaps, but it is a great opportunity for you to practise feeling the story and attuning to your partner. The more practice you do, the easier the process will be to use when tensions are running high.

Feeling the story is worth the time and effort. Once you've got the hang of it, it will reduce the amount of time you are in conflict or disagreement with your partner. Conversations with your partner will become more meaningful and succinct because you are getting straight to what you each need – attunement and validation. The hard work you put in now to get good at feeling the story will pay off with rewards and an easier time later.

The only exception to feeling the story is if your partner is being aggressive, which is pretty much an exception to most of our skills in this book. We do not accept aggression or violence in relationships. You must always protect yourself if you are at risk. Instead of using feeling the story when someone is being violent or aggressive, set boundaries and remove yourself from the situation immediately.

 **TIME FOR ACTION**

Tell your partner about the task of feeling the story. Explain it to them. You learn further through explaining a process to someone else. Share this chapter with them. Then practise on your partner. Afterwards, ask your partner to practise feeling the story on you.

When you are the listener, allow your partner to talk about something in their life – preferably something not related to the relationship at first. They could talk about their day at work, their experience at a social event, even a disagreement with a friend or family member. Try out the two steps of feeling the story.

Listen and put aside any of your interpretations, judgements or viewpoints. Hear what they're saying and feed the story back to them. You might say, 'It sounds like you had a busy day at work today. You first had three meetings in the morning and your boss was grumpy. Then you didn't have time for lunch because you had two deadlines to meet this afternoon.' Report back the story and check if you got it right. 'Have I got your story right? Am I missing anything from your story?'

Then do the second step of identifying their feelings. For example, 'It sounds like it's been stressful today. You felt kind of pressured in those meetings', 'You were anxious to meet the deadlines in the afternoon' and so on. Check if the feelings you feedback were accurate – 'Have I got your feelings right? Did I miss any of your feelings?' Allow your partner to give you feedback. When they give you feedback, go back and repeat it. 'I didn't get that quite right. You were angry at your boss for being so aggressive in those meetings.'

If needed, look back at the list of feelings provided earlier in this chapter. You can use this list as both the storyteller and the listener. Remember the key phrases to start: 'It sounds like ...', 'What I'm hearing is ...', 'You are feeling ...' Being willing to try is the key ingredient. Good luck.

Finding the time for feeling the story

Couples often state time is a barrier to feeling the story. No doubt you have a busy schedule and numerous external demands on your time and attention, and this may limit the time and energy available to you to practise feeling the story. Time constraints will always be a barrier for any of the strategies in this book. It's a tricky problem when you have a full life, and we explore time and relationship investment in detail in chapter 6.

For now, it is important to understand that to get used to the process of feeling the story, you'll need to carve out time to practise. Otherwise, you will never get good at this skill. And this is one of the most important skills you need for your relationship. Your relationship will thank you if you make a little bit of time most days to use feeling the story with your partner. This could be over dinner or while going for a walk together – wherever you are able to speak to one another about your lives. Feeling the story is the first step to feeling connected with your partner so it is worth it.

Before we finish the Feeling the Story love link, let's revisit the couple Juan the pilot and Julie who works in finance from earlier in this chapter. If we were a fly on the wall and watched them argue before they learnt the feeling the story skill, what would we have seen? Perhaps Julie would bring up an issue about their renovation (for example) with a hint of frustration on the morning Juan was due to fly out for five days. Juan would quickly become defensive and they would inevitably end up yelling at each other. The conflict would then shift to both Juan and Julie putting their respective walls up. They would separate without goodbyes, both upset for several days before reconnecting by phone thousands of kilometres away from each other.

When we conducted feeling the story in session, the following stories and emotions emerged:

- *Julie's story:* Julie had been feeling vulnerable since the death of her mother. Julie and her mother were very close. She would have dinner with her mother every time Juan was away and they would talk on the phone most days. Julie was able to deal with the grief better when Juan was around. She felt safe and held by their relationship. When he was away she felt more anxious and alone. She wanted to talk more about this with Juan but was worried about burdening him and did not want him to worry about her, especially when piloting a plane. When Juan was away for work she felt his absence and had stronger feelings of grief. Every time they argued, Julie felt guilty and promised herself she wouldn't get frustrated the next time. Julie had hoped to spend quality time with Juan the day before he left to ease some of the loneliness and grief. However, Juan had been going off to play squash most evenings more and more in recent times. Julie felt neglected but did not want to seem controlling and, therefore, did not raise it with Juan. Julie loved Juan and was struggling with the fact that she needed more closeness but lately they seemed more and more distant.

- *Julie's emotions:* Julie was suffering from grief following the death of her mother. Julie was feeling vulnerable and less secure in life generally. Julie at times felt neglected and alone in the relationship, and felt frustrated. Julie felt a yearning for closeness and safety.

- *Juan's story:* Juan did not love his job as a pilot the way he used to. The novelty had worn off and he was craving a life with more routine. He felt guilty about having these feelings when he was in such a privileged position. He had been working hard to stay positive and have gratitude for his position. However, he felt Julie was making it much worse. He stated he was starting to feel anxious in the days leading up to his departure. He had noticed that Julie would bring up many issues the hour before he had to leave. They would end up in a big fight and he would go off to work in a bad mood. He was starting to feel resentment toward Julie. He loved her and missed their close relationship with less conflict. He had started to play squash more to deal with stress and to avoid more time together when they might argue. He just could not understand what was going on with Julie but he was tired of it and his patience had gone.

- *Juan's feelings:* Juan was feeling unsettled at work. He had feelings of confusion and guilt that were career related. Juan was experiencing anxiety, and was worried about their next fight. He was feeling resentment toward Julie and was stressed and angry. He was also starting to avoid the relationship. He felt sad about the loss of their close relationship and confused about why it was happening.

Through the feeling the story process, Juan and Julie's conflict resolved and was replaced by care and compassion. This was only possible through both Juan's and Julie's willingness to hear and feel each other's story.

Summing up

In this chapter, you have discovered that the need to be validated and attuned to is a core human need. Without this, you'll struggle in relationships and feel unsatisfied in life. Empathically attuning to one another can stave off and even solve conflicts in your relationship.

You have learned that a fundamental component of getting you and your partner's need for validation and attunement met is willingness. Without this, your relationship will fall down. You have also learned the simple but challenging two-step process of feeling the story to improve your connection.

Stop jumping to solutions in your partner conflicts, disputes or even just when your partner is speaking to you. Stop getting stuck on who's right and who's wrong. There are always two stories to the experience – no-one's right and no-one's wrong. Stop being obstinate in conversations with your partner. Wilfulness doesn't get you anywhere. Start seeing that every niggle, disagreement or conflict has two stories going on at the same time. Start accepting this and take the time to understand each of these stories.

Before anything else, you need to feel your partner's story. You need to attune to and validate their experience. This will increase your connection and set you up for better communication and more effective conflict resolution.

In the next chapter, we delve deeper into the challenging but also growth-enhancing space of conflict in your relationship. You'll learn to go even deeper to understand the two layers of your experience during conflict. This will enhance understanding and reconciliation.

You will identify your typical ways of coping in conflict, which will be self-educating and enhancing. You will learn how to resolve seemingly unresolvable problems, and how to de-escalate conflict and increase positivity in your relationship.

Link five

Conflict Compass

You have arrived at the enormous chapter. This chapter is significantly bigger than the rest, and arguably juicier – but try not to get overwhelmed by its sheer size. Conflict occurs in all relationships and is one of the main reasons couples struggle. Hang in there. We've included lots of exercises and skills in this chapter to help transform your relationship into one that's more cohesive, peaceful and connected.

A good relationship is not without conflict. Rather, a healthy relationship is one that can navigate conflict to deepen understanding and connection. Conflict is a reminder of the presence of two individuals in a relationship. Inevitably, these two individuals will have differences in opinions, needs, desires and priorities. One should not subsume the other. There is room for both. Harnessing conflict for good cherishes this presence of two individuals. You can be your authentic self and allow your partner to be theirs. This approach to conflict means you will learn more about yourself and your partner.

We see conflict as a cycle within the relationship. It occurs between the two partners and is an interaction based on more than what meets the eye. When the cycle is understood, conflict can be caught early on and cut through faster, so you have less stress and more joy in your life.

Although the reduction of conflict results in more peace, some conflict is beneficial because it can lead to growth in your relationship. Therefore, the goal isn't to eliminate conflict altogether but, instead, to understand the conflict cycle and express needs and feelings in a way that promotes care, empathy and cohesion.

We define conflict as a state of disagreement, tension or discord between partners. When we speak about conflict in this chapter, we are talking about the maladaptive conflict patterns that occur in relationships. We are not talking about domestic violence. If you are suffering from domestic violence, we recommend you seek professional help.

Healthy conflict involves open and respectful communication, empathy, compromise, validation of one another, and finding mutually agreeable solutions to the issues at hand. Conflict can be productive when done in this calm and kind way, which you will learn how to do in this chapter.

Conflict can be managed well

There is no single experience of conflict. Conflict can be hot and fiery with lots of words, but it can also be ice-cold, detached and silent. It can also feel like surrender and submission.

Conflict is a relationship killer when it isn't managed well. You must learn how to manage it so your relationship has better flow and you feel more often like a team. When managed constructively, conflict can lead to increased understanding and growth in the relationship. However, when handled poorly, it can lead to increased tension, resentment and the deterioration of the relationship.

World-renowned researchers and clinical psychologists Dr John and Dr Julie Gottman have spent decades researching couples. They are the co-founders of The Gottman Institute, where they outline their Gottman Method Couples Therapy. Through their research, the Gottmans found conflict occurs in most couples. But, more importantly, they found how the couples *turned up* to conflict predicted their relationship satisfaction and the likelihood of relationship success or breakdown. Healthy and happy couples approach conflict in a gentle way. The interaction has low physiological arousal and is focused on listening and understanding. Repair and apologies are present, as is an emphasis on de-escalation and compromise.

While the Gottmans research confirms that conflict is inevitable in your relationship, it also emphasises that couples must learn to manage it in a positive way. Unless you learn a healthy way to approach it, you will remain feeling stuck.

In this chapter, we outline the secrets to managing conflict well. You can gain insight and understand conflict resolution is not just about finding a solution to the problem at hand. Rather, it is the art of expressing and understanding the true source of the conflict. We also cover the unconscious ways you engage in conflict that can impact your conflict cycles, helping you grow understanding and empathy for yourself and also take more responsibility and create change. And throughout the chapter, we provide strategies to help you cut through conflict immediately – you won't even need to wait for your partner to start or to be on board.

Understanding conflict and 'conflict topics'

As we are writing this, the Australian Open is in full swing. So, with tennis on the brain, imagine you are turning up to a tennis match with your partner. When you step onto the court, you and your partner become opponents. Your main goal for the interaction is to win. And there can only be one winner. Each shot is calculated in the hope of winning the point. Alternatively, you are run ragged as you defend your opponent's attacks. You find yourself locked in rallies, breathless to win the point and gain advantage. A poorly placed shot can be jumped on by your opponent, driving their point home.

It's not hard to see the similarity between tennis and relationship conflict.

Couples come to therapy hoping the therapist will take the role of the umpire – ultimately deciding the winner in any given match and the overall champion in the tournament of their relationship.

Both tennis and relationship conflict hold the sentiment of there being a winner and loser. Resolution only occurs when the winner is determined. The problems with this are no-one likes to be the loser and no-one is seeing eye to eye on points scored. Moving out of this cycle to consider reconnecting is difficult, with both partners often tempted to keep pressing forward with more point scoring. There is often so much hurt no-one is willing to let go.

As mentioned, conflict is inevitable in relationships, and you can be in conflict about a multitude of things. We call these 'conflict topics'. These conflict topics are triggers for conflict, yet they are not why you fight. We will address this later in the chapter.

Some of these conflict topics include:

- *Differences in perspectives:* You may have different views and priorities on how to live and what is most important in life – for example, religion, culture, work–life balance, parenting, lifestyle, health and financials.

- *Differences in needs and baggage:* This refers to your attachment needs. Attachment needs are the basic emotional needs all humans have as children that need to be met by caregivers so they grow into healthy well-rounded adults. Schema therapy (refer to the previous chapter) provides a helpful summary of these needs:
    - to know you are loved and important
    - to feel safe and protected

- to have the freedom to express feelings, thoughts and needs and be met with nurturance and understanding
- to be allowed to engage in age-appropriate tasks and receive useful, non-critical feedback
- to be allowed to play and explore
- to have appropriate limits set that are age-appropriate and responsive to you.

These needs may not get met in childhood, and may continue to be neglected in adult relationships. Therefore, such unmet needs will spill over into your current relationship, causing tension. This is what we call 'baggage' – your vulnerabilities, insecurities, fragilities and susceptibilities that you bring with you to the relationship. We provide much more detail about these vulnerabilities in chapter 7.

- *Differences in expectations:* You may have different expectations about the relationship, future plans or roles within the relationship.

- *External pressures:* Demands outside of your relationship can put pressure on the relationship. These can include work pressures, financial troubles, cultural norms, societal issues, health challenges and family issues.

These conflict topics are like the first serve in tennis, setting off the ensuing conflict match and resulting in power struggles and disconnection. A power struggle is when you and your partner are vying for control, influence or dominance in any number of the conflict topics just mentioned. This creates tension, as each of you seeks to assert your preference or authority, or to get your way. Disconnection refers to when resolution in these conflict topics feels impossible and you slowly move apart from one another. You might avoid the issue because it is uncomfortable or seems impossible.

The longer conflict is unresolved, the more damage is done to the relationship. This accumulates over time, leading to resentment and disconnection. Conflict has the potential to poison your relationship if you don't understand how it manifests in your relationship.

In our clinical practice, we see couples clashing over conflict topics all the time. Couples are overwhelmed and stuck in disagreements. So much conflict can be present that it ends up being the dominant theme in the relationship. All conversations between these couples are about proving who was right and who was wrong in the last argument. The couple are locked in a never-ending tennis tournament. Tallying the points as they go, they become fierce rivals, lost in conflict topics. Neither win – they both just lose each other.

Our couples tell us, 'I don't know why we fight about everything. I know we always fight about stuff, but I'm not sure which conflict topics are relevant to my relationship. It feels like we are constantly in opposition to one another.'

Conflict can be overwhelming. You are not alone. Everyone finds themselves in conflict at some point in relationships. Even if you can't identify the conflict topics in your relationship, don't fear. In the next section, you'll cut underneath these conflict topics to uncover the real reason you are in conflict.

 **TIME FOR ACTION**

For now, reflect on your relationship and the conflict topics you get stuck on. Take some time to consider the following questions:

- What are the common things you and your partner argue about?

- Does the conflict tend to be about your differences in perspectives? If so, what things in particular do you have different views on and how are these differently prioritised?

- Does the conflict tend to be out of differences in needs and vulnerabilities? If so, whose needs and vulnerabilities are going unaddressed?

- Does the conflict tend to be about differences in expectations? If so, what are these expectations about? Expectations about the future, the relationships, roles? How are your expectations different from one another?

- Does the conflict tend to be related to external pressures? What external pressures can you identify? Are you experiencing pressures from work, extended family, religious ideas, cultural norms or health complaints?

- Does it feel like you and your partner are in a game of tennis? How often do you feel you are a team versus being opponents?

Maybe the conflict in your relationship covers more than one of these conflict topics. This is okay, you are just being curious here.

The goal of this reflective exercise is to step out of the power struggle and diffuse the conflict by observing it from an external position. This exercise is to build awareness and insight only. You will learn how to manage conflict later in this chapter.

You might be stuck in a tiebreaker with your partner. No-one is willing to concede a point and the argument continues forever. There's so much hurt and exhaustion as a result of this match and all the others prior. If you are stuck in a stalemate with your partner, you need to shift focus to your own values. Ask yourself, 'How do I want to be as a person? What matters most to me? Am I achieving this in my relationship?' When you connect with what matters most to you, you gain intrinsic motivation to change. This moves your focus away from point scoring towards integrity with yourself.

Reflect on whether you engage with your partner in the same way you engage with other people you care about. If the answer's no, then go back to your values. What values do you embody when you engage with other loved ones that are missing with your partner?

Always remember, the relationship is bigger than any one conflict. When it feels stuck, try to look at change within yourself. You are the one with the power to create change in the dynamic of your relationship.

The one simple reason you are in conflict

Underneath the conflict topics outlined in the previous section are secondary conflict emotions – and getting stuck in these is the real reason you and your partner keep fighting. Secondary conflict emotions are any emotions on the spectrum of anger, from frustration to rage, as well as emotions encompassing passivity, submission, avoidance or detachment. Secondary conflict emotions are intense and overwhelming. They dominate your experience. They are what you notice in the conflict and what your partner experiences of you. Your secondary conflict emotions clash with and often activate your partner's own secondary conflict emotions.

Although secondary conflict emotions are what is being expressed, and felt intensely by you and your partner, something more important is occurring. Secondary conflict emotions are not feelings of vulnerability. Secondary conflict emotions occur when an unmet and unexpressed inner vulnerable feeling is occurring. You will naturally flip into secondary conflict emotions when you feel hurt or vulnerable, even without conscious awareness. This means beneath your secondary conflict emotions are your inner vulnerable feelings.

For example, if your partner is angry and critical, this is their secondary conflict emotion. You will only see and experience anger and criticism from your partner. You won't see their inner vulnerable feelings. Therefore, you will react to the anger and the criticism rather than the real experience underneath – their inner vulnerable feelings. If you do not become aware of the inner vulnerable feelings beneath the secondary conflict emotions, the true source of the conflict is not known and, therefore, cannot be resolved. Conflicts going unresolved will negatively impact your relationship.

The following diagram shows this interaction. The emotions in the outer circle – the secondary conflict emotions – cannot exist without the inner vulnerable feeling within it. While the person in this example feels abandonment, the outer world only experiences and reacts to their anger.

Secondary conflict emotions and inner vulnerable feelings

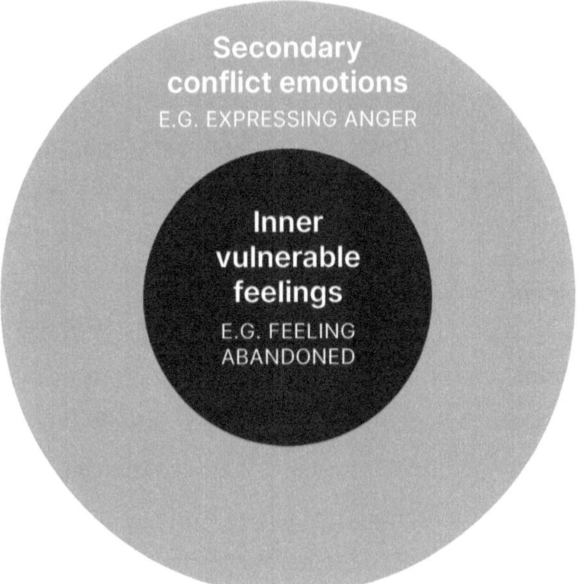

In our work as couples therapists, we have collected innumerable client stories around this. The couple are locked in heated conflict seemingly about the same topic. But beneath the surface different hurts and needs are not expressed and taken care of. The following diagram illustrates this further.

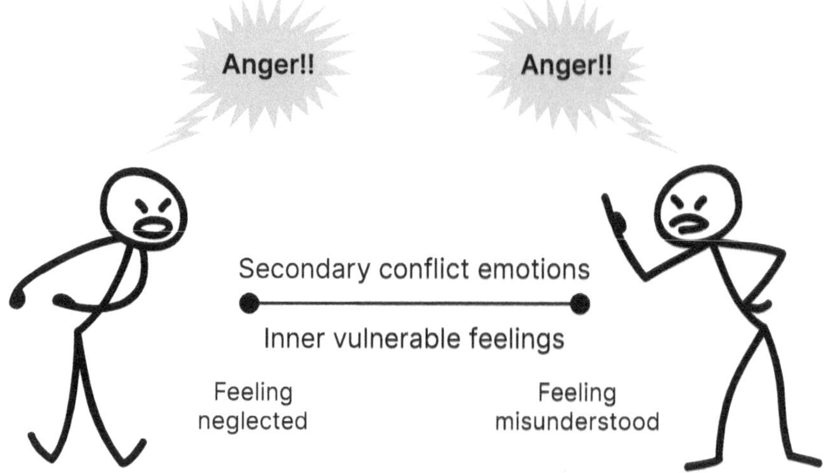

In the example shown in the figure, anger is being met with anger. In this typical situation, anger continues to escalate, causing more damage until one person shuts down. When you are communicating 'above the line' – that is, focusing on the secondary conflict emotions – you are in conflict and will never reach a resolution or reconnection. To resolve the conflict, you and your partner must be able to express and understand each other's inner vulnerable feelings. This can only occur once your emotional state is 'below the line' and out of the secondary conflict emotions. This allows you to be open and willing.

Being below the line is more about body language and tone than it is about words. Saying the right words while being frustrated means you are still above the line in secondary conflict emotions and not in a position to take care of each other. At times, you might need to take a break and agree to reconnect later to allow some space for you both to cool down. When you are able to address your invisible hurts and needs, the conflict is de-escalated. You are able to understand each other and address the real issues related to your inner vulnerable feelings.

Let's take a look at a specific example in Helen's couples therapy.

Looking beneath the emotions

Paul and Michelle were recovering from an affair Paul had in the past. Right before one of their therapy sessions, Paul and Michelle had an argument about the relationship satisfaction survey in our My Love Your Love app. (The survey is designed to show progress and also keep the relationship authentic in times of strain.) Paul and Michelle came into our session stuck in their secondary conflict emotions. They were angry and detached from one another, and the feelings were palpable in the room. No-one needed to speak for me to know something big had just happened. Michelle had seen Paul's score on the relationship satisfaction survey – and it was very low. Michelle immediately became cold and rejecting of Paul. She remarked that continuing with couples therapy was pointless, seeing as he was so miserable. Paul responded in kind, becoming frustrated and annoyed with Michelle. She too had scored her relationship satisfaction very low. He pointed this out dismissively, scoffing at her.

At first glance, they appeared to be fighting over the same topic – the survey results. My first step was to de-escalate from the secondary conflict emotions. I did this by simply pointing out they were in their secondary conflict emotions and expressing my genuine interest and care in wanting to understand what was really going on for them (their inner vulnerable feelings). Even in therapy, resolution and reconnection was not going to be possible until both of them had moved out of their secondary conflict emotions.

When they looked beneath their secondary conflict emotions and at their inner vulnerable feelings, it became clear they were fighting over very different things. Once they were able to identify each of their inner vulnerable feelings, and validate these, they were able to get somewhere.

When Michelle saw Paul's dissatisfaction on the survey, she felt scared and insecure for the future of the relationship. She felt helpless and hopeless to change it for the better. What Michelle had really needed in that moment was some reassurance and hopefulness from Paul.

Ultimately, her secondary conflict emotions were unable to effectively express this for her.

When Michelle, instead, reacted with coldness and rejection, Paul felt hurt and attacked by her. He'd tried to be transparent and open with the survey, which was something he'd been trying to do to improve trust. He didn't understand her cold reaction, particularly as she also had scored very low on the survey. What Paul needed in that moment was kindness and curiosity. Like Michelle, Paul's secondary conflict emotions did not accurately represent his true feelings and needs in that moment.

In therapy, Paul and Michelle explored their inner vulnerable feelings and subsequent needs beneath their secondary conflict emotions to see what was really going on for each other. They were able to attend to these inner vulnerabilities and provide each other with what they each needed. This resolved the conflict.

Initially, Paul and Michelle's secondary conflict emotions were battling one another, hiding the real cause of the conflict. The conflict topic was around the survey score. Rather than being the *cause*, however, the survey score was the *trigger* for the conflict.

Working through your emotions to get to the inner feelings

When a conflict has occurred and you and your partner are feeling upset, you need to start by each owning your secondary conflict emotions. When we say 'own your feelings', we mean take responsibility for your feelings and acknowledge them without blaming others for how you feel. The next step is to acknowledge how you and your partner's secondary conflict emotions are interplaying and impacting one another. After this, you can go deeper to inner vulnerable feelings and get to the cause of the conflict. If this process seems overwhelming don't worry – we give you a structured process to follow later in the chapter when we discuss 'reach out to repair'.

Something we hear all the time is, 'I don't have any inner vulnerable feelings. I'm feeling angry and frustrated. These are my true feelings and so I should express them.' Feelings of anger and frustration are real and often intense to experience – and easy to identify because the emotion of anger is motivating and energising. The function of anger is to protect yourself, so it's physiologically activating and can feel empowering.

Although it dominates our experience, whenever you feel anger, an inner vulnerable feeling is always beneath it. Connecting with that inner vulnerable feeling is much harder and more uncomfortable because you are more exposed and vulnerable when you do so.

Here is a simple example from Helen.

Getting beyond secondary conflict emotions in everyday life

Road rage is something you can perhaps relate to. Personally, my encounters with road rage often unfold when I find myself running late, tense with stress and agitation. With one eye on the clock, I navigate through the relentless traffic. Then, seemingly out of nowhere, a slow-moving vehicle materialises in my path. Frustration and anger swiftly take hold. My hand hovers over the horn. I find myself muttering expletives under my breath. My secondary conflict emotions are well and truly present.

Peeling back these intense emotions reveals a deeper, more intimate layer of vulnerability. Stepping back within myself, I find stress and worry about being late. Tricky emotions of guilt and incompetence for not meeting my responsibilities are also floating around. These inner vulnerabilities, masked by my secondary conflict emotions, reveal a more genuine narrative of personal turmoil. It also means the focus for my attention needs to be within, taking care of my inner vulnerable feelings, rather than external, blaming and acting out against the other drivers and traffic more generally.

It's okay to verbally represent your feelings of frustration and anger, passivity or detachment. You can do this by naming such feelings – for example, 'I'm feeling frustrated right now.' But it's not okay to express them physically or behaviourally – for example, through raising your voice, slamming doors and so on. This turns the perfectly authentic feeling of anger into aggression, which can cause interpersonal damage.

To help you get below your secondary conflict emotions and name the underlying inner vulnerable feelings, the following table provides a list of the most common emotions and feelings.

Common emotions and feelings

Common secondary conflict emotions		
Anger	Avoidance	Coldness
Compliance	Condescension	Contempt
Defensiveness	Disconnection	Disgust
Dismissiveness	Frustration	Fury
Grumpiness	Holding back	Irritation
Mocking	Over-rationalisation	Point-scoring
Running away	Scoffing	Shutting down
Silent anger	Submission	Wall up
Common inner vulnerable feelings		
Abandonment	Afraid	Alone
Anxious	Confused	Defective
Excluded	Fragile	Frightened
Helpless	Hurt	Incompetent
Lonely	Lost	Misunderstood
Not good enough	Not heard	Overwhelmed
Powerless	Rejected	Sad
Self-conscious	Sensitive	Small
Undervalued	Unlovable	Unloved
Unprioritised	Unsupported	Weak

♥ TIME FOR ACTION

Reflect on a recent conflict with your partner. This conflict could be something simple like your partner not doing the dishes after you cooked a meal for you both.

Work through the following process to identify your and your partner's secondary conflict emotions and inner vulnerable feelings:

1. Choose the secondary conflict emotion you experienced and the secondary conflict emotion you experienced of your partner. For example, your secondary conflict emotion could be annoyed and frustrated. Your partner's secondary conflict emotion could be defensive and dismissive.

2. Go deep and think about what your inner vulnerable feelings were, and have a guess about what your partner's inner vulnerable feelings might have been. Your inner vulnerable feelings, for example, might be feeling unimportant and deprioritised. Your partner's inner vulnerable feelings might be feeling criticised and small.

Use the preceding list of common emotions and feelings and the flow diagram overleaf to help with this process.

You might get stuck in your secondary conflict emotions, even though your partner has expressed their inner vulnerable feelings. What do you do? It takes hard work, vulnerability and consistency to learn to identify inner vulnerable feelings. Don't give up. To help you get underneath the secondary conflict emotions and identify your inner vulnerable feelings, ask yourself these questions:

- 'What am I left with?'
- 'What does it say about me?'
- 'What is so bad about it?'

Try to be specific and get to an 'I' statement about the conflict.

Processing secondary conflict emotions and inner vulnerable feelings

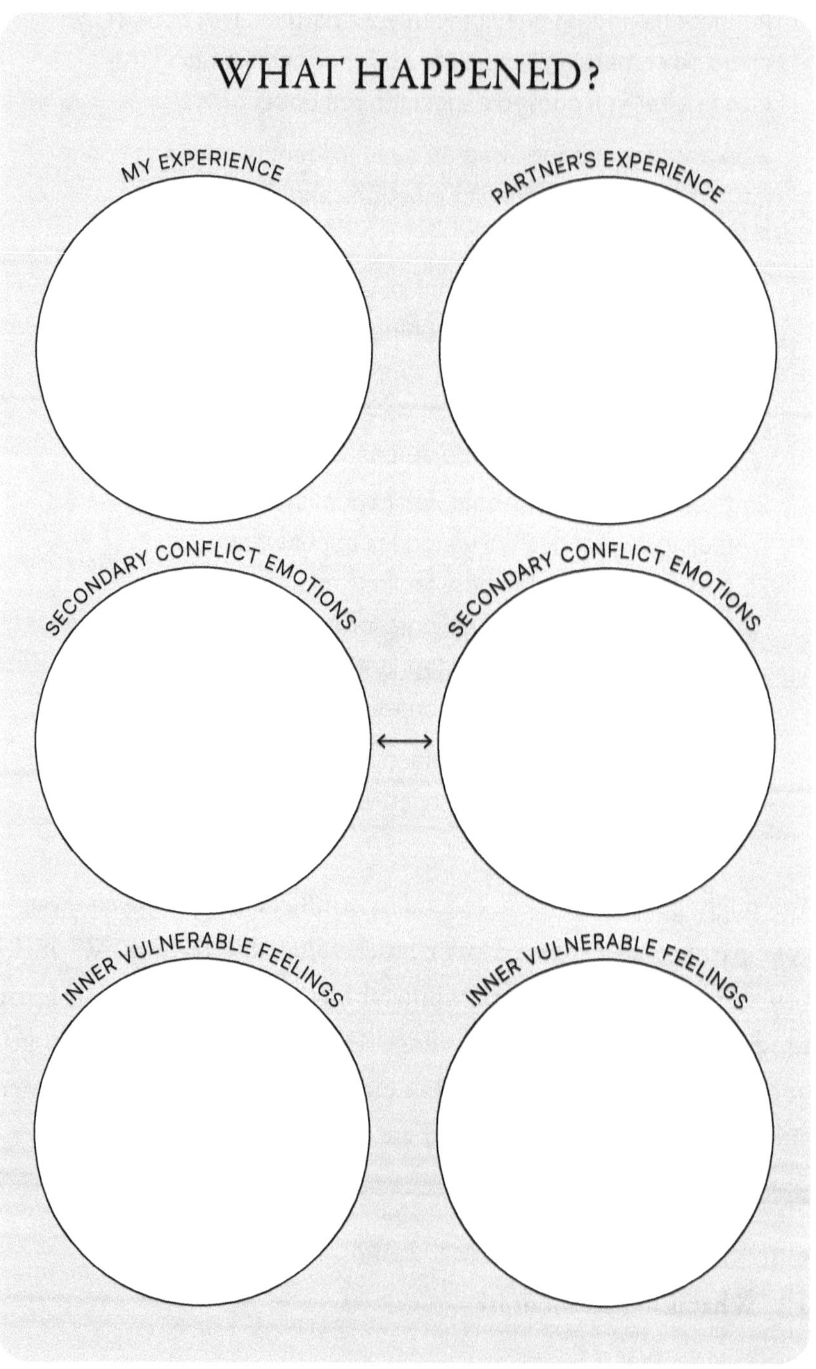

For our example about the dishes, you could use these questions to uncover the following insights:

- *'What am I left with because my partner didn't clean up the kitchen after I cooked?'* I had to do it. I'm left with the task.
- *'What does it say about me that they didn't do this?'* I'm not very important. I'm the maid of the house.
- *'What is so bad about the fact they didn't clean up the kitchen?'* I feel unloved.

Now you have arrived at the inner vulnerable feeling. By expressing 'I feel unloved' instead of anger and criticism, you are more likely to have a different response from your partner and a different outcome from the interaction. And, most importantly, you have expressed your genuine experience, irrespective of your partner's reaction, which builds your emotional awareness.

Meet your conflict personas

Our concept of conflict personas makes understanding secondary conflict emotions easy and relatable, and offers a point of change. Conflict personas are forms of aggression, submission or detachment and, therefore, are your secondary conflict emotions personified. These personas refer to a mind state or state of being. While they are a part of who you are, they're not all of you and don't represent your inner vulnerable feelings. The function of conflict personas is to protect or defend you, but they are maladaptive.

Your conflict personas developed from how you learned to survive in your family of origin and previous relationships. Every single human has some form of conflict persona. Conflict personas, like secondary conflict emotions, take over your whole being in the moment, consuming you. They dominate your feelings, thoughts and behaviours.

We have created the following list of the conflict personas we see in couples:

- *Micromanager:* The Micromanager is the part of you that seeks security when you are stressed or vulnerable. This conflict persona is all about gaining control – of yourself, your environment and your partner. The function of the Micromanager is to provide a sense of certainty and safety. This may be to compensate for a sense of being devalued. The Micromanager aims to prevent mistakes and the anticipated ensuing criticism, as well as the humiliation and guilt that go along with these mistakes and anticipated criticism. The overall aim is to protect you from underlying feelings of inadequacy, shame, and being undervalued or overwhelmed.

- *Angry Attacker:* The Angry Attacker is about protection and staving off any threats. It works to prevent perceived mistreatment, abuse or humiliation. The Angry Attacker can become active if you believe you are being invalidated, feel threatened or are at risk of being hurt. The Angry Attacker often is a sign an underlying need of yours is not being met, but it is expressed in an uncontrolled and ineffective display of anger. The Angry Attacker can be a way to assert control and entitlement. Getting one over your partner may feel safer and more in control, but it prevents your partner from expressing their needs or emotions and hides yours.

- *Cold/Hot Wall:* This conflict persona might not speak many words but it communicates loud and clear you are upset and activated. As the name suggests, the Cold/Hot Wall is communicated through iciness or anger. In the Cold Wall, you express very little emotion but send a clear message there is a problem. The Hot Wall has a similar function but is far less subtle. When active, the Hot Wall communicates on your behalf: 'I have a wall of fire around me; come near me and risk getting burnt'. The Cold/Hot Wall is active when you feel hurt, invalidated or entitled to something you have not received from your partner. It can be difficult for you to express your needs or vulnerabilities so shutting off from the other can feel safer. It may also help you move away from any feelings of rejection or abandonment.

- *Self-Sacrificing Partner Pleaser:* The Self-Sacrificing Partner Pleaser works to avoid conflict or feelings of guilt that might arise if you were to take care of your own needs. This conflict persona responds to a deep fear you will be rejected or abandoned, or face punishment from your partner or others in general if you were to express your needs or feelings.

- *Persistent Conflict Resolver:* The goal of this conflict persona is to fix the problem and move on at whatever cost. There are two types of the Persistent Conflict Resolver. The first is the anxious type, where the function is to protect you from an underlying fear of abandonment or rejection. It is marked by anxiety and fear. The second is the entitled type, which works to compensate against feelings of defectiveness and emotional neglect by ensuring your partner agrees with you and comes over to your position.

- *Conflict Avoider:* As the name suggests, avoidance is the agenda of the Conflict Avoider – and this includes the avoidance of direct fiery arguments, or the avoidance of any discomfort, disagreements and emotions in general. The Conflict Avoider functions to keep you safe. Emotional arousal and expression (and vulnerability more generally) is deemed bad, dangerous and threatening.

- *Suspicious Detective:* This conflict persona attempts to keep you protected by containing your partner and exposing any perceived or real threats or malicious intentions. Often beneath the Suspicious Detective is the fear of being made to feel defective and being controlled and overpowered, leading to feelings of rejection, betrayal, inadequacy and powerlessness. Your own underlying insecurity in yourself and the relationship can evoke the Suspicious Detective. This can be a common conflict persona for people who have been the victim of an affair or abandonment in current or previous relationships.

- *Superior One-Upper:* This conflict persona inflates your sense of worth, power, influence and abilities, scaffolding you against any threats to your value, image or status. Often far beneath the Superior One-Upper are feelings of unworthiness, inferiority, shame, weakness or defectiveness. When this conflict persona is around, you might become condescending and mocking, and use your partner's flaws or vulnerabilities against them.

You must not ignore your conflict personas. Conflict cannot be resolved when you are stuck in your conflict persona. The longer they are front and centre in your life, the more damage they're causing to your relationship.

Here is an example of a conflict persona in action with one of Shahn's clients, Kevin.

Conflict personas can form in childhood

Kevin has a strong Self-Sacrificing Partner Pleaser conflict persona, and this plays out negatively with his partner, Danielle – sometimes over something as seemingly simple as dinner plans.

Kevin values his social connection with his friends and had wanted to catch up with them for a long time. He made plans to see his friends on the upcoming weekend. However, Danielle told him her parents, who lived out of town, were in Sydney that weekend. They'd invited them to dinner at a lovely restaurant and she wanted Kevin to attend.

On hearing this, Kevin experienced a variety of feelings. Deep down, he wanted to see his friends. However, he had a strong sense of guilt when he considered asserting his own needs. He also experienced anxiety and fear that Danielle would be rejecting or angry if he stuck to his original plans.

To avoid feelings of guilt, anxiety and fear, and to make Danielle happy, Kevin sacrificed meeting up with his friends and agreed to go with Danielle to dinner with her parents. He mentioned nothing to Danielle of his real desire to see his friends.

Why did Kevin do this?

His Self-Sacrificing Partner Pleaser took over at that moment. By looking at his past, we could discover why this conflict persona had such a hold on him.

Kevin grew up in a family in which his father was a prominent and domineering figure. He would become angry and rejecting if Kevin or his brother expressed a need or desire that was in conflict with his own. Kevin's mother was passive and allowed her husband to take the lead within the relationship and the family to avoid his angry moods. She encouraged Kevin and his brothers to do the same. Kevin learnt early on to suppress his needs to avoid conflict and rejection in the home. This was adaptive within the environment and because Kevin was a child with limited power.

This response carried over to the present day in his relationship. Although Danielle expresses her disappointment and frustration with Kevin at times, she is not his father or anything like him. Yet Kevin's Self-Sacrificing Partner Pleaser automatically and subconsciously acts as if Danielle is.

This example with Kevin demonstrates how his conflict persona developed and how it once helped him in the context of his childhood. However, he is now an adult with more power and the self-sacrifice no longer serves him – in fact, it makes things worse. It means Kevin cannot express his needs and Danielle is left none the wiser.

You may say to yourself, 'My conflict persona keeps me safe', 'My conflict persona keeps things in control' or 'It gets things done.

Without it, my relationship wouldn't be going anywhere'. Unfortunately, a conflict persona solution is a maladaptive solution. It's a solution, but it's not a solution that is most productive to your best interests. Conflict personas also do not have the relationship at heart. Instead, they encourage a conflict persona dance with your partner – which we talk more about in a moment.

♥ TIME FOR ACTION

Using the list provided in this section, choose your conflict personas. Reflect on which conflict personas your partner might have. When reflecting on each of your conflict personas, the following questions can help you understand where your conflict personas have come from and how they're functioning for you now.

Ask yourself:

- 'When did my conflict persona start to appear in my life and what role did it play then? What role does it play now?'
- 'How is my conflict persona trying to help me? What is it trying to protect me from?'
- 'What messages and rules does my conflict persona have about me, others and the world?'
- 'What situations does my conflict persona come out in?'
- 'What emotions and body sensations do I experience in my conflict persona?'
- 'How do I behave and what negative outcomes occur when I am in my conflict persona?'
- 'What are my inner vulnerable feelings beneath my conflict persona and what do I actually need based on these feelings?'

These questions can help you understand why this conflict persona is here and what it is trying to help you with. This knowledge builds insight and empathy for yourself. It also highlights the unhelpfulness of your conflict persona and how it's covering up your true experience – your inner vulnerable feelings. Explore and understand your conflict persona so you can diffuse from it and connect with what's underneath.

You might feel like you're opening yourself up for criticism by admitting you have a conflict persona, which in turn may tempt you to deny their existence. You might refuse to engage with this part of the book. However, knowing your conflict personas will help you. Identifying your conflict personas is not about making you feel bad or ashamed of yourself. Rather, it will help build empathy for yourself. You have to get to know something before you can change it. Looking at areas for self-improvement is character building and a sign of strength.

Conflict personas were there to help and, at one time in your life, they did help you. Without them, you would have suffered further. You needed them to literally or metaphorically survive the experience. However, if you keep letting them run the show, you'll keep your true needs hidden from your partner. You'll have more conflict and less peace and joy. You'll end up feeling even more alone.

At the end of the day, you are responsible for the behaviours that occur when you are in a conflict persona. Be kind to yourself when looking at your conflict personas and accept that everyone has them. It's courageous to take ownership of your conflict personas and you will grow when you do.

Finding your conflict persona antidotes

Conflict may occur over many topics, but only a limited number of what we call 'conflict dances' are on repeat in your relationship. These dances occur when one or both partners flip into conflict personas and the conflict personas interact.

Common conflict dances include the Micromanager with the Conflict Avoider, the Angry Attacker with the Persistent Conflict

Resolver, or the Superior One-Upper with the Self-Sacrificing Partner Pleaser. We will give you examples of these dances through this section.

What is your conflict dance? Which conflict personas do you and your partner slip into and how do these interact?

Both you and your partner are responsible for relationship conflict, because conflict is an interaction. The conflict dance is the secondary conflict emotions reacting to one another. Unfortunately, your inner vulnerable feelings are not part of the dance steps. This means that the real truth of the interaction for both you and your partner isn't revealed or attended to.

A way to step out of your conflict dance is to use the conflict persona antidotes. These are strategies, actions or approaches that can be used to counteract or alleviate the negative effects of conflict personas. These antidotes promote understanding, care and boundary-setting within the relationship, and help mitigate the tensions and disagreements that can arise as a result of a conflict persona. They also come in two types: self-antidotes and partner antidotes. Self-antidotes are simple things you can do to address your conflict persona, while partner antidotes are things you can do to address your partner's conflict persona. You will always have an option to disrupt the conflict dance and begin to engage in a healthy way.

Antidotes are not magic solutions that will solve your problems instantly. They're ways to engage and circumvent the conflict dance so you both have an opportunity to reflect on your secondary conflict emotions and inner vulnerable feelings. Using these antidotes with either yourself or your partner can feel challenging, but it will get easier with practice and the reward will pay off with persistence.

In the following sections, we outline the self-antidotes and the partner antidotes for each conflict persona. As you read through, keep in mind you can always create antidotes tailored to your own experience and needs.

For the Micromanager

Self-antidotes:

- If you realise you are in your Micromanager conflict persona, stop everything! The Micromanager is all about pressure, analysis and action, so you must stop and check in with your body and feelings. What can you feel in your body? Try to find any inner vulnerable feelings lurking beneath the surface. Name what sensations and emotions you can sense in your body. Don't ask anything of yourself or your partner for a period of time. Once you have calmed down and given yourself some space, speak to your partner about what is happening. Always start from your inner vulnerable feelings.

- If you want your partner to do something, ask nicely. Resist the urge to insist or demand. If you are asking in a sickly-sweet way or a polite but cold way, you are still in your conflict persona. Back off and wait until you can connect with your inner vulnerable feelings.

- Your discontent may not be about the thing you are requesting of your partner. Rather, you are likely feeling left out, inadequate or hurt about something else. If this is the case, engage your partner in a meaningful way. Ask them to join you in an activity focused on connection – for example, go for a walk together, buy ice creams, or play basketball at the local park.

- The pause is essential when stepping out of the Micromanager. If you are overwhelmed and stressed, this is not the time to address whatever issue is bothering you. Take time out. Even wait until the next day. Then talk about what happened with your partner in an open way, so you can come up with a collaborative solution.

Partner antidotes:

- When you notice your partner is in their Micromanager persona, first check in with how you are feeling. In particular, notice if you are stuck in any secondary conflict emotions, or if you have gone into one of your own conflict personas. Try to get to your inner vulnerable feelings. How is your partner's Micromanager leaving you feeling? Once you identify your inner vulnerable feelings, approach and invite your partner into a discussion. It might go something like this: 'I'm feeling a bit controlled at the moment. I feel like I'm losing my autonomy, can we make time to talk about this?' or 'Hey, I'm feeling controlled, what's going on for you? I'm interested in how you are feeling underneath.' Use the Feeling the Story love link (covered in the previous chapter) to understand one another.

- Try out the 'own your shit' skill, which we outline later in this chapter. Acknowledge any truth in what your partner's Micromanager is accusing you of. Are you letting the team down? Does your partner have to over-function for your lack of action? If you acknowledge the truth in what your partner is saying, you take the steam out of the Micromanager. This allows your partner to access their own inner vulnerable feelings.

For the Angry Attacker

Self-antidotes:

- If you feel a belly full of fire, your Angry Attacker is here. Take some time out. This could be 30 seconds to a couple of hours. Develop insight into the Angry Attacker and commit to the idea that nothing positive can be gained from it. The Angry Attacker is damaging to both you and your partner. During your time out, acknowledge the Angry Attacker will not get your needs met. Take the time to connect with your inner vulnerable feelings and write them down – labelling emotions helps process them. The very act of doing this is reflective, which indicates you are moving out of the Angry Attacker.

- Visualise your partner as a child version of themselves. Imagine how they might feel to have this angry energy heaped upon them. Develop empathy by identifying some emotions they may be experiencing as a result of your Angry Attacker. You can't have empathy and be in the Angry Attacker at the same time, so this very action will help put the fire out.

- Visualise yourself as a child version of yourself. What is the little child feeling beneath the anger? What vulnerable feelings is the Angry Attacker trying to prevent you from experiencing? What needs is the Angry Attacker trying to get met? Try to identify and express these feelings and needs – first to yourself, and then to your partner once you have calmed down.

- If you are struggling with the options provided here, try engaging in an activity to release the built-up tension. Try things like hitting the gym, singing loudly or going for a run. Changing your focus to an unrelated activity is another way to calm down – for example, listening to an interesting podcast or having an unrelated conversation with a friend. The change of focus can often act as a circuit breaker, allowing you to access your inner vulnerable feelings and increase your capacity to return to the issue from a calmer space.

Partner antidote:

- You must not engage in a content discussion with the Angry Attacker. You won't get anywhere. The Angry Attacker is not easily reasoned with and will likely escalate if faced with reason.

- Remember, beneath their anger your partner is in emotional pain. If you attack back, withdraw or surrender, neither of you are going to get your needs met. Consider the idea that everyone is motivated by their own attempts to feel good or escape pain. This can help you develop compassion and an empathic reaction to respond from a calm and healthy space.

- You may be aware that something is going on beneath their anger but all you see is what is in front of you. Tell your partner in a calm way you know they are distressed. You are going to give them some space because you don't want to engage with the anger. However, you are there for them and you want to understand. Don't leave things open-ended. Explain you will come back to them when the anger has lessened – for example, 'I want you to know while I am giving you space, I care and will check in on you to see if you want to talk in about 30 minutes' or, 'I want you to know I care and I want to understand what is going on for you. Whenever you are ready to talk, let me know and I will do my best to understand and hear what's going on for you.' When your partner is ready to talk and the Angry Attacker is less present, show compassion and curiosity. When things are calm, let your partner know you feel fearful or attacked when their Angry Attacker is around – for example, 'I need to let you know when you are upset in that way I feel afraid.'

- It is not okay to be the subject of any type of abuse – whether it is verbal, psychological or physical. Boundaries are very important here. You may need to tell your partner you can't talk with them while they are in their Angry Attacker. Your safety is paramount and moving out of the situation might be your best move. When in a safe place, you can choose your next move, which may be to text your partner and let them know you are open to talking but not while they are in their Angry Attacker persona.

For the Cold/Hot Wall

Self-antidote:

- Start with some reflection. Insight allows change. Acknowledging you are in this conflict persona is a must. Imagine you are a third person watching this scene play out on a TV screen. What would they see? Remember this person would not know your history or your thoughts. They'd just see your behaviour and body language.

- Once you've identified you are in your Cold/Hot Wall, label and name your inner vulnerable feelings. Go back and check out the list of inner vulnerable feelings earlier in this chapter. Journaling what is going on for you can help you process the emotions and come out of your wall.

- Now comes the hard part. Acknowledge that while the Cold/Hot Wall might have helped you in your past, it is no longer helping you get your needs met, and is instead leading to more disconnection and hurt. Let your partner know you feel activated by something. It's okay to ask for space and time if you can't talk about it right away. But you must specify a time frame for coming back and checking in with them. Letting your partner know something is happening for you is crucial to letting some of the wall down. Eventually you will need to talk through with your partner what happened.

Partner antidote:

- The Cold/Hot Wall can trigger a range of emotions, including rejection, abandonment and resentment. You might find yourself moving into your own conflict persona. While this is tempting, it will lead to a conflict dance. Instead, hold up an emotional mirror to your partner to reflect back to them what you see – for example, 'Hey, it seems you might be upset at the moment. I am not sure what is going on but I am happy to talk about it

when you are ready. I would like to be part of the resolution for
whatever is going on, even if it is just to offer support.'

- Stay calm and open. It is not your job to guess what is going on
for your partner, or to make everything better. It is okay to tell
your partner how the Cold/Hot Wall is making you feel – for
example, shut out, alone, disconnected and anxious. Sitting with
discomfort is challenging yet it is more effective in the long run if
you don't join in the dance.

For the Self-Sacrificing Partner Pleaser

Self-antidote:

- Guilt is a common emotion in this conflict persona, and you must
distinguish between its two versions: justified guilt and unjustified
guilt. Justified guilt is an appropriate emotional response to
a genuine wrongdoing or violation of your values. Justified
guilt motivates you to acknowledge and take responsibility for
your actions. It communicates the need for repair. Unjustified
guilt is not warranted by your actions or circumstances, and is
experienced guilt without a reasonable basis. Although you have
behaved in accordance with your values and needs, the guilt
persists. This unjustified guilt is driven by your internal world
and, in particular, your assumptions, expectations and predictions
of how the other person will respond negatively to you. When
you experience justified guilt, it is healthy and appropriate to
apologise and repair. However, when you experience unjustified
guilt, you must resist the urge to apologise, comply, surrender or
stop the behaviour that has triggered the unjustified guilt. When
this persona is active, you avoid expressing your needs or position.
You self-sacrifice to your partner to avoid feelings of guilt or
anxiety around perceived conflict.

- Instead of self-sacrificing or trying to please your partner, you need to sit with difficult emotions and persist with whatever it is you want to do or assert your genuine needs and position around the evoking situation. Both guilt and unjustified guilt feel the same. Therefore, you must determine which guilty feeling you are experiencing to come out of this conflict persona.

- Ask yourself, 'What would I suggest a friend do if they were in this current situation?'

- Ask yourself, 'If my partner told me right now they can guarantee not to harbour any anger or disappointment towards me in this situation, what would my needs be? What is stopping me from asserting my needs?'

- Resisting the Self-Sacrificing Partner Pleaser feels like you are being mean or nasty. In order to get through this, you have to sit with anxiety and unjustified guilt. The good news is the more you balance your needs and your partner's needs, the more the uncomfortable feelings will subside over time. Your value in the relationship will go up. And both of you will experience greater contentment and satisfaction.

Partner antidote:

- Although your partner might be trying to please you, it can still be frustrating. In particular, it can be difficult to know what they want. Be patient and calm. This will help to avoid triggering their anxiety.

- Give them reassurance you are happy to meet their needs in an equitable way.

- It's okay to draw a line in the sand and insist they take responsibility for their own needs – by saying, for example, 'I am not choosing this time. I'd like you to take care of your needs. And I will support your decision.'

- Getting your own way might feel good. However, this is having a negative effect on your relationship, impacting how attracted you feel towards your partner and how much you value them. To balance this out, you must create opportunities to take care of them or do nice and special things for them that encourage their worth.

- If and when your partner brings up their needs, be supportive and responsive. Practise feeling the story (chapter 4). Encourage and celebrate them looking after themselves – for example, if they request to take time out from the family to do an exercise class. Even if this adds responsibility to you, find a way to do it.

- It is worth noting that if you and your partner discuss each of your needs and positions around any given situation and then in an informed way end up choosing one partner's position, this is no longer self-sacrificing. Coming out of this persona is all about speaking up and moving away from self-sacrifice to collaboration and being a team.

For the Conflict Avoider

Self-antidote:

- Bring awareness to the presence of your Conflict Avoider. When you do this, you will feel the tug of avoidance. Acknowledge this internal resistance. Ask yourself, 'What am I afraid of if I approach this rather than avoid it?' Then face it. Approach your partner. Start with something like, 'I want to tell you something but I'm scared of your reaction.'

- Take a big breath and approach rather than avoid. Remind yourself this short-term pain will result in long-term gain for you. It is better to deal with your partner's upset now rather than their upset later *plus* their feelings of betrayal because you didn't tell them about it. You will stop being the one 'in trouble'.

- Before approaching your partner, ask yourself, 'Have I done something wrong?' If you answer yes, then you need to fess up. Ask yourself, 'Am I about to do something wrong?' If the answer is yes, don't do it! If you persist with avoidance, you will perpetuate the conflict dance. On the other hand, if the answer is no to both those questions, remind yourself there is no need to avoid based on your values. If your partner has a negative reaction, they might need to work on their baggage activation. Avoiding further is just keeping a problem in the relationship hidden.

Partner antidote:

- When your partner's Conflict Avoider is around, express your inner vulnerable feelings. Opting for your own conflict persona (commonly the Angry Attacker or Micromanager) will fuel the cycle of avoidance. You may end up in a 'parentified' relationship, where you take on the role and responsibilities of a parent to compensate for your partner's avoidance. The problem here is that you will be perceived as boring and controlling and they will act as the rebellious child – avoiding now, getting in trouble later.

- Reassure your partner you will be kind to them when they are forthcoming. Express a willingness to work collaboratively to meet their needs or requests. Rather than expecting your partner to suddenly spill exactly what they want, be curious. Ask them what they want. Understand why it is important to them. Do this in a gentle way.

- When your partner speaks, especially about how they feel, stay calm. You need to make a safe space for them to express themselves. Avoid criticism and be aware of your own reactivity because this will scare them off. Validate your partner's feelings to help them learn it is safe to express them.

- Before expressing your own thoughts and feelings, ensure you clarify and understand what they are asking or telling you. Use feeling the story (chapter 4) to hear their story and understand their feelings. Only after this, should you communicate how you are feeling. Pay particular attention to your inner vulnerable feelings.

For the Persistent Conflict Resolver

Self-antidote:

- Be aware of your Persistent Conflict Resolver. Take a step back, literally. Remove yourself from your partner. Remind yourself that sometimes saying less is more helpful. The relationship is not over because your partner is asking for space.

- Repeat back what your partner has asked of you (for example, some time and space).

- Write down your thoughts concerning the argument. This will allow you to pause on the conflict because you won't lose the important points you want to share with your partner. Then put them aside.

- Ask your partner for a time to come back to the issue at hand. Respect this by not bringing it up until the agreed time has arrived.

- You don't have to agree on everything or find a solution for everything. You will learn how to hold two truths at the same time later in this chapter.

- The desire for your partner to agree with you on a topic can be overwhelming. But forcing them to a verbal agreement doesn't mean they do agree or value your position. They may be doing so out of submission. In time, they will resent your persistence.

Partner antidote:

- Be kind and calm. Remember they are anxious underneath. Assure them you love them and want to resolve this but need some time and space first.

- Give your partner a specific time when you can commit to addressing the conflict. Keep this time.

For the Suspicious Detective

Self-antidote:

- Remind yourself no-one is perfect and part of being a human is making mistakes. Neither you nor your partner will get it right all the time. People are intrinsically flawed. To love someone means loving them warts and all.

- The concept of impermanence is helpful here. Everything is in a state of change and nothing lasts forever. It is a myth to think you can lock down a relationship as completely safe and trusted. The more you try to do this by controlling the relationship, the more insecure you will feel and the more controlled your partner will feel – and the more they will feel they have to hide from you. Relationships are ever-evolving and to be in one is to take risks. There are no guarantees, no matter how much you desire it. Forcing and controlling behaviour ultimately destroys relationships.

- When in your Suspicious Detective conflict persona ask yourself, 'Am I jumping to conclusions?' Ask a trusted friend whether they come to a different conclusion. Try to only use facts, not your interpretation, when talking to your friend.

- Try to put yourself in your partner's shoes – how would you feel to be on the other end of all this mistrust?

- Although your Suspicious Detective wants to protect you from harm and keep you safe, it is getting in the way of meaningful connection and putting your relationship at risk.

- Remind yourself – your partner is going to be much more responsive to your vulnerability than your suspicions. Try to get underneath your secondary conflict emotions to your inner vulnerable feelings and express these instead. You will get a much better and more caring response from your partner.

Partner antidotes:

- Speak your truth. Honestly discuss your boundaries. Be clear on what you are okay and not okay to compromise in the relationship. Avoid lies. You do not need to change your truth to avoid your partner's Suspicious Detective coming out. This is something they have to work on. If you find yourself telling white lies and covering up things, you could be in your Conflict Avoider persona. You will eventually be ensnared in the Suspicious Detective's trap.

- Own your shit. If you have done something the Suspicious Detective is accusing you of, own it. Only own the specifics of what you have done, not anything else the Suspicious Detective has made up.

- If your partner attempts to drop the Suspicious Detective and starts to express their inner vulnerable feelings, stop and listen. Validate these feelings. They might still be a little angry when they do this, so stay calm. Remind yourself, this is their coping mechanism, not them as a whole. Try to attune to their vulnerability.

- If your partner has a Suspicious Detective persona as a result of a previous affair you had, tell your partner that you are responsible for their Suspicious Detective. This can be a compassionate way to recognise the suffering they experience in this conflict persona. In general, make sure you are completely transparent and consistent.

- If your partner is stuck in the Suspicious Detective, reflect back what you see and how it makes you feel – for example, 'I'm feeling attacked and ridiculed when you keep questioning me about my intentions.'

For the Superior One-Upper

Self-antidotes:

- You must notice and label this conflict persona. Call it out. Notice how it makes you feel. Don't beat around the bush with this conflict persona. Owning your Superior One-Upper may invoke feelings of shame. Be kind to yourself. But remember – until you own it, it will continue to dominate.

- Take a break. If you notice that you can't shift out of the Superior One-Upper, ask your partner for a time out. It is better to take a break than allow the Superior One-Upper to let fly. There will be a lot less mess to clean up later.

- Remind yourself that although your Superior One-Upper is trying to increase your worth, it is only destroying it. If left unchecked, this persona will push away the people you love. Those who stay will be there out of submission not respect.

- Try to get beneath the urgency to feel better than your partner. Deep inside, a little child part of you feels inadequate, inferior and defective. Try to connect with this side of yourself and be kind to it. Remind your inner child that you are worthy because you exist and that is enough. That little child part doesn't have to be better, more successful, more beautiful to be worthy.

- Practice empathy. Imagine how your partner is feeling and thinking. Think about what it might be like to be in their experience. Remind yourself that no-one's experience is more important than another's.

Partner antidotes:

- Remind yourself that this is their Superior One-Upper persona. It is not a reflection of you. The Superior One-Upper's agenda is to make you feel small, silly and stupid. You are not these things. The persona aims to activate your own sense of defectiveness so they can feel better about themselves. Remember this – you are okay and allowed to speak up for yourself.

- Communicate your discomfort with their Superior One-Upper's condescension and one-upmanship. Share with your partner how it leaves you feeling – for example, 'When your Superior One-Upper is around I'm left feeling small and silly. I'm not okay with this.'

- Set a limit. Engaging with their Superior One-Upper is futile because this conflict persona doesn't play by the rules. When you notice this conflict persona is here, gently state you won't be engaging with it – for example, 'I believe your Superior One-Upper has joined us. This part of you can be critical and mean so I can't speak to you while you're in this conflict persona. I'm happy to talk about the issue when you can connect with the other side of you that I love and respect.'

Stepping away from the conflict dance

If you become aware of your conflict personas and the conflict dance you and your partner are caught up in, you'll be able to resolve all those pesky conflict topics. By using the antidotes provided in the previous section, you will change the dance steps to a more cohesive number – one in which your inner vulnerable feelings can be addressed and taken care of. But if you don't, you will stay stuck in your dance. The unresolved conflicts will pile up and resentment and detachment will grow.

As an example of this, let's take a look at a couple Shahn was seeing.

Letting go of conflict personas to find cohesion

Kylie and Leo were often in a conflict dance. Kylie has a Micromanager conflict persona and Leo has a Conflict Avoider conflict persona. When Kylie's Micromanager was around, she focused on control to make her feel safe. Leo's tactic, on the other hand, was to avoid. This helped him feel safe. In this example, their conflict dance commenced when Leo's friends invited him to the pub the following week.

Although he wanted to go, Leo said nothing to Kylie because he worried she would not be supportive. The day of the event, he dropped into a conversation with Kylie that his friends were at the pub up the road and he would just go say hi for a little while – and then scampered out the door. Kylie, feeling hoodwinked, was frustrated from the get-go. She suspected Leo had known about these drinks for a while, and now she was also left to care for their small child.

As he left, Leo told Kylie he'd be home in an hour. An hour passed with no sign of Leo, so Kylie texted him, asking him where he was and reminding him he was meant to be home by now. Leo texted Kylie back – 'I'll be home in 10' – thinking to himself, *I'll just finish this beer then head out*. But alas, one of his friends returned from the bar with another beer for him. As 10 minutes passed and he was not home, this dance continued. Kylie upped her demands and threats. Leo continued to avoid, pushing out his return time and eventually not replying altogether. Eventually, Leo begrudgingly returned home. They had a big argument and went to bed angry with each other.

Our therapy focused on addressing both Kylie and Leo's conflict personas. Through this work, Kylie learnt to delay and resist her Micromanager's control response when she felt challenged by Leo. Practically, this meant not sending persistent text messages to Leo, checking in on his whereabouts or reminding him of his responsibilities. Resisting the urge to control meant she had to express her inner vulnerable feelings instead. This represented her experience more accurately. When Leo expressed his desires and feelings, Kylie had to work on staying calm and just listen. She often had to agree to something that left her feeling a little bit out of control.

On the other hand, avoidance was the target with Leo. He had to work on being more upfront with Kylie. White lies were banned because they simply kept pushing back the truth. For example, when he wanted to attend something, he worked on telling Kylie immediately about the event and his desire to attend. Leo had to practise identifying his own secondary conflict emotions and inner vulnerable feelings. Due to his avoidance of all discomfort, Leo was not aware of his inner world. Leo had to express himself even in the face of Kylie's Micromanager.

By letting go of their conflict personas, Kylie and Leo were able to find more cohesion in their relationship.

Conflict is the interplay of your conflict personas. When reflecting on Kylie and Leo, neither was right and the other wrong – both had understandable needs beneath their conflict personas. Rather, the dance was the problem. This dance maintained the conflict, and allowed it to return time and time again. You must break the dance to see real change and cohesion in your relationship.

You might be wondering, 'If conflict is a dance, how can I be the only one trying new steps? Don't we both need to know this new dance for our conflict to change?' You must take ownership. This is empowering. Otherwise, you will feel hopeless and powerless. When you change a step in the dance your partner will be forced to do something different. Something will shift.

 **TIME FOR ACTION**

Think of a recent conflict and try to map it out. Add a blow-by-blow account of what happened, what feelings you had, and actions taken. Include both your secondary conflict emotions and your inner vulnerable feelings. You can use the flow diagram opposite to help you map your conflict dance and how you might remove yourself from it.

Stepping away from the conflict dance

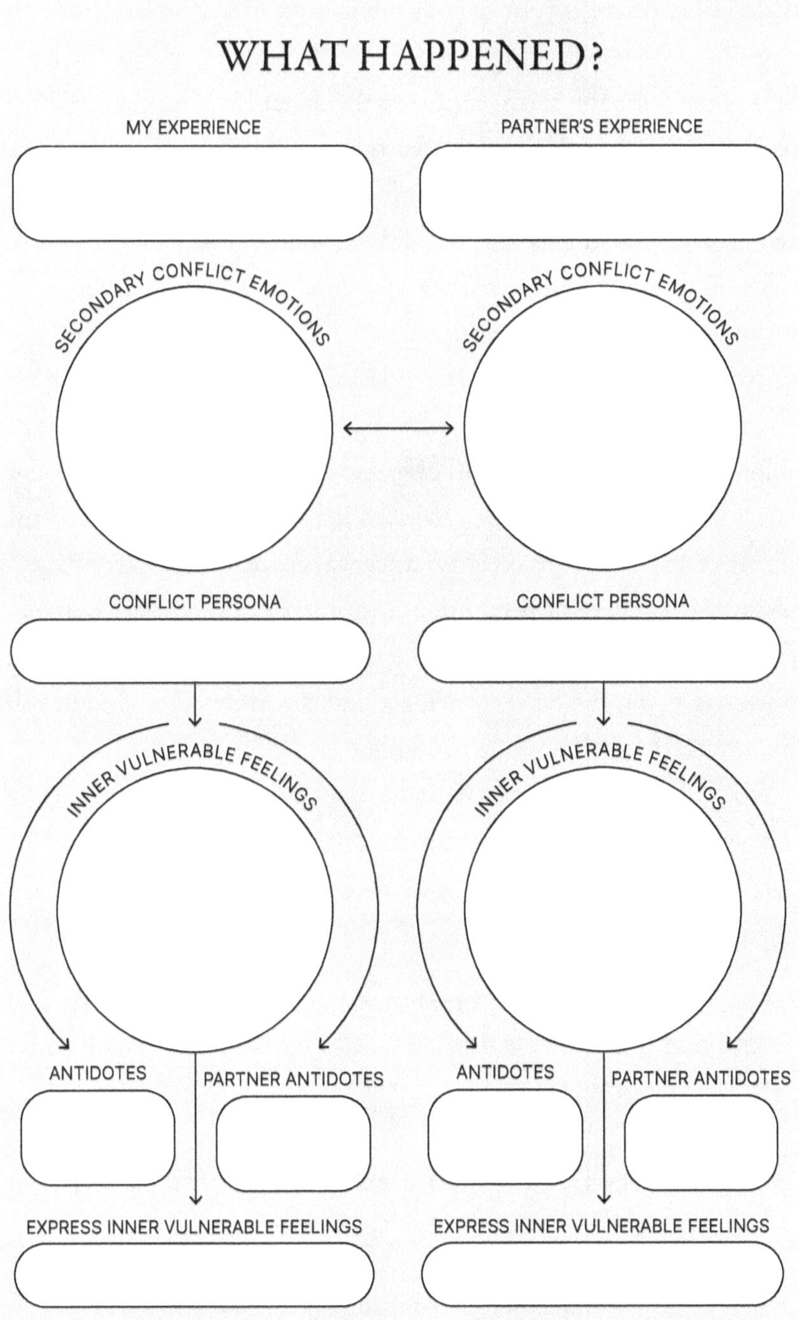

Retrospective work is important

The conflict dance is your default interaction in your relationship. So it's going to keep returning – and it's challenging to change the dance steps in the moment. If you can't stop the dance from happening, make sure you go back later. You will learn the skill 'reach out to repair' to identify each other's secondary conflict emotions and inner vulnerable feelings later on in this chapter. Take ownership of your part in the dance. Talk honestly about what happened, focusing on feelings and the interplay between you both.

Retrospective work involves coming back to your partner and talking about the conflict in a calm space. It is when you discuss inner vulnerable feelings and conflict personas after conflict. You can't expect to be perfect from the get-go. When you do retrospective work, you are teaching your brain alternative ways to act when in conflict. As your brain learns healthy communication results in a better outcome, you will become calmer when conflict arises. The more you practise retrospective work, the better you'll get and the more automatic healthy communication will become in conflict.

To explain this further, Shahn outlines a conversation he had with Michael, who had anger management problems.

Making time for retrospection

Michael: My Angry Attacker keeps coming out and causing all sorts of problems. I need you to help me stop it from happening. I have read the anger management books and nothing is working. Should I just keep taking time out when angry?

Shahn: Michael, as we discussed, if you feel your anger rising then taking time out to avoid further damage is always a good option. However, this alone is not going to tame your Angry Attacker conflict persona. A lot of anger management strategies teach you how to

prevent or defuse anger but they're not getting to the source of
the issue.

Michael: What do you mean? How do I change the source of the issue?

Shahn: Throughout your childhood you learned that you only received
attention from your busy parents when you screamed and acted out.
This wired you in a way that your Angry Attacker believes it has to
come out to get your needs met.

Michael: Okay, but how does that information help me stop the
Angry Attacker?

Shahn: That is just an explanation for the origin of your Angry Attacker.
To tame it, we need to teach your brain there is another way of
communicating. Unfortunately, we can't expect you to never get angry
again because the behaviour is ingrained. However, we can get you
to commit to owning the behaviour each and every time it occurs.
Each time the Angry Attacker comes out, you need to own it and
acknowledge the impact it has on other people. Then you need to
express your inner vulnerable feelings. For example, you need to go to
Anne and say, 'I know my Angry Attacker was just out, and I am sure
this made you feel scared and hopeless. I want you to know I am sorry.
What I was feeling underneath my anger was neglect. When you and
the kids had plans without me, I just felt left out.'

Michael: That sounds hard and I am not sure I will feel like doing it.

Shahn: It will be hard but it is the only way. If it takes you a week to
go back and speak to Anne, that's okay. Each time you practise the
retrospective work, you will be able to do it sooner the next time your
Angry Attacker comes out. It will eventually be the next day, the next
hour and then the next minute when you can do the retrospective
work. If you keep doing the retrospective work, you will one day reach
the point of change and express your feelings in a healthy way. With
practice, your brain will choose the better method of communication.
You will feel the Angry Attacker rising, but you will be able to temper it.
Then, everything will get better.

The two truths: Ending the relationship tug of war

Samantha and Emir have been together for over 10 years and have established a life together in Melbourne. Because they were young when they first started dating, they have grown into themselves together. Emir has established his own successful business, while Samantha has explored different career options through study and work. Their relationship has had the usual ups and downs but they have a lot of love and warmth for one another.

But Samantha isn't happy. She wants to move overseas. She has wanted this for a long time and is now advocating for it to be something they must make a decision on. And she's not backing down. Emir has little interest in living overseas and wants to stay living in Melbourne. Samantha and Emir are at a loss. They've discussed this topic time and time again. There have been tears, raised voices, doors slammed. They have agreed to take breaks from it. But still it festers. They are at a stalemate after going around and around on this issue. They just want different outcomes to the problem. Sadly, they are considering whether they need to break up over this issue.

When making decisions, couples fall into the dead-end relationship tug of war of who is right and who is wrong. Our 'two truths' exercise is a step-by-step guide to help you reach solutions together without there being a winner and a loser. You may be wondering how Samantha and Emir could possibly come to a win–win outcome. Don't worry – we come back to them later in this section.

Avoiding power struggles and the need to be right

In relationships, you can get locked into power struggles and tend to see arguments as, 'I'm right and they're wrong'. Power struggles are when you and your partner are disagreeing over something in which a decision needs to be made, and being in this tug of war feels like you are in a deadlock – stuck with nowhere to go. You may feel the need to dig your heels in further the longer it goes on. Or you feel like you have to surrender and let your partner win.

The two truths concept will help you move away from the dead-end, right/wrong relationship power struggle. It is a strategic and empathic approach to resolving conflicts and reaching mutual solutions. The concept guides you towards navigating power struggles and indecision by acknowledging the existence of two opposing truths within a given disagreement. This methodology emphasises the importance of understanding the inherent value behind each individual's position. It might feel like you are arguing over the same topic. But, in reality, the issues within this topic are different for each partner. The apparent disagreement stems from the different meanings associated with a shared topic or problem.

So while the conflict appears to be topical – such as, 'Should we spend money on travel?' – the tension is occurring due to a clash of needs or values. These are your and your partner's truths for the topic – for example, the desire for safety and security versus the desire for adventure and spontaneity. Two different truths are at play.

Our two truths exercise comes from the philosophy of dialectics – a method of philosophical inquiry and discussion that involves examining and resolving opposing ideas to arrive at a higher level of understanding. A dialectic is when two seemingly conflicting positions are true at the same time, so dialectics is a way of thinking and reasoning that acknowledges the dynamic and often contradictory nature of reality. It seeks to synthesise conflicting elements to reach a more comprehensive and nuanced perspective.

Our two truths tool is a way to arrive at decisions around complex problems. You can use it when you are in opposition but are able to speak kindly and respectfully to one another. It is not a tool for when conflict is heightened.

The two truths exercise can be used on endless topics – anything from which family you should spend Christmas with, to how often you should see the in-laws, or how much money you should or should not be saving. 'Should we get a puppy? Should you go out with your friends on Saturday night? Where should we go on holidays next?' Its uses are endless.

The two truths exercise

Here are the five parts to our two truths exercise:

1. *Identify the problem:* Together, define and agree on the problem.

2. *Identify the two positions in opposition to one another:* You have one position (what you want the outcome of the problem to be) and your partner has another (what they want the outcome to be).

3. *Acknowledge the two truths:* You need to identify both of these truths and then discuss them. Each position has a truth. The truth is the value and meaning beneath your position – the why to your position. It doesn't need to be logical, and neither is right or wrong. You have a truth and your partner has a truth in relation to the problem identified. Before you can move on to the next point, both partners must be able to feed back the truth behind each other's position.

4. *Decide together whether to compromise or come over:* Explore solutions in an open and curious way before committing. The solution options are either 'coming over' or 'compromise'. This means only three options are possible for a solution: you come over to your partner's position, your partner comes over to your position, or you find a compromise somewhere in the middle. Coming over is an act of love and must be communicated as such. It cannot be an act of sacrifice or resentment. One partner willingly joins the other in their position. You are not giving up your truth when coming over. You still hold your truth, but

you decide you are comfortable in coming over to your partner's desired outcome. When your partner comes over to you, you must show your appreciation and commit to reciprocating coming over in the future. Compromise means that both parties give up something and meet somewhere in the middle. Compromise must occur when both partners feel they cannot come over for the other. For a genuine compromise, both of you will give up and gain something. Neither partner will get their position (desired outcome). When choosing to compromise, you should brainstorm as many options as possible even if they seem silly or out there. Then explore the pros and cons of each compromise option.

5. *Choose your solution:* Together, with the knowledge of each other's truth, you choose one of the three solution options and do it wholeheartedly together.

If you don't understand the underlying truths in the problem, resentment can breed. Decisions can feel coerced, rather than being made as a team. This skill is life-changing. You will not only be able to make decisions together, but also have more understanding of one another and grow closer together.

Let's go back to Samantha and Emir, explained by Helen.

Finding compromise through the two truths

As Samantha and Emir are in Melbourne, I see them in our clinical practice via videoconferencing. We used the two truths exercise in session to work through their issue of Samantha wanting to move overseas and Emir wanting to stay in Melbourne. In just one session they were able to understand the truth beneath their separate positions. They visibly warmed to one another and could understand where each was coming from. This was despite them having very different positions and truths.

Together, they unpicked Samantha's truth for wanting to live overseas. She valued and needed adventure and exploration. She currently felt stuck in life and had for some time. Living overseas had always been on her bucket list. Emir's truth, on the other hand, was that he thrives with routine. He was anxious about not knowing what would be ahead, and financial security was one of the most important things for him. The truth behind Samantha's position was the need for adventure and exploration. The truth behind Emir's position was the desire for stability and the feeling of anxiety with change.

They brainstormed possible solutions, including potential compromises. Initially, Samantha and Emir found this hard. They were so stuck in their separate positions and found seeing anything else difficult. But with me, as the therapist, offering some pretty silly and outrageous as well as mild options, they got into it and came up with a range of compromises.

By doing the two truths, Samantha was clear she was unable to come over to Emir. She couldn't let go of her dream. Therefore, the solution had to be a compromise or Emir coming over to Samantha. In the end, they chose a compromise. This compromise was a commitment to living overseas for a minimum of one year. After six months, they would reassess how it was going. And Emir got to choose their destination.

In this example, neither Emir nor Samantha stayed in their position and neither got their desired outcome. However, they were able to shift to a compromise with each other's truth in mind. Coming to this decision was not possible until they had developed compassion and understanding for each other's truth.

Some decisions feel impossible. This was the case with Samantha and Emir. You might feel you are losing yourself if you shift your position. But by understanding the truth behind your and your partner's positions, you can grow empathy and move towards a workable solution that recognises and respects each other's truths.

Our clients often tell us, 'I'm letting my partner walk all over me if I let go of my truth and position.' Your truth never has to change. You never have to let go of your truth. You only let go of your position. You keep your truth but change your position out of love and respect for the relationship. If you are always coming over to your partner, then, yes, you are being walked all over. Or if your partner is always coming over to you, you are walking all over your partner. You need a balance between you and your partner coming over to one another.

♥ TIME FOR ACTION

Now you can try the two truths exercise with your partner:

1. Identify the problem.

2. Identify the two positions. Your position is what you want the outcome of the problem to be and your partner's is their desired outcome.

3. Acknowledge the two truths. Identify the value or truth to your position. Ask yourself, 'Why is this position so important to me? What does this mean to me?' Share your truth with your partner. Listen and understand your partner's truth.

4. Decide together whether to compromise or come over. Here you have three options: you both compromise, your partner comes over to you or you come over to your partner's position.

5. Enact the decision whole-heartedly. If you are coming over to your partner, do so fully! If your partner is coming over to you, be appreciative. If you are compromising, do so with grace and willingness.

You can use the worksheet overleaf to help you map out your responses.

Putting your truth and positions aside to hear your partner's position and truth can be difficult. Such differences can be uncomfortable to sit with. Often your ego gets in the way. You want to be right. It can be confronting to find your partner thinks and feels differently to you. It's human nature to want to be right and, therefore, feel uncomfortable with differences. Be kind to yourself. This is a challenging exercise.

Uncovering the two truths and finding solutions

THE ISSUE/PROBLEM/CONFLICT

PARTNER 1 POSITION

PARTNER 2 POSITION

PARTNER 1 TRUTH

PARTNER 2 TRUTH

PARTNER 2 COMING OVER

COMPROMISE

PARTNER 1 COMING OVER

OUR CHOSEN SOLUTION

It takes effort to accept each other's truths. To accept your partner's truth doesn't mean you like it or approve of it. To accept their truth is to acknowledge and embrace it, without resistance or judgement. They are allowed to have their truth – like you are allowed to have yours. Acceptance of each other's truth means you can each be your authentic selves in the relationship. To accept the presence of two different people yet still remain cohesive is enlightening and empowering.

A healthy relationship is not one without conflict

Relationships are in constant flux. Conflict can be positive, the vessel for change. By navigating conflict well, the tension in your relationship system will be reduced, helping you flow better as a couple and feel less constrained as an individual. With this in mind, who started the conflict is irrelevant. As the ultimate goal is to create positive relationship growth, both partners need to look for points of change and diffusion.

In this section, we run through the fundamentals of how to do conflict well, including steps and strategies. We start with 'reach out to repair' – a process of turning towards your partner, rather than away from them, to resolve conflicts. Next, we outline the gratitude letter – a way to show love and gratitude for your partner and the relationship as a whole. Finally, we walk you through 'own your shit', which tackles defensiveness and promotes willingness to take responsibility where appropriate.

Reach out to repair

After conflict, it is helpful to identify your and your partner's secondary conflict emotions and inner vulnerable feelings to understand what the conflict was really about. This needs to be done before you can move towards resolution. When you are able to communicate your inner vulnerable feelings, you and your partner will be taking a huge step toward connection, empathy and love.

Here's how to reach out to repair after conflict:

1. Identify and label your secondary conflict emotions.

2. Identify and label your inner vulnerable feelings. Dig deep and ask yourself why you might be so upset. Think about the impact the issue has had on you and how it leaves you feeling. Try to focus on you – not your partner and what they have done.

3. Express to your partner your inner vulnerable feelings and acknowledge your secondary conflict emotions.

4. Go one step further and identify your partner's secondary conflict emotions (this is the easy part). Then take a guess at what their inner vulnerable feelings might be. Check these with them.

5. Don't forget to practise feeling the story (chapter 4) when your partner is expressing their inner vulnerable feelings and secondary conflict emotions.

Gratitude letter

The gratitude letter is exactly what it sounds like – a letter you write to your partner outlining the things you love and are grateful for in them and the relationship. Often, particularly in conflict, you do not reflect on the good aspects of your partner, their positive influence on you or the value you gain from your relationship. It's easy to get bogged down in the negatives of the relationship, which means you get stuck seeing your partner and relationship through a negative lens. This feeds conflict. The gratitude letter does the opposite. It brings attention to the positives in your partner and what they bring to the relationship. This, in turn, can bring down your defences.

You can use the gratitude letter following an argument or conflict. Whether the issue is resolved or not is irrelevant because the gratitude letter works to change the mood of your interaction. It refocuses you, away from the content of the conflict and onto what you love and value in your partner. It is an act of love and kindness, helping you cut through all the nastiness of the argument and get straight to what matters. The gratitude letter is a way of coming back together to reconnect, which feels good.

When writing your gratitude letter, focus on why your partner is important to you. Reflect on what you have learnt from them and the things you love most about them. Take a moment to reflect on how your partner might be feeling after the latest conflict or argument and affirm your commitment to them and your relationship as a whole. Steer away from any content-focused comments surrounding the conflict.

When receiving a gratitude letter, you must see it as an act of love and kindness on the part of your partner. Your partner has gone to the effort to write you this letter so please try to open your heart to it and the sentiments within.

Own your shit

When in conflict, it is easy to feel criticised or attacked, and so respond with defensiveness. Defensiveness is a protective response in the face of perceived threat or criticism, shielding you from perceived attacks to your self-esteem, identity or relationship. Through denial, counter-attacks, deflecting, excuses, blaming or avoidance, defensiveness aims to preserve your sense of safety and worth. Yet, defensiveness instead hinders connection, communication and problem-solving, and escalates conflict.

The 'own your shit' approach circumvents defensiveness and de-escalates conflict. Owning your shit means taking responsibility for your part in the conflict, argument or situation. This might be your behaviour (intentional or not), your mistakes or your insensitivities.

Owning your shit requires genuine vulnerability. You are putting your hand up to acknowledge your humanness. You stuff up sometimes. Owning your shit doesn't mean you are conceding to your partner or offering to take all responsibility for the conflict. Rather, you are taking ownership of your part in the negative interaction. Owning your shit doesn't mean you should be punished or shamed for your behaviour – by your partner or yourself. It is a growth strategy in which you increase your self-esteem and integrity by looking inward, accepting and taking responsibility for yourself and your behaviour.

Some examples of behaviours you might need to own include the following:

- not doing a domestic chore or any domestic duties
- not doing what you said you were going to do
- coming home later than you said you would
- drinking more than you said you would
- talking rudely to your partner
- yelling
- criticising or mocking your partner
- being rude to your partner in front of friends
- ignoring your partner
- being in a conflict persona
- snapping at your partner
- not prioritising the relationship.

Owning your shit works best when it goes both ways. It's not helpful if one partner always owns their shit, and the other never does. This will lead to feelings of resentment and frustration. However, it's also not 'tit for tat'. Just because you've owned your shit at this moment doesn't mean your partner has to. Sometimes, it may be only you who has something to own. It's more important that, over time and arguments, a sense of equity develops in how much you both own your shit.

Here are the four simple steps to owning your shit:

1. *Bring awareness to your experience of defensiveness:* Notice the urge to defend or fight back. Observe your body tensing up.

Identify feelings of anger or frustration. Tune into your body sensations and what your mind might be telling you. Label this experience as defensiveness: 'I am feeling defensive.'

2. *Listen out for the truth in what your partner is saying:* This is challenging. You may not want to admit it. Feelings of guilt or shame can turn up here. Be kind to yourself but also take responsibility. Ask yourself, 'What is my partner accusing me of? Am I responsible for anything in this disagreement or interaction? Have I done something or not done something that wasn't helpful or nice, even if my intention wasn't bad? Am I letting the team down or not pulling my weight in some way?'

3. *Take responsibility for those parts that are true.* What can you take responsibility for in this conflict or in what your partner is saying? Own what is true in your partner's criticism of you. You do not need to take responsibility for those parts that are not true.

4. *Express an interest in how your partner might have felt due to your part in the problem.* Have a guess how your partner may have felt as a result of what you said, did or didn't do.

Doing conflict well

Reach out to repair, the gratitude letter and own your shit are all acts of kindness. Such positive action often leads to positive outcomes. When you soften, show kindness and take responsibility, your partner is more likely to mirror you. Here is Helen's personal example of our gratitude letter.

Practising what we preach

Shahn and I get stuck in conflict just like the rest of the world. In this particular incident, we were in a complete stalemate. We had talked it out, disagreed with one another, and then decided, 'Right, we'll just stop talking about it'. The tension between us was palpable.

Although we'd conceded to just avoid the whole thing, it felt awful. I was preoccupied with our argument; going around and around in my head, trying to come up with new ways to prove I was right. It was exhausting and distracting. This continued for a couple of days. Then one evening as I finished work, I saw a text come through from Shahn. My stomach dropped and I thought, *Oh no, here we go again.*

But it was a different kind of message. It was our gratitude letter in the form of a text message. In this message, Shahn cut through the conflict by expressing how much gratitude he had for me and our relationship. He noted this conflict had been challenging and he could imagine that I was feeling hurt and misunderstood. He acknowledged how important I and our relationship were to him. The conflict felt so big at the time, yet as I write this I'm struggling to remember exactly what we were arguing about for those couple of days. What I can remember is Shahn's message.

Your relationship is so much bigger than any dispute. When I received Shahn's gratitude letter, I immediately softened and we were able to come back together with care and love. When one person softens, the other often follows. It was a big step for Shahn to offer this gratitude letter to me. He had to put his ego and position in the argument to one side to choose care and connection. And I'm very appreciative of it.

Our clients often say to us, 'Well my partner isn't reaching out to me to resolve our dispute or making an effort to bring positivity into the relationship. Why should I?' You can only control your own behaviour. That's it. If you don't do something, nothing's going to change. Positivity breeds positivity. When you show a willingness to resolve conflict and take responsibility, your partner might also feel safe to do so. Approaching your partner with tenderness, showing care and taking responsibility are courageous and show vulnerability. They are not signs of weakness but great strengths. Strengths that can help heal a relationship.

Familiarity and resistance to discomfort work against you. It's not uncommon to get stuck in the same negative conflict cycles.

Humans have a natural tendency to be drawn to the familiar, even when the familiar isn't good for us. This is particularly relevant when circumstances are challenging. Doing something different can feel uncomfortable and even wrong. But discomfort is a good thing. It means you are expanding. Growth and positive change only arise when you step out of your comfort zone and embrace new ways of thinking and behaving. Just because it feels strange or uncomfortable, doesn't mean you shouldn't persist. Over time, the new behaviour will become easier and will become the new familiar. Your relationship will be much better for it.

Ensuring your base camp and boundaries are intact

Veechi and Giovani's relationship was sailing through the six-month mark. They got along well and had a meaningful connection. But a storm was brewing beneath the surface. Giovani, with his last-minute approach to dating and socialising, unknowingly cast a shadow over their otherwise budding connection.

Giovani's dating style reflected his spontaneous nature. He would surprise Veechi with last-minute date invitations. While this brought an element of excitement in the early stages of their relationship, Veechi found it increasingly challenging to align her schedule with Giovani's spontaneous whims.

Despite Veechi's efforts to plan ahead and extend invitations for them to meet up, Giovani often found himself agreeing to her proposals at the eleventh hour. Veechi, though understanding of his free-spirited personality, couldn't shake off the growing frustration. The problem wasn't just the spontaneity, but also the impact it had on her sense of worth and ability to commit to other plans.

Veechi found herself waiting anxiously for Giovani, uncertain if their plans would materialise. This made it difficult for her to commit to other social engagements, leaving her feeling stuck and unfulfilled. She began to question the level of importance she held in Giovani's life and whether his last-minute approach was a reflection of his priorities.

Veechi and Giovani's experience touches on boundary issues. We cover boundaries – and, in particular, the importance of setting up boundaries within your relationship – in chapter 2, but here's a quick recap. Boundaries establish the rules and guidelines that promote mutual respect, emotional safety and individuality within a relationship. They assist with communication, conflict resolution, trust building and maintaining your own identity. Importantly, they are not one person's boundaries or preferences. Boundaries are mutually satisfying and provide respectful limits agreed on by both parties.

Boundary violations range from relatively minor infringements to more extreme behaviours. What counts as a boundary violation is dependent on your relationship and your agreed boundaries. Here are some examples:

- being on the phone a lot
- drinking alcohol every single night, or consuming alcohol beyond the agreed boundary
- speaking negatively about your partner to other people
- being overly flirtatious with others
- saying yes to a third party without consultation to your partner
- having an emotional or sexual affair
- restricting autonomy, saying no and having negative reactions to requests for individual pursuits
- making unilateral decisions that affect the relationship.

Dealing with boundary violations

Boundary violations are common in relationships and can have serious consequences, particularly if left unchecked. Learning how to deal with such boundary violations is necessary for the integrity of your relationship. While ending a relationship at the first sign of a boundary issue may be tempting – and may feel safer – it might be a way of avoiding responsibility in the interaction. Likewise, not addressing boundary violations out of a fear of conflict will only serve to decrease your value in the relationship. Instead, addressing boundary violations requires a graded approach.

We find a helpful and healthy approach to boundaries is to liken them to a solid wall with a door in it. A healthy boundary is solid and sturdy like a wall. But the wall always has an opening (the door) through which you are able to reconnect.

To explain this, let's go back to Veechi and Giovani. Veechi was Shahn's individual client.

Setting a clear boundary

After numerous evenings spent waiting for Giovani, Veechi brought this up in her therapy with me. Through our discussion, Veechi decided it was time to address the issue directly with Giovani.

Veechi expressed her feelings honestly to Giovani, explaining how the lack of planning made her feel unimportant and constrained. Giovani, initially taken aback by Veechi's revelation, admitted he hadn't realised the toll his behaviour was taking on her. He committed to being more considerate of Veechi's need for a balance between spontaneity and planning. He understood that while his free-spirited approach was part of his charm, it shouldn't come at the expense of Veechi's wellbeing.

A healthy boundary was agreed on: Giovani needed to decide on their plans for the weekend, in particular Saturday night, by the Thursday before. The 'door' in the boundary was agreeing to plans by Thursday. Veechi and Giovani came to this together. If Giovani failed to commit by Thursday, Veechi would plan and commit to friends. This was her solid wall.

Such a boundary was important because it promoted Veechi's self-respect and need to feel valued. Upholding the wall was just as important as accepting the 'door'. Whether or not she had plans for the weekend, if Giovani contacted her on Friday to meet up, Veechi would say no. Veechi enforced the boundary only one time before Giovani's behaviour changed.

Being transparent with your partner about boundaries in your relationship and their consequences is essential. Further, the boundary may be presented by one of you to address a particular unmet need, just like it was for Veechi. But being flexible and welcoming the other's input means a more sturdy and respected boundary can be built.

Enforcing boundaries with a stepped approach

Putting in boundaries is difficult and boundary violations can ruin your relationship. If a boundary violation is impacting your relationship, you must take a stepped approach to trying to resolve it. If you don't take a stance against boundary violations, you are non-verbally communicating that you accept the negative behaviour in the relationship. Even if you verbally complain without action, you are not actually enforcing boundaries.

The following list is a guide to a stepped approach of enforcing boundaries. Start at the top and work your way down. The number of times you should enforce a particular boundary violation in each step is unspecified. Do it based on what you think is fair and reasonable. If you are feeling frustrated at the lack of change, it is time to take the next step. Only proceed to the next boundary management step if the step you are on is not successful in maintaining the boundary.

Work your way through the following steps during boundary violations:

1. *Notice the boundary violation:* Which domain is it in? (Refer to chapter 2 for a recap on relationship commandments and domains.) What commandments are being compromised? How is it impacting you and the relationship? Does this violation represent a potential shift in a domain? With your

partner, point out the commandment violation and discuss the impacts. Then, talk to them openly about a potential shift in the domain. Do they want to change something or are you both still aligned? Re-commit to each other and discuss ways to limit the boundary violation.

2. *Have a chat with your partner about what inner vulnerable feelings are evoked by the boundary violation:* Tell them you feel disrespected and uncared for. Ask them if they can curb the behaviour and, in turn, ask if you can do anything to make it easier for them. For example, if partner one keeps cancelling on family commitments at the last minute, this leaves partner two in an awkward position. Partner one can commit to being reliable while partner two can agree to limit family commitments or encourage a day a week where partner one goes out with friends to feel more independent.

3. *Use the two truths exercise to enhance understanding and empathy:* Does the boundary need to be adjusted to honour both or one of your truths? See if either of you can come over or compromise. (Refer to 'The two truths: Ending the relationship tug of war', earlier in this chapter, for more on this exercise.)

4. *Use the emotional mirror:* The emotional mirror is a metaphorical concept in which one partner shows interest in the other's feelings while simultaneously setting boundaries around certain behaviours. It involves holding up a 'mirror' to reflect and communicate how a specific behaviour is affecting the relationship, and is a healthy boundaried response rather than a reactive conflict persona response.

   You can use the emotional mirror to set limits around the boundary violation and associated behaviours. For example, if your partner approaches you in anger, instead of reacting in a conflict persona or with defensiveness, you hold up the metaphoric emotional mirror. You stay calm (not joining them in a conflict dance). You explain to them that you are not prepared to talk to them about the issue while they're angry (this is the solid wall). However, you really want to know what is going on for them and you are there to talk about it when their emotions are 'below the line' (this is the door in the solid wall). If necessary, you walk away while reminding them you will only interact with them once they cool down. You may think this will make your partner angrier; often, however, it doesn't. While people can escalate initially when they are given boundaries, if you stay in position and hold this healthy boundary, their behaviour becomes more obvious and they start to respond positively. (See 'Using the emotional mirror', later in the chapter, for more detail on how to use this approach.)

5. *When feeling calm, explain to your partner you are feeling betrayed by the boundary violation and are starting to lose trust in the relationship:* Do not engage in further conversation or conflict about the boundary violation at this point. Instead, set a boundary by removing yourself physically and partake in a value-driven behaviour involving supportive people in your life. After this, engage back with your partner to express the impacts of the boundary violations on yourself and the relationship. For example, say partner one suggests to partner two that they go out for dinner on Friday night, but partner one has a history of cancelling couple plans to prioritise work outside of business hours. This causes significant relationship distress because little time is given to the relationship. Partner one then cancels their dinner plans. Partner two calmly communicates they feel betrayed and are losing trust in the relationship. They also communicate they need some space and won't be available until Saturday afternoon. Partner two then visits her supportive parents on Friday night. On Saturday

morning, partner two meets a friend for a coffee and a coastal walk. The value-based behaviours of connecting with family, friends, nature and exercise allows partner two to value herself in a way partner one is not. The space and time is a consequence of the boundary violation. It communicates, 'You can't have me unconditionally – I have value'. When coming back together, partner two discusses the impact the boundary violations are having on her and the relationship, and informs partner one she can't stay in a relationship where she is not valued.

6. *Leave:* Leaving the relationship is the ultimate limit if the boundary violation continues to occur without improvement. While it is not a desired outcome, it should always be the last step in mind. Without this, you are communicating to yourself and your partner that you are willing to be mistreated.

When addressing boundary violations, you might feel you are creating tension or conflict where it didn't already exist. Tensions might ensue when you bring up boundary violations. But it is worth it. How you manage the boundary crossing can minimise the damage significantly. More importantly, addressing boundaries will sustain the health of the relationship. Without this, you will continue to fall into relationship traps that undermine the integrity of your relationship.

Boundaries and maintaining them are a key component of a successful, fulfilling and lasting relationship. Here is a personal example from Helen.

Setting boundaries with love

Early in our relationship, I would get upset and distressed on occasion. When in conflict, I thought I was expressing my feelings and vulnerability in a healthy way. I was being honest and open about my experience. Yet, until Shahn pointed it out, I was unaware that I was actually coming across as angry and attacking.

Shahn pointed this out gently. He explained he could tell I was upset and wanted to understand what was going on for me. But he couldn't work with this angry side of me. He had all the time in the world for my vulnerability but not for my unbridled anger. This was confronting. I didn't want to hear what he was saying. I felt embarrassed that I was so out of tune with my emotions. I felt guilty for the impact my behaviour had on him. And I felt frustrated that my needs I was advocating for weren't getting met. Yet the core of Shahn's message was loving and supportive. He did want to meet my needs but my anger was getting in the way of him doing so.

By working on the expression of my distress in a healthy way, I could get my needs better met. By Shahn using the emotional mirror with me, I learnt it was safe in our relationship to express my true vulnerabilities (my inner vulnerable feelings). My secondary conflict emotions were only getting in the way and hurting Shahn. When I did express my inner vulnerable feelings, Shahn stopped, listened and validated as he said he would.

Helen's story demonstrates how managing boundaries is not punitive or critical. It is an act of love and support, allowing your and your partner's needs to be better met. Her story also shows a boundary violation may not come from sinister intentions. You might not even realise you're violating a boundary. If you set a boundary, you need to follow through. Shahn said he had all the time in the world for Helen's vulnerability, so he had to honour this when she was vulnerable – otherwise, she would never have trusted in safely expressing her inner vulnerable feelings.

Using the emotional mirror

A common dispute we hear from our clients is, 'My partner will get upset if I try to manage a boundary violation on their part.' This can be daunting, especially if you are more self-sacrificing. You have no guarantee your partner will respond well to you reinforcing a boundary – in fact, they likely won't initially. But you have to start. It's uncomfortable for both parties, but it gets easier the more you do it. Remember – boundary management is not critical or punishing. It is an act of love for the relationship, so you both feel valued and your true selves in your relationship.

To help with this act, we invite you to try the emotional mirror. As mentioned, using the emotional mirror means demonstrating an interest in how your partner is feeling, reflecting back to them their behaviour in question and setting a limit around the particular behaviour. The emotional mirror assists in you staying as calm and neutral as possible by reflecting back the negative energy you are receiving from your partner. This can protect you from flipping into a conflict persona. By staying calm and empathic, the boundary crossing is more obvious.

Here's how to use the emotional mirror:

1. Identify the behaviour that has crossed your couple domain boundary and the relevant relationship commandments. Be specific.

2. Identify the impact of the behaviour on you.

3. Show care, empathy and willingness to address the underlying issue.

4. Set a limit.

5. Enforce the limit. This might involve removing yourself from the situation.

As an example, consider Sebastian and Luke. Luke has a habit of talking to Sebastian disrespectfully. Luke comes from a family who tend towards dismissiveness. They don't dwell on things and use the 'get over it' approach. This apparently works in his family of origin. But by engaging in this way with Sebastian, Luke is breaching the commandments of the campfire (care and warmth) and the walkie talkies (coming together to communicate respectfully). This leaves Sebastian feeling hurt. He's willing to talk about the issue, but not in this dismissive way.

The emotional mirror for Sebastian sounded like this: 'Luke, when we are in conflict, I'm noticing you speak to me like you and your family speak to one another. Although that's okay for your family, it's not okay for our relationship because we've agreed to speak kindly and respectfully to one another. When you speak like that to me, I feel hurt, demeaned and lost with where to go. I want to understand what's going on beneath this need to shut it down and tell me to get over it. Something must be going on for you and I want to understand it, but I can't when this dismissive statement is being thrown at me. I can't talk about the issue when you are saying these things to me, so please come back to me when we can talk about this in a more caring way.'

When you move away from a conflict persona dance by re-establishing a boundary, your partner's behaviour may initially escalate. Unconsciously, this escalation is designed to move you back into your familiar conflict persona dance. You must anticipate this and maintain your new dance steps. If you hold steady, your partner will have to adjust their steps as a reaction to your new behaviour.

Summing up

Congratulations! You made it through the enormous chapter. In this mammoth chapter, you have gained insight into conflict. It is inevitable and, if done well, can be an avenue for deeper connection and understanding. Conflict can be about anything, and you've explored the numerous conflict topics most relationships find themselves tangled in. Yet you've gained understanding into the two layers of emotions that cause and maintain conflict. You've learned about secondary conflict emotions, which may have felt like the only experience of the interaction, and explored inner vulnerable feelings, which tell a richer story of the interaction.

You've met your conflict personas and seen how they dance with your partner's. While conflict personas were once your friends helping to protect you, you know they are now working against you. You've explored the antidotes to use with your own conflict personas and antidotes to use with your partner's conflict personas. These will help break your conflict dance. You've learned how to resolve conflict and come to mutual solutions using the two truths exercise. And you've discovered how to be brave and engage in proactive actions to break the conflict cycle, mastering the gratitude letter and owning your shit. Finally, you've learned how to respond to boundary violations in a loving way.

Stop waiting for your partner to be the bigger person. Stop thinking conflict will cease only when your partner understands where you are coming from. You must start reflecting on and taking responsibility for your own emotions and behaviours, and see your role in your relationship's conflict dance. When you do this, you have the power to break the cycle of negative feedback loops.

Now you know how to navigate conflict in your relationship and harness it for good. Your relationship is well on the way to a more peaceful and authentic connection. You are creating more positive cycles and feedback loops that will have a positive effect on the other love links. In the next chapter, we help you have deeper connections with your partner. We move away from the negative lens of conflict and into the exciting and relationship-enhancing space of values, building joint goals and getting to know one another on a deeper level.

Link six
Deep Connections

Linton and Elaine came to our clinic in distress. They couldn't understand how they'd got to this point in their relationship. They were both high achievers and had met many relationship goals. They built their dream home. They had kids in private schools. They often had dinners with friends. They were doing well as parents and financially. But something was missing. They said they'd felt like roommates for a while and couldn't understand why. Linton said that they'd run out of love and it was normal. He'd read something about the seven-year itch and they'd made it past that milestone twice so maybe that was just it.

Linton and Elaine were living parallel lives. On the surface, they had achieved a lot together. However, they did not have an intimate relationship on any level. At the end of the night, they'd go into separate rooms to either scroll on their phones or watch TV. There was no desire and little emotional intimacy. This did not occur overnight. Their disconnection was the culmination of many years of relationship neglect.

This story does not have a happy ending. While Elaine was keen to try to re-engage in the relationship, Linton had checked out. Elaine knew their relationship was not perfect, but had no idea Linton had been contemplating exiting the relationship for a long time. Linton and Elaine broke up. They had lost each other.

Deep connections are the profound and meaningful bonds established between individuals in a romantic relationship. They are like the threads weaving through the fabric of your relationship, binding you and your partner together in a tapestry of shared moments, emotions and dreams, creating a beautiful and resilient bond. They support the growth of a lasting relationship and are its basis as it thrives. These connections are characterised by a strong emotional and psychological intimacy, allowing partners to understand and appreciate each other's thoughts, desires and experiences. Deep connections involve a sense of vulnerability and trust, and foster open and honest communication, empathy and support within the relationship.

In this chapter, we outline the value and consequences of how you spend your time, and the importance of continuing to learn about and understand the inner world of your partner.

We then cover the power of doing exciting and new things together, and the effect this will have on your relationship. We also explore how creating space for autonomy keeps the mystery and excitement alive while helping you both feel more satisfied and free in your relationship.

Throughout this chapter, you will learn practical ways to form deep connections and unlock the power and positive influence of this sixth love link.

The power of a deep connection

Partners in a deep connection feel secure, heard and valued by one another, creating a solid foundation for mutual growth and companionship. Quality time together is intentional and focused. Space is carved out to connect, experience new things together or to promote autonomy. To form and maintain a robust bond with your partner, you have to take a multifaceted and balanced approach. For example, investing quality time in shared values is as important as creating space for autonomy in your relationship. Deep connections promote shared intimate experiences, for mutual and individual growth. As covered in chapter 3 (the Magic Moments love link), it's important to be present and committed to the moment when fostering a meaningful relationship. Magic Moments are the small gestures of kindness and connection that set the tone for the relationship. Deep connections go deeper. They are the key foundations that establish the direction of your relationship, based on values, emotional intimacy, aspirations and goals.

The Deep Connections love link is not about watching streaming services together. Watching a TV series is a time for mutual relaxation at best. In excess, it can be unhealthy self-soothing. Don't worry – TV has a place in your relationship. It can be fun and interesting to discuss a show together. However, this is not the quality time we're talking about in deep connections. Creating deep connections requires higher quality interactions. You need to be listening and attending to each other above all other distractions, and approaching interactions with curiosity. Deep connections are also formed when engaging in a new experience together or creating time for one another to pursue high-value interests.

When you engage in deep connections, you carry the good feeling with you beyond the interaction. This good feeling stays with you for the rest of your day or longer, and it influences your life outlook. This is the difference between engaging in deep connections versus relaxing. When you watch a show or eat your favourite food (or both at the same time) the good feeling ceases as soon as it is over.

If you have formed deep connections in your relationship, you are safe to be authentic and vulnerable. You're not concerned about feeling judged by your partner because you're confident they accept you unconditionally.

Having meaningful conversations, discussing dreams, fears and aspirations, and sharing vulnerabilities brings a closeness between partners. Authenticity is important. This means discussing hard topics or differences in a respectful way and is the opposite of avoidance or holding a wall up. It is about embracing what you love and accepting different opinions.

Finding time for deep connection

Deep bonds are formed in many ways. One example is through a flowing conversation to understand each other's inner world and build a feeling of validation and togetherness. Another might be carving out time for each other to do something enriching, such as a social, creative, sporting or intellectual pursuit. This action promotes a sense of gratitude, freedom and deep appreciation for the relationship. Further, creating time for excitement or new hobbies together promotes a positive association to the relationship. Deep connections make your relationship stronger.

This might be sounding like a whole lot of mumbo jumbo. 'Why should I care about this?' you might be wondering. 'Is it worth it?' Yes, it is! Without growth within your relationship, it's highly likely to end or at best be mediocre.

As a couple and couple therapists (and the authors of this book), it probably comes as no surprise that we make time for our relationship and forming deep connections. Connecting every day is one of our top priorities, but this can mean many things. It might be as simple as taking our dog Indie (indie_the_alaskan_klee_kai is on Instagram if you'd like to meet the cute little guy) for a walk without distractions so we can check in with each other. It's having at least one meal together each day and going to bed together each night without the distractions of technology. We also embark on many joint projects. These vary and can be anything from business-related activities, to seeking out adventure and travel together. The point here is that as a couple we work toward connection and goals. This allows for shared experience and mutual growth. Further, prioritising the relationship means we are each other's number one. For example, if we have something planned together, we stick with our plan unless something very important arises.

We've also pursued shared common interests that have been new and exciting. For example, we've taken dance lessons. We both enjoyed this, even though one of us was much better than the other. (Helen couldn't stop laughing at Shahn's awkward moves.) We love hiking, and have planned and completed many hikes together in new environments. Exploring the world together is very important because we both share the value of exploration and adventure. For us, our relationship bond is strengthened because we meet the needs for this value within the relationship.

We also take time to promote our own autonomy. For example, we're comfortable saying to each other, 'I'm going out with my friends and I'd rather go alone than as a couple.' We see friends as individuals and as a couple. We understand the need for autonomy and don't get offended when one of us needs some individual friend time. There is a freedom in being able to say, 'I need some more autonomy time' without fear it will lead to conflict. In our relationship, this is easy – not because we value autonomy so much, but because we prioritise our relationship and spend lots of quality time together.

We also make time to support each other's activities. For example, time is scheduled for Helen to pursue her hobby of agility training with Indie and for Shahn to pursue his freediving training.

When you invest in each other, you form deep connections. You do this by connecting with your partner and sharing common goals and values, while still allowing each other to feel free in the relationship.

Time is precious, invest it wisely

The time you put into your relationship today will influence your relationship tomorrow. To have a strong relationship now and into the future, you must move it up the priority list. Do you and your partner create time for each other? If you don't, you're not alone. Most couples have good intentions that do not come to fruition. This occurs because it is easier to engage in activities that bring immediate comfort or pleasure. For example, having a glass of wine takes less effort than going for a walk with your partner. It is easier to have a meal in front of the TV than to put effort into a conversation. Spending hours on your phone or online is easier than taking those dance or cooking lessons together. The problem here is that you can end up regretting choosing comfort over a high-value relationship activity. The cycle of choosing what's easy or comfortable keeps you in a rut. However, you won't regret doing a high-value relationship activity over comfort because afterwards you are left with a sense of connection and mastery.

Determining the value of your activities

We want to help you gain control of your relationship and life so you can start to thrive. With that in mind, we invite you to think about the behaviours you engage in on a regular basis – either solo activities or those you do with your partner. These behaviours will fall into three categories: high-value, low-value and no-value activities. High-value activities are in line with your values and the version of your best self. Some examples are spending meaningful time with your partner (whether it is a conversation or an activity such as playing pickleball), time with friends and family, doing activities that look after your health, putting effort into study or career, focusing on charity work or a cause, developing mastery in a hobby, or putting effort into a business idea or other project such as a herb garden at home. High-value activities are meaningful in your life. They might be hard to do and take work, but you come away with a strong sense of mastery. You don't regret time spent on these activities or wish you had been doing something else.

Perspective is important when it comes to working out what a high-value activity is for you. For example, some people feel doing the dishes or cooking dinner are not high-value activities. However, if you're doing this for yourself, your partner or your family, we consider they *are* high-value activities. Imagine if no-one ever did the dishes. The people in the house wouldn't be able to eat. The action of cooking and cleaning improves the lives of people around you. Some activities have higher value than you realise.

As implied, low-value activities bring less to your life. For example, let's say you're into gaming. We are not saying gaming has no value. (Playing EA Sports FC Online, formally known as FIFA Online, is one of Shahn's guilty pleasures.) But it has less value than high-value activities. Even though you may get some mastery and enjoyment from the activity, you don't carry a good feeling for long after the activity is completed. Other things in the low-value category include watching sports, going to the movies and online shopping. We're not saying they have no value. Low-value activities can be pleasurable and good for you in the right doses. However, they don't provide the same level of meaning you might get from spending quality time with your partner or family.

To be clear, low-value activities can be very enjoyable and healthy if they get less attention than high-value activities. While a low-value activity may interest you, it does not stack up in terms of importance when compared to your relationship. If you invest too much time in the lower value activities at the expense of high-value activities, you will feel listless, anxious and low in mood. Low-value activities might bring you a sense of pleasure in the moment, but you rarely walk away from them with a positive feeling when done in excess. Also be aware that some high-value activities can slip into the category of low-value activities if they become obstructive to your relationship or health. For example, if you are staying late at work most nights or always working on the weekend, you will no doubt be neglecting your relationship. The once high-value activity of putting effort and time into work has now become destructive.

No-value activities do not add long-term positivity to your life – for example, mindlessly scrolling on a feed, mindless snacking, drinking too much alcohol or smoking. Where's the value in these activities? No-value activities are bad habits that help you escape a feeling but add no value to your life. Investing too much time in a no-value activity can have serious consequences, such as physical and mental health and relationship problems. No-value activities can be low-value activities in excess. So they could include binge watching TV or excessive online shopping. When the behaviour becomes harmful to your relationship or health, it has transformed into a no-value activity.

Finding the right balance

It's easy to fall into a life where you engage in a whole bunch of low-value or no-value activities. The more stress in your life, the more you will lean toward low-value or no-value activities to compensate. For example, if work is busy and your relationship and home life is stressed, you will have a greater desire for immediate relief. Therefore, you're more prone to engaging in no-value activities such as excessive phone use, porn, gambling, watching endless amounts of TV, or misusing marijuana, alcohol or other vices. It's then easy to develop a habit in these activities. You fall into the trap of believing that these activities are where life is enjoyable. When in this trap, you are metaphorically holding your breath each day until you can inhabit the no-value bubble. Any relief from a negative mood state, however, is temporary.

The streaming rut is an easy one to relate to – indeed, we can relate to this. We've had busy periods trying to balance family, school homework and business, and feeling exhausted day after day. Flopping on the couch and spending the last two to three hours of the night watching Netflix felt like a way to zone out and recover.

Let's be clear – watching TV can be unwinding time. We enjoy watching a good series together. However, it goes beyond leisure when you spend too much time doing it. It also takes away precious time from high-value activities – even if the high-value activity is as simple as getting more sleep!

Two to three years ago we were stuck in a Netflix rut, watching more than a couple of hours each night. We both enjoyed the warm bubble of escape. However, we also noticed we felt a bit dirty and grumpy afterwards. That much TV was in opposition to our values. It was then that we came up with the Netflix addiction exercise. We worked out that we had been watching three to four episodes a night over the preceding two weeks. We then worked out how many episodes we would watch over a year if we kept the same pace. The result was staggering – watching four episodes of TV a day, we'd watch a staggering 1460 episodes per year. If the average season runs for 10 episodes, that's 146 seasons! And that's a lot of time and a lot of TV! With that calculation in mind, bursting the Netflix bubble was easy. Together, we identified other high-value activities we would rather be engaging in, and were able to make a commitment to these and hold each other accountable.

These are the high-value activities we put in place of the extra TV hours:

- 15 to 20 minutes of yoga stretching each night – a must for anyone who wants to keep going to the gym over 40!

- Prioritising sleep – bedtime ritual commences eight and a half hours before wake up time.

- Night-time reading in bed – and, of course, no devices in our bedroom.

The compounding effects over the last few years have been amazing. Even on a practical level, we are physically more flexible, better rested and well read.

When you think about how finite life is, time becomes valuable because it's irreplaceable.

You can't be productive all the time. Even if you are motivated, leisure and recovery is necessary to get the most out of your brain. When it comes to leisure and recovery, however, you might not think about high-value activities. High-value activities are often associated with effort, discomfort and work, whereas no-value activities are easy and offer immediate reward. For example, it's a lot easier to binge-watch TV than it is to have dinner without distraction with your partner. The problem here is that no-value activities are not as recharging as you might think. Once you turn off the TV or gaming device, put the phone down or sober up, you are out of the comfort bubble and all your stress is waiting for you.

When engaged in no-value activities, you are not resting. You are just deferring or masking your stress. This can be a major cause for disconnection in your relationship. You'll have more interactions in a stressed state and the call of the no-value bubble will be more appealing than connecting with your partner. You might also underestimate how recharging high-value activities are. For example, spending the last 15 minutes of your day doing yoga with your partner is much more restorative than watching more TV. Giving each other a massage or going for a walk calms your mind much more than doom scrolling. Over time, if you associate your relationship with high-value activities, you are learning that your relationship brings meaning and wellbeing to your life. You will find that your unconscious brain understands that high-value activities have a better pay-off. At this point, they become a habit and are much easier to choose.

The culmination of too many no-value activities over time can be destructive. Ill health and dissatisfaction are waiting. They can be relationship interfering and lead to relationship distress. If no-value activities such as addictions or unhealthy habits feel out of your control, seek professional help while also working on your relationship.

 **TIME FOR ACTION**

You and your partner don't have to be perfect. It is more about improving your average over time. Consider how you spend your time on any given day. Now write down all your activities under one of the following three headings: 'High-value activities', 'Low-value activities' and 'No-value activities'.

Which activities are getting most of your time? If you are spending more time on low-value and no-value activities, how has this affected your relationship over time? How will this affect your connection and health, and your ability to grow and explore together? What can you work on reducing? What can you introduce to foster deeper bonds? What can you and your partner do for stress reduction so that you are more engaged with each other?

As a couple, the aim is to spend most of your time engaging in high-value activities. When you achieve this, low-value activities such as enjoying a movie, watching the game or splurging on some internet shopping are more enjoyable because you have the right balance of mastery and pleasure.

Don't become 'parallel partners'

Your relationship has to be a priority if you want to establish deep connections. Some couples engage in high-value activities as individuals to the detriment of their relationship. On the surface, it looks like they are doing great. They may be kicking goals as parents, in their career, financially and in health like Linton and Elaine were. However, somewhere along the journey, they've parted ways and have less in common. They don't have enough crossover, connection or common interests and values.

We use the term 'parallel partners' to describe people in this pattern. They are living in a manner that is parallel to one another.

Differentiating parallel partners from partners who have deep connections is important. Parallel partners may seem fine, but their relationship is too far down the priority list. Token efforts are not enough. As a 'parallel partner' you feel lonely in your relationship. You may seek connection and comfort from outside your relationship. To break this dynamic you must start reconnecting with your partner.

You no doubt have many competing demands in your life, which means your relationship is at risk of being pushed down the list of priorities and eventually neglected. The following is a typical day in order of what gets the most time for many of our couples:

1. work
2. commuting, running errands, dropping off and picking up kids
3. phone time – including social media, email, news or work emails
4. family commitments
5. health-related activities
6. watching streaming platforms, TV and movies
7. another no-value activity
8. life admin and chores
9. the relationship.

For some couples, phone time is number two on their list. (You can check your screen time reports to see your daily average time spent on your phone.)

Your relationship should be your number one priority. If you want to change the direction of your relationship, you have to give it more time. If your relationship is running well, everything else will be better – including parenting, your mental health, self-pursuits or career goals. A relationship with deep connections offers you far more benefits than a neglected relationship. Your relationship doesn't need to get the most time – that's not practical or necessary. However, it should be high up on your priority list and should come before low-value or no-value activities.

Take time out each day to spend together – for example, catching up while making dinner, going to bed at the same time, or having a chat to check in on each other. Create rituals to ensure this quality time is also regular – for example, family or couple dinners most nights of the week at the table with no devices, taking an evening walk on weeknights after dinner, doing a regular scheduled hobby together, and a weekly brunch with just the two of you. You must shift and minimise activities of less value. Once you prioritise the time, keep it as sacred as possible. That means not prioritising other activities during your scheduled connecting time, unless absolutely necessary.

Investing now in your relationship's future

Your relationship may be in more trouble than you realise. This is not uncommon. We experience this with the couples we see on a regular basis. Deep connections safeguard your relationship by fostering and protecting your bond.

You might have heard of the boiling frog metaphor, where a live frog is first placed in a large pan with cool water. The frog is comfortable and won't instinctively jump out. It might even swim around enjoying the water. When the water is gradually heated, the frog is blissfully unaware. It doesn't notice the small incremental temperature change and so doesn't jump out. The poor frog is pretty much cooked by the time it realises it's too hot to stick around. But it's too late – it does not have the energy to save itself.

Although proven to be a myth – the poor frog would jump out – this is still a helpful metaphor for relationships. Like the frog in water, you float along in your relationship thinking everything's okay. The busyness of life takes your relationship out of focus. Also, your partner fails to raise any concerns, so you assume all is fine. Yet, one day you wake up and the relationship is cooked. You feel alone and the relationship is at risk of death by disconnection. In this situation, often one partner decides it's time for change. They're not feeling connected or attracted and are struggling to stay. This can come as a big shock to the other partner who thought life was sailing along.

Sometimes it's what you're not doing that causes problems in your relationship. The lack of relationship investment initiates the fracture. Common thoughts resisting this are, *I don't have time*, *I'm too busy* or *I can't get motivated*. These are signs that your relationship is already at risk.

 **TIME FOR ACTION**

Go back to your list where you grouped your activities into high-value, low-value or no-value. Now write down the approximate minutes or hours you spend on each activity – for example, eight hours of work, one hour of commuting, one hour cooking and cleaning. How much is your screen time? Some estimates put screen time in the United States and Australia as between three and five and a half hours a day! How many minutes are you spending on your devices?

If your relationship is getting a lot of time then great, you are investing in its future. If not, reflect on how your low- or no-value activities stack up in real time – in actual minutes and hours – compared to the time you are engaged with your partner.

If digital tech is stealing your attention, you're not alone. Indeed, the odds are stacked against you because an army of software engineers are working hard to get your attention. A great strategy to improve relationship investment is to create boredom. Yes, that's right – boredom! It is the most underutilised resource you can use to create new habits. Consider this, if you removed all the technology from your home, how would your life change? Imagine – you have no access to your phone, TV or computer. After completing your chores, you would no doubt soon be bored. What would you do? Chances are, you would be more likely to play board games, have conversations, read books, go to the gym, go for a walk together or start a dance class together. It's summer and the beach is an hour's drive away but you and your partner go anyway because you have nothing else to do. Removing access to no- or low-value activities opens up high levels of motivation to do high-value activities. Why? Because humans don't like to be bored. And this is great for your relationship and social life because humans don't like to be lonely! No-value activities mask loneliness. Removing them means you will naturally want to connect more.

Creating space for high-value activities must be an agreed joint effort. One partner can't drag the other to it. Start by discussing your values and come up with a plan together. Create a space where you're motivated to connect – for example, go on a road trip with mobile data switched off. Incorporate no technology time between 7 pm and 8.30 pm on weekdays or a bigger chunk of time on the weekend.

This world has so much busyness. Everyone's holding their breath, just getting through the grind. Everyone is tired. You must be brave to create space. For example, give yourself permission to work less if it's possible. Shave off some of the children's afternoon activities so everyone has more free time. Even the kids will benefit from less busy time and more family time. Look at what's on your plate and see what you can scrape off. You must create the time and invest in your relationship or risk relationship death by disconnection.

Working with your partner

Perhaps you're thinking, 'I want to spend time with my partner, but I can't get them to commit.' If your partner won't commit to spending time together, they're breaching one of the relationship commandments. Be open and transparent, and talk to them about your concerns and how it's affecting you. For example, do you feel bored, lonely, stagnant, uncared for, or have low attraction levels in the relationship? Get to the vulnerability of what you're feeling and express this using 'I' statements. Then get curious and ask how they feel. Ask your partner to set a low bar with you. Rather than making a huge change, commit to something you can do a couple of times a week – for example, a meal without distraction or a new hobby one hour a week together, such as a cooking class. Or start going to bed together at the same time and having a catch up and snuggle before you go to sleep.

If your partner is resistant, embody in yourself what you want in your relationship. Limit or stop engaging in low- or no-value activities with your partner and increase your own high-value activities. For example, get off your devices and start reading a book, spend more meaningful time with other important family members, go for a walk or to the gym, arrange to meet friends or engage in your own hobby. Start doing new things. Create an obvious change in lifestyle. Your partner will sense the gap between you and experience discomfort as their low- and no-value behaviours become more obvious. Your self-esteem will improve as you move toward a life in line with your values.

As your world expands, you send the message you can thrive on your own. This increases your value and gives your partner a choice. They can step up to improve deep connections or face an increasing distance. If they move to join you, that's wonderful! By focusing on yourself, you have created the positive relationship you desire. If this does not motivate them to change, you could be outgrowing the relationship. Your partner may have good intentions but can't effect change. If this is the case, a triangulation may be blocking your relationship growth. We cover what triangulations are and how to break them later in this chapter.

One exception to the relationship-investment rule is worth highlighting here. A relationship with solid, deep connections can endure periods with reduced connection. In certain situations, the relationship may need to drop down the priority list in terms of time – for example, you might have to bunker down for work, care for a loved one, or take part in or support a solo quest such as training for and completing a marathon. One of the underpinning philosophies of the eight love links is to stay open and flexible. If you both feel such a period is necessary, talk about it with your partner. Make time to check in with each other's experience. When you have spare time, be sure to prioritise each other. You don't want these periods to become the norm – they should be worthy exceptions that are beneficial for one or both of you.

A final word on time …

One of our favourite authors is Dr Irvin Yalom, an American existential psychiatrist and a professor of psychiatry at Stanford University. Dr Yalom has written countless books, both fiction and non-fiction, including a wonderful book called *Staring at the Sun* on death anxiety. When it comes down to it, confronting death is all about embracing life. Dr Yalom references the philosophy of Nietzsche in this book, including the idea of 'eternal recurrence', as a way to contemplate your life. Nietzsche's 'eternal recurrence' suggests when you die, you will live the exact same life over and over again for all of eternity – all of the ups, all of the downs and everything in between. You can't change the experience; you must live exactly how you did on the first life cycle.

Now imagine you've just become aware of this secret. You can't change how you have already lived up until this point. You'll live from your birth to this day over and over. However, you are in the first life cycle. How would you now live moving forward, knowing you have to live your life on repeat over and over for the rest of eternity? What would you keep doing? What would you stop doing? What would you do more of? What would you start doing to change your eternal fate?

Removing triangulations

One of the main barriers for deep connections is triangulations. We learnt the concept of triangulation via the work of psychiatrist

Dr Murray Bowen, who developed Family Systems Theory from the mid-20th century. Triangulations are influences – including people and objects – outside of your relationship that create disharmony. For example, let's look at Abraham and Xia. Usually, they have a positive relationship. However, every time Abraham's mother visits they end up fighting. Before the visit they are united. After the visit they are divided. Xia feels abandoned and Abraham feels defensive. While Xia likes her mother-in-law, she feels she visits on a regular basis without notice – on weeknights and weekends. They have even missed date nights because Abraham feels guilty about putting in boundaries with his mother. They've had plans to go out, and then his mother turns up. He is worried setting boundaries with his mother will upset her and she will withdraw from their relationship. Xia is left feeling devalued in their relationship. She feels frustrated with Abraham and on edge because she is unable to relax each night, unsure if his mother will turn up. Abraham feels stuck in the middle and is angry at Xia for putting pressure on him.

The following figure first shows how the relationship looks when the couple are in a 'healthy relationship'. They are in line and connected with one another. In the triangulated relationship, a third point has come in and split the pair. Abraham and Xia are no longer united. Abraham has united with his mother and Xia is left out and alone.

You can substitute Abraham's mother in this example for any other person. For example, say both parents are united until their child acts out. Parent two tries to set limits with the child while parent one comes to the defence of the child, and now the parents are triangulated. Parent one has aligned with the child and parent two is left on the outer. This dynamic can also occur with work colleagues, ex-partners, siblings and friends.

A healthy relationship versus a triangulated relationship involving another person

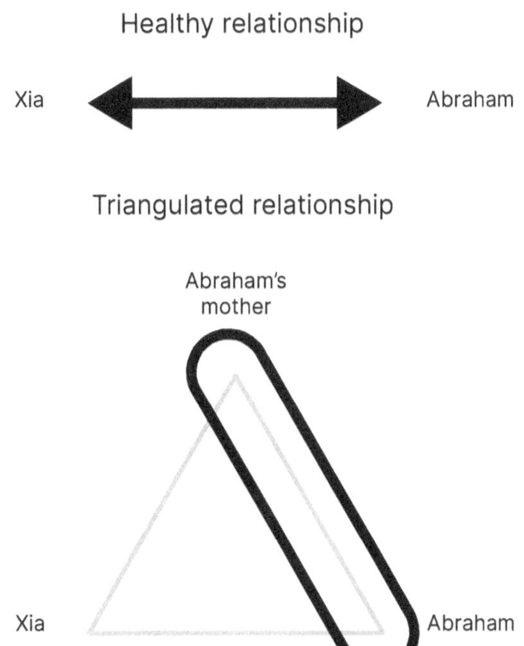

Object triangulations occur when a partner chooses to align with a non-human object in a way that leaves the other feeling isolated. An object can be, for example, excessive work, substance use, gaming, excessive exercise or over spending. Anything done in an obsessive way can cause triangulations. One partner is habitually choosing something outside of their relationship which is causing conflict. This is shown in the following figure, where the behaviour of gambling is severing the relationship connection.

Some triangulations are more serious than others; however, they all cause disharmony and are worthy of attention. Left unresolved triangulations can fester into serious resentment.

A healthy relationship versus an object triangulated relationship

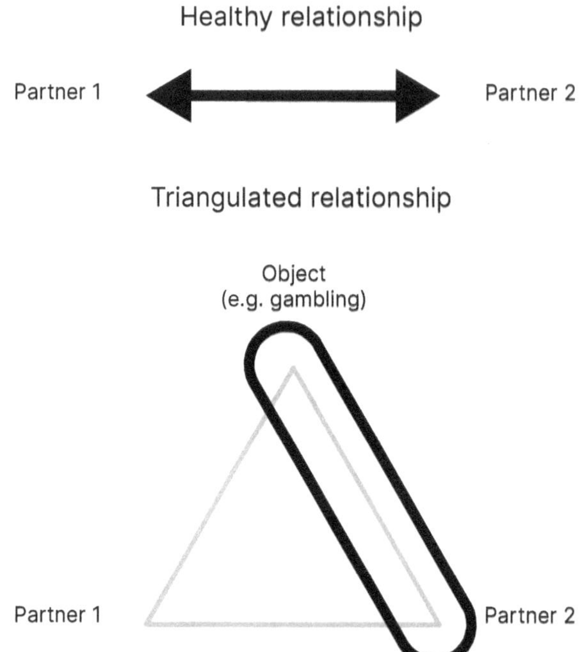

 **TIME FOR ACTION**

Identify any triangulation in your relationship. Draw a few triangles and write down your and your partner's name at the two lower points of the triangle. Then add any people or objects that cause triangulation to the third point at the top. Now answer the following questions:

1. Who is getting isolated in the triangulation?

2. How does the isolated partner feel when they are triangulated?

3. How does the other partner feel when they join the third triangulation point?

4. Why is the triangulation occurring? Is it a form of coping? Is it pressure from a family of origin dynamic? Is it conflict avoidance or self-sacrificing?

5. What are the relationship consequences of the triangulation?

6. What is the true position of each partner without outside pressure or influence?

7. Now go back to chapter 5 and use the two truths exercise to form a joint position. Discuss what needs to happen in order to break the triangulation. How can you do this as a team?

8. How would the relationship benefit if the triangulation ceased?

In the case of Abraham and Xia, here are the answers to the preceding questions:

1. Xia is getting isolated. Abraham is choosing to appease his mother at the expense of his relationship with Xia.

2. Xia feels abandoned and undervalued. She feels anxious about having free time at home without any boundaries with Abraham's mother. Xia also feels a building resentment.

3. Abraham feels terrible. He feels anxious. He does not want to upset his mother and is fearful of her reaction. The culture of his family of origin has always been one where people come and go from each other's houses. However, he also feels very stressed about Xia's reaction. Further, he would also like fewer visits from his mother. After work, he just wants to rest and recover. So he feels burdened.

4. The triangulation is occurring because Abraham feels guilty and anxious at the idea of establishing boundaries with his mother.

5. The relationship between Xia and Abraham is suffering. Resentment, distance and frustration are building.

6. Xia does not mind her mother-in-law visiting. However, she would like it to be less frequent with some prior notice.

Abraham, ideally, would also like fewer visits from his mother. He values time alone with Xia and is tired of the stress caused by the triangulation.

7. Xia and Abraham agree on a compromise. Abraham will ask his mother to text them the day before she intends to come over but he won't ask her to attend less. They will reassess how it is all going in a few months.

8. Abraham and Xia can be a team again. They will not feel split and can better plan their time.

Getting on the same page and breaking triangulations can be difficult. You have learnt the powerful two truths exercise and stepped approach to boundary setting in chapter 5. If you need to resolve a triangulation, go back to this chapter and put the strategies to work! Once you have an agreed plan, discuss how you might put the boundaries in place. Anticipate when boundaries might need to be reinforced and have a joint plan to support each other.

Knowing your partner's inner world

Knowing the inner world of your partner builds compassion and brings you closer together. The inner world of a person is not static and, instead, evolves and changes. By staying open to your partner's inner world, you remain open to discovering new aspects of their identity, beliefs and desires. This allows for adaptation across the lifespan. While this might seem obvious, many couples fail to continue to get to know each other.

Light conversations and chats are great for relationships, but they are not the sorts of interactions that bring a deeper understanding of each other. To do this, we mean being open and curious about each other's values, beliefs, emotional experiences, history, fears and hopes.

There needs to be a strong sense of safety without judgement or criticism as you bring all your attention to your partner's experience. You're checking in with them about their inner thoughts and feelings, and being curious about their experience without adding or trying to influence, with the exception of being invited to do so.

Knowing your partner's inner world will make your relationship more resilient in difficult times. Life is filled with challenges and relationships are not immune to them. Partners who understand each other's inner worlds are more equipped to weather the storms together. A deep understanding of each other's strengths, vulnerabilities and coping mechanisms enhances resilience, and invites more compassion, patience and support.

Knowing each other's inner world establishes a profound sense of belonging and acceptance. Wonderful relationships are without fear of judgement or rejection. They foster a sense of belonging and create a solid foundation for trust and transparency. As such, the relationship is sacred and maintaining boundaries and trust in the relationship becomes effortless. You have less need for rebellion and are more aware of your partner's wellbeing, which essentially safeguards you from acting in a way that might be more hurtful or disrespectful toward them.

As an example of this, here is a couple's anecdote from Helen.

Staying open to internal shifts

I saw Martha and Jin in our practice in Sydney. Martha's mother had been diagnosed with dementia, and Martha was thrust into caring for her while also confronting and grieving the loss of her mother's personality. Through this journey an internal shift occurred. She became aware of her own mortality. Martha started wanting new experiences and to work less. Jin continued on as usual, working and taking care of the kids, unaware of Martha's internal shift. Yet her shift became a source of tension in the relationship.

They started to fight over money, their lifestyle and quality time together. Resentment was building. They couldn't articulate what had gone wrong, but were both feeling resentful and defensive. Prior to Martha's mother becoming ill, they had got along well.

Through couples therapy, Martha was able to get in touch with her inner world. Prior to her mother's illness, Jin and Martha had shared goals based on growing wealth. While Jin's motivations had stayed the same, Martha's had shifted away from growing wealth to more meaningful connection and life experiences. Neither party was in the wrong. They were both just struggling to communicate the intrinsic motivation behind their position.

Jin was not aware of the shift in Martha's inner world and this meant they didn't have the information they needed to make the best decisions for their relationship. Once Jin learnt more about Martha's inner world, he was able to have more empathy and compassion for her position. He could identify with many of her internal shifts and, as a couple, they were able to adjust their lifestyle. This made them stronger.

Importantly, neither Jin nor Martha is wrong in this example. Both are responsible for communicating. The path to a good relationship is always staying open to underlying motivations and vulnerabilities within yourself and your partner.

Breaking through to connection

Discovering your partner's inner world may sound challenging. You might also be wondering how you will know if you're achieving a deep connection. When you have deep connections, you'll feel a sense of calmness. You'll feel supported, part of a team, and with a sense of what is important. You'll feel held by the relationship. Have faith in the process. Keep up with the investment in the relationship. One day you'll notice, almost by surprise, that you're feeling confident, secure and content in your relationship.

If you are out of the habit, spending quality time with your partner can feel awkward. Sometimes it can be a struggle to go deep and have meaningful conversations. This doesn't mean your relationship is not capable of having them. It just means you need help getting the ball rolling.

Try asking each other the following questions to help facilitate deeper conversation:

- What makes you feel joyful like a little kid?

- You are at the end of your life. What would you regret not doing?

- Would you like more independence or more couple time in our relationship?

- What is your saddest memory as a child?

- Tell me about one of your most positive memories – when was it, who were you with and why was it so great?

- List three things you would like to achieve as an individual over the next 12 months (for example, read more books, achieve a promotion, improve on a relationship or parenting, improve your individual pollution footprint, go to the gym each week or eat more vegetables).

- Tomorrow you find out that you can no longer work in your field of work ever again. However, you have an endless budget to retrain in whatever you like and your living expenses (bills and enough money to enjoy life) are covered until you are ready to work. What would you do?

- What is the thing you worry most about on a day-to-day basis?

- What attracted you most to me when we first met?

- What was your proudest moment as a child?

- What has been the saddest time in your life so far?

- When you are in your final years and you are looking back on your life, what are some things you hope to have experienced with me?

These questions are from Getting to Know More of You in the Deep Connections section of our My Love Your Love couples app. They are just a sample – we've included more than 100 questions (and counting). Asking these questions is a wonderful way to elicit meaningful conversation and to rediscover each other's inner world. Go ahead and try it. We use these questions when we feel disconnected with nothing much to say to each other. It does wonders!

Another activity to get you started is to write a list of three desires (non-sexual) or concerns you are not sharing with your partner. Ask them if they'd be willing to do the same in the spirit of curiosity. Come together and discuss what's on your list.

Create a habit of connection where you check in with your partner and their opinions on a regular basis. You provide no solutions, only curiosity. Have a ritual, such as a weekly brunch, to confirm the habit. It may feel awkward and unnatural at first but remember – you need to throw out the window the idea that things should come naturally. Habits feel natural. This occurs when you've been practising for a while.

Doing exciting things together – grow and prosper

Research conducted by Arthur Aron, a professor of psychology at the State University of New York, concluded that couples who grow together, stay together. He and his colleagues formulated the self-expansion model, which suggests that individuals seek to expand their sense of self by broadening their experiences, knowledge, outlook and competence so they can thrive in life. Novel and exciting experiences lead to self-expansion and, in general, this then leads to high levels of contentment and happiness. When this growth occurs within your relationship, you also experience greater love and deeper bonds.

When you meet your partner, your world expands without effort. You experience new people, cultures, opinions, activities and geographical locations. This self-expansion deepens your bonds and your sense of self. Your life becomes richer as a result of your partnership. Sooner or later, however, self-expansion via the relationship runs dry. The new becomes the familiar. Self-expansion stops and the relationship can feel less satisfying. Couples who experience their relationship to be stagnant or mundane are much more likely to break up.

Creating novel and exciting experiences together fortifies your relationship, because you continue to experience self-expansion as a result of the relationship. You continue to grow as an individual, which makes your relationship more valuable.

The act of continuing to do new and exciting experiences together is what facilitates growth. For example, say you decide as a couple to take up tennis. Through this joint activity, you learn and grow. However, after a period of time, tennis is no longer novel. By all means, continue playing tennis – it's great for your health and a fun activity to do together. But you must add new experiences to get new points of self-expansion. You must commit to being the couple open to new experiences rather than the couple who just plays tennis.

Understanding the impacts of self-expansion

Perhaps you're wondering, 'Is it really important to try new things together?' Yes! Don't leave yourself in stagnation, with a greater chance your relationship will fail. The research is conclusive – if you continue creating excitement together, you will value each other more and have a greater bond. Self-expansion not only safeguards your relationship but also increases attraction in your relationship. This is one of the reasons couples report having more sex when travelling.

In 2022, Arthur Aron and fellow researchers reviewed the self-expansion model in close relationships based on the last 20 years of research. Here is what they found:

Engaging in self-expansion activities improves relationship satisfaction and quality. Higher sexual desire for a partner is associated with higher overall satisfaction in a relationship.

Their review highlighted some further insights:

- Boredom in a relationship is attributed to a lack of novelty and stimulation, and linked to lower pleasure and arousal in relationships. When people are bored in a relationship, they tend to seek out new activities driven by their inherent motivation to self-expand. This means, if self-expansion is not occurring in the relationship, individuals will seek it outside of the relationship.

- Relationships that don't promote self-expansion can also lead individuals to focus on alternative partners. This can harm monogamous relationships, causing lower satisfaction and higher risks of infidelity. People who experience lower self-expansion in relationships may find computer interactions more appealing when these programs offer self-expansion. In other words, a lack of self-expansion in the relationship encourages you to move towards other stimulating activities and further away from your relationship.

- On the other hand, self-expansion in relationships limits attraction to other people, because thinking about moments of self-expansion in current relationships can reduce brain activation when people see attractive faces. This reduces desire to focus on alternative partners. Putting it simply, if you feel your relationship is great because it facilitates a life where you continue to grow, you will not feel the need to look for a new partner. Your relationship will be too valuable. This makes self-expansion a protective factor against infidelity.

- Self-expansion opportunities in a relationship can influence individuals even after the relationship ends. If a relationship doesn't promote self-expansion, a break-up can provide new opportunities for personal growth leading to higher life satisfaction. However, if the relationship facilitated self-expansion, a break-up leads to a sense of self-contraction where individuals feel they've lost a part of themselves.

The overall takeaway from Aron's research is that individuals seek self-expansion, and have an innate desire to grow and evolve. If this is not facilitated within your relationship, it becomes more attractive to break up. However, the opposite is also true. If your relationship does facilitate self-expansion, you'll value it much more. On average, you will experience higher levels of sexual intimacy and safeguard your relationship against infidelity.

Adding in some novelty

Adding self-expansion activities to your relationship may sound like too much work. Novelty does not have to be the norm, however. Rather, it must be the exception. Travelling to a new destination, completing new projects, attending live music, trying an adventure sport, visiting a museum or theatre, dining at a new restaurant, doing a cooking class or trying a new experience together doesn't have to be something you do every single day or even every week. You just have to do such activities occasionally to keep the spontaneity and excitement alive. You can still have your favourite restaurant. This can be comforting and affirming for your relationship too. Just keep in mind that your relationship will need injections of excitement, joint learning and accomplishment to stay strong.

Making a list of all the things you've learned as a result of meeting your partner that's led to your individual self-expansion can be helpful, and is also an excellent exercise in gratitude.

As an example, here's Helen's list of all the things she's learned from meeting Shahn:

- I gained a window into Kurdish culture.
- I have explored Newcastle, Australia, where Shahn's family live.
- I became a step-parent to two children.
- I learned that someone could be there with kindness and care each day, day after day.
- I learned to trust in myself to start a business and do something outside the box.
- I learned to trust that I could be successful, and this success wasn't just something that other people got to experience.
- I learned how to take a risk in life, in investments and in things that are scary, such as starting an Airbnb in the Blue Mountains or a relationship app.
- I learnt about martial arts when Shahn was doing kickboxing and even learnt to partially enjoy the UFC.
- I've learnt to enjoy watching football (soccer – no other variety).
- I've experienced the fear and joy of riding on the back of a motorcycle.

And here's Shahn's list of what he learned from Helen:

- I was introduced to different philosophies and ways of thinking about social justice, the world and the earth in general.
- I discovered parts of southern New South Wales and the culture of those areas.
- I explored parts of London visiting Helen's family.
- I explored Hong Kong and Reunion Island (off the coast of Africa) visiting her friends.
- I learnt more about feminism.

- I had no idea of what living off-grid was like until I spent time with Helen's family. I learnt what it's like to live off the land using solar power and other self-generating energies.

- I learned more about the environment and animal rights.

- I learned it's possible to have a partner where I can let go and be myself without judgement or any fear of guilt. This has allowed for the greatest sense of autonomy and freedom I've felt in a relationship.

- I've learned to be part of a book club and to read more.

- I've learnt the true value of partnership in joint ventures and adventures.

 **TIME FOR ACTION**

Now it's your turn. Write down all the things you've learned as a result of meeting your partner that's led to your individual self-expansion.

Once you've made this list, make another list of new points of self-expansion you've created together. These are things you've discovered together as a result of your relationship – for example, travelling, moving to a new area, starting a sport together, renovating a home or becoming pet parents. Now answer the following question: does your relationship currently have enough excitement?

However you answer, still try the following. Make a wish list of things you'd like to do with your partner using the following three categories:

1. *Easy done new experiences:* For example, a cooking class, visiting a new restaurant, hiking a new local walking trail, or going to an art museum.

2. *Big couple goals:* Base these big couple goals on a shared value. For example, if you have a shared value of physical movement, maybe take up salsa lessons. If you have the

shared value of entrepreneurship, consider starting a side business. If you have the shared value of exploration, plan your dream trip – even if it might take years to save for. If you are both adrenaline junkies, start an extreme sport such as mountain biking, skydiving, snowboarding or freediving. If you have the joint value of mindfulness, start a garden project or commit to six months of yoga. The kinds of big couple goals you could work toward are endless.

3. *Exciting activities:* For example, skydiving, adventure sports, going to concerts or festivals, watching a live sporting event such as the F1 or a grand slam, going to a live gig, or enjoying a camping trip.

If your partner is open to the eight love links journey, invite them to read this chapter. Express with gratitude the growth you have experienced as a result of your relationship, and have them do the same for you. This feels amazing! (We are talking from experience. You just read the list we created for each other.)

Discuss with your partner the self-expansion that has occurred as a result of meeting each other. How did it feel to have these experiences as a result of meeting or creating them together? When was the last time you did something new together? Now look at your wish list. What is the most appealing? What is easy to tick off, and what might need a bit more effort? Commit to making time for planning, meeting and achieving some of these novel experiences. Over the next three to 12 months do things from your 'easy done new experiences'. This is a minimum. Also try one of the experiences from your 'big couple goals' and 'exciting activities'. Don't hesitate. Even planning a simple date together can be exciting.

Maybe you're thinking, *We can't afford to invest in anything like this at the moment.* Money can help with creating new experiences, but it's not necessary. Plenty of low-cost activities and hobbies are available, such as road trips, hiking, visiting nature spots, creating new recipes together or planting a small herb pot. Get your self-expansion groove on!

Free to be me in we

Mohammed and Elise were in a co-dependent relationship, with fear and anxiety keeping them from self-exploration. Placing security above autonomy, they felt stuck and had many conflicts. Both felt threatened by the other leading an independent life, but also felt dissatisfied in their relationship. They fought. They felt stuck in a rut. They were bored and said they were 'rotting together'.

Both Mohammed and Elise needed to focus on autonomy to rebalance their relationship and to bring a sense of desire and excitement back. Despite some apprehension, they saw the logic of this formulation. This was a slow journey because they both felt a sense of abandonment when the other was being independent. They needed to create positive associations with autonomy. In therapy, a graded exposure project encouraging autonomy commenced. Initially, simple exercises of separation were practised, such as going out of the house or room to make phone calls to friends and family. These exercises increased to activities such as meeting a friend for a coffee, starting new individual hobbies and eventually going away alone with friends for a weekend.

Both Mohammed and Elise were great participants in therapy, learning to sit with their vulnerable feelings. This was hard at first but became easier over time. The changes in their relationship were remarkable. They began missing and desiring each other again. They had more appreciation of the time they spent together, and found it exciting to hear about each other's new experiences. Their attraction grew. Although they had more time apart than ever before, they still spent the majority of their time together as a couple. However, the resentment and boredom were gone. They experienced higher self-esteem and greater trust in the relationship. All of their gains were created through increased autonomy.

Great relationships support individuality and allow time for personal pursuits, hobbies, platonic friendships and life explorations. When unencumbered in a relationship, couples report high levels of life satisfaction. They also value and find their partners more attractive.

Assuming you have safety and security within your relationship, you will experience positive outcomes from encouraging individuality. You have more to talk about as you learn about each other's experiences. And it's true what they say – absence makes the heart grow fonder. You can enjoy the break and look forward to seeing your partner again. If you and your partner have individual pursuits, you are sending the message that you can survive and thrive as an individual. This means you are a valuable asset, increasing attraction. Neither party feels held back. The relationship becomes a base to continue to grow and explore as an individual creating a positive association to the relationship.

Interdependence rather than co-dependence

Having a sense of autonomy within your relationship means you are free. Your authenticity and personal identity is preserved. Your relationship moves away from feeling controlled or stifled to having deeper bonds and desire within it. Individuality means the freedom to express ideas, desires and opinions without fear and judgement. It also means the ability to explore hobbies, interests and a social identity as an individual.

'Free to be me in we' is not about making unilateral decisions. It's not breaking the relationship commandments or boundaries, or putting your relationship at risk. 'Free to be me in we' is about transparency and good communication. It's encouraging each other to have individual experiences. It's tolerating any vulnerabilities or insecurities you experience when your partner expresses opposing values or life desires.

This leads to a healthy form of interdependence, where partners support individual growth and wellbeing. It's attractive because the relationship is based on choice, not obligation. Creating more room for autonomy can be as simple as making individual time for hobbies, friends and learning. Couples who do this well communicate openly and enjoy spending time together. However, they are not threatened by individual time. They're comfortable with both couple and individual socialising. They can voice desires and differences, but still make decisions that are respectful within the boundaries of the relationship.

Making time for each other's autonomy is important. You'll live in a relationship without resentment or boredom – and with more mystery!

Embracing differences with respect

Individual differences and autonomy can add depth, excitement and personal growth, making the relationship more attractive and fulfilling. The key is to embrace these differences with respect and understanding, creating a balanced and supportive partnership. Feeling a sense of discomfort or vulnerability is common when a partner expresses a desire for more autonomy. This is related to a need for safety through predictability. Divergence from the norm can be challenging. However, the solution is to work on the resistance and sit with the anxiety.

Sitting with anxiety refers to the act of experiencing the feeling without attempting to avoid or suppress it. It involves observing the physical sensations, thoughts and emotions associated with the anxiety, while maintaining a stance of curiosity and non-resistance. The goal of sitting with anxiety is not to eliminate anxiety altogether, but to develop a healthier relationship with it. Once your partner has autonomy and comes back to the relationship, you will feel better. You learn your anxiety isn't always correct because your partner does return and it was okay for them to separate from you after all. Your unconscious mind learns autonomy is positive for the relationship because reduced tension and greater positive mood states is associated with it. Getting more comfortable with autonomy will increase trust and self-esteem.

The exception is when infidelity has occurred and the relationship remains fractured. Transparency and repair takes precedence over autonomy for as long as needed. With time, you will need to gradually move back toward encouraging autonomy within the boundaries of the relationship. If infidelity in the relationship hasn't been processed, focus should be on strengthening the trust bonds for as long as it takes. 'Free to be me in we' is not the priority in the context of infidelity.

 **TIME FOR ACTION**

If you feel you don't have enough autonomy in your relationship, do this exercise. Start by determining some individual values – either come up with your own or select from the following list:

- animal welfare
- arts
- career
- discipline
- entrepreneurship
- environment
- friendships
- health
- hobbies
- mindfulness
- music
- sport.

From this list, pick one value and create a goal within it. Talk to your partner about your desire to pursue this. Ask them to help create space and time for your goal. Offer to do the reverse for them.

The amount of time you invest in personal pursuits might fluctuate. You can do small periods of time often or doses of it when you feel the need. When you and your partner create space for each other to focus on personal pursuits, you will feel more gratitude in the relationship.

Summing up

In this chapter, you've learned to get the best out of your relationship by bringing it up the priority list and investing in it and each other. The Deep Connections love link is all about continued growth and self-expansion. More than just doing new things together, deep connection is about knowing the inner world of your partner. It involves creating space for your partner's individual identity. Through deep connections, you foster companionship, trust, compassion, teamwork and belonging. You create mystery, excitement and sexual attraction.

Stop putting your relationship at the bottom of your priority list and start moving it up today. It is time to shake things up. Even small deviations from your current routine can lead to higher levels of satisfaction.

Imagine you're in the last weeks of your life and you're presented with a photo album of all your life moments. As you flick through this album, you see the time you spent at work, family and relationships. But you also see the time you spent on social media and TV. Your photo album is filled with posts and memes that aren't meaningful to you. It's filled with TV series and movies that are long forgotten but take up pages and pages of your life album.

Is this the reality of your life?

Now imagine the photo album you would rather be looking through. What would the pages be filled with? What needs to change?

Don't waste another page! It's time to start creating the pages you want now.

If you need more help, download the My Love Your Love app. The Deep Connections module can make it easier for you through facilitating more than 100 'getting to know more of you' questions, covering topics around vulnerabilities, fears, hopes and dreams. It'll also help you discover joint values and how to plan and achieve big couple goals.

Now you know that having a good relationship is about not just reducing conflict but also taking your connection to the next level by investing in the relationship and each other. A great relationship is a solid base for a beautiful life.

In the next chapter, we show how you've been carrying emotional baggage your whole life, picking it up from your family of origin and previous relationships. This baggage has more of an influence on you and your relationship than you realise. We outline how to identify your baggage and the baggage of your partner, and offer strategies to help you carry this baggage in a way that fosters compassion and care for one another.

Link seven

Baggage Claim

Karen and Ben are in their 20s and married. Karen held a steadfast belief that, as partners, they should share every moment together. She advocated for this, and so most of their time while not working was spent together. Although Ben enjoyed joint activities with Karen, he also wanted to pursue his own interests, separate to Karen. When Ben expressed a desire for solo activities, Karen's Micromanager conflict persona emerged. She would insist on limits around this separate time. For example, her Micromanager wanted multiple contacts throughout the period he was away from her, with a clear return time. When he tried to negotiate on these limits, Karen would end up upset and distressed, becoming panicked and desperate. This left Ben feeling constrained and overwhelmed. His Self-Sacrificing Partner Pleaser would take over, and he would give up on his need for autonomy. As time went on, Ben's resentment grew until his Self-Sacrificing Partner Pleaser gave way to an explosive Angry Attacker. Neither Karen nor Ben understood why this topic was so loaded.

Karen and Ben were in a conflict dance. (Refer to chapter 5 for a reminder of the conflict personas and the conflict dance.) For Karen, something more was going on deep inside her; a vulnerability was getting triggered. Addressing Karen and Ben's conflict personas would be helpful. But unless they understood what was happening deep below the surface, this conflict dance would keep returning.

In this chapter, we help you go deep within yourself to understand your vulnerabilities (baggage). We outline the different types of baggage and help you select those relevant to you. You'll see how unclaimed baggage adds a load to your relationship and can burst open at any time, adding to your conflict dance. We help you claim any lost baggage and unpack it to better understand where it has come from, improving your self-awareness and increasing your self-growth in the process. We provide ways to take care of your own baggage so you'll feel better and reduce tension in your relationship. And we outline ways to help your partner carry their baggage, diffusing conflict and bringing you closer together.

Claiming your baggage may be uncomfortable and hard work. But it's worth it.

Why 'baggage'?

Each partner brings to the relationship their own vulnerabilities, insecurities, fragilities and susceptibilities – what we call 'baggage'. This will inevitably emerge within the relationship context, causing tension and disconnection. You must identify, understand and take care of your own and your partner's baggage.

Vulnerabilities are aspects of your emotional or mental state that make you more susceptible to experiencing distress, challenges or negative outcomes. For the remainder of the chapter, we refer to vulnerabilities as baggage.

We understand that 'baggage' is a loaded and judgemental word. You may even find yourself flinching at this term, and have an instant negative reaction to it. But hang in there. Why it's a helpful term – and why Baggage Claim is an important love link – will become clear.

Baggage serves as a metaphor for your emotional vulnerabilities within the relationship context. Colloquially, baggage is associated with negative aspects carried from the past that impact your current behaviour, attitude or ability to connect with a partner. It leads to challenges such as trust issues, communication problems or difficulty in forming deep emotional connections. Seen as a source of complications, people are quick to reject partners based on past baggage. If you've ever been rejected by a potential partner because you 'carry too much baggage', you will understand the hurt this brings.

Your baggage is dragged around from your past into your current relationship. It is largely subconscious, only drawing awareness when it bursts open within seemingly innocuous interpersonal interactions. If you are lucky enough to have insight that the source of the rift is your baggage, you might be tempted to reject or avoid it. Claiming your own baggage is confronting so, of course, avoidance becomes the path of least resistance.

Rejecting your own or others' baggage is not only hurtful but also futile. Everyone has baggage. It is part of who you are. If you turn your back on it, it will inevitably burst open and cause trouble.

So why would we choose such a loaded term?

You already know the concept of baggage. It's relatable. We are simply reclaiming the concept of baggage. Here, baggage refers to the accumulated emotional and psychological experiences, wounds and learned perspectives you carry with you from your family of origin and past relationships. Your relationship is burdened with this invisible weight. When your baggage bursts open, your thoughts, feelings and behaviour are all affected. This overshadows the present with historical patterns of responding. While this sounds negative – and when left unchecked, we know it can have serious negative impacts on your relationship – we see baggage as an opportunity for growth, both individually and as a partnership. Navigating baggage together can foster a deeper connection, ultimately strengthening the relationship bond. What this means is you need to know how to deal effectively with your own and your partner's baggage.

Claimed versus rejected baggage

When your baggage arrives, you have a choice – you can reject it or claim it.

Rejected baggage is ignored, lost or unclaimed. You still haul this baggage around with you, but you pretend it doesn't exist. Over time, it becomes a heavy load on you and your relationships.

Claimed baggage, on the other hand, means you take ownership of it. You unpack it and learn ways to carry it so it doesn't weigh you down.

By inspecting your baggage, you'll discover how it's been fuelling conflict and disconnection in your relationship. This will increase your self-knowledge, enhancing self-growth. You'll also better understand your partner, bringing you closer to one another. Past wounds will be healed.

Let's revisit Karen and Ben, who Helen saw for couples therapy.

Lost baggage from childhood

Therapy dived deep into Karen and Ben's conflict dance. It became apparent Karen was carrying lost baggage beneath her Micromanager, which we identified as her abandonment baggage. (We go through all the different types of baggage later on in this chapter.) Her abandonment baggage was bursting open when Ben sought his independence.

Karen grew up with a father whose job required constant travel. He often missed important events such as sporting finals, birthdays and graduations. Due to the nature of her father's work, dates of travel would change with little notice. She experienced a persistent worry he would not be there. And although her mother was around, Karen felt closer to her father. When he was around, he was warm and loving towards her. She felt lonely and adrift when she needed his soft touch but he wasn't there to provide it. Her father's unreliable presence created an attachment anxiety for Karen. She learnt she couldn't rely on him when she needed him.

This experience in childhood and the wound it created was getting triggered in the present with Ben. For Karen, when Ben sought his own space it felt like he was abandoning her. Those same feelings of anxiety and loneliness from her childhood arose. Not knowing what to do with such feelings, her Micromanager emerged in an attempt to get her needs met from Ben. Unfortunately, this meant her abandonment baggage never got addressed and Ben's own needs were stifled.

Having identified the role of Karen's abandonment baggage in their conflict dance, this became a focus of therapy. Our therapy focused on building insight into this baggage and why it was bursting open. Building insight increased Karen's empathy for herself and for Ben. Likewise, Ben had a better understanding as to why Karen was struggling with this particular issue. He could turn up to her baggage with kindness and understanding.

They then increased the time they were apart through small graduated steps to increase her window of tolerance to the abandonment anxiety. ('Window of tolerance' is a psychological term referring to the optimal state of arousal where you can effectively cope with stress. It's a range between hyperarousal (overwhelmed, anxious) and hypoarousal (numb, detached). Staying within this window allows for adaptive responses to challenges.) The aim was to expand Karen's window of tolerance, helping her to regulate her emotions.

By gradually increasing their time apart, Karen learnt she could confront and overcome her abandonment feelings. She worked hard to resist what her abandonment baggage and Micromanager were telling her to do. She resisted hard and fast rules around their time apart, and avoided text messaging Ben when he was away. Instead, she practised tolerating her feelings and speaking kindly to the part of herself that felt anxious and abandoned.

Ben was sensitive to her abandonment baggage. He upheld flexible boundaries around their time apart. He clearly communicated his commitment to Karen and the relationship regularly.

Following these steps, Karen and Ben were much happier and had a better connection when they were together. Ben was free to be himself and do his own things. And Karen learnt that she could be on her own safely, knowing Ben would return.

When you lose, ignore or reject your baggage, problems from the past arise in the present. You act in ways influenced by the weight of your baggage, which affects your relationships, often subconsciously. You may not realise how your baggage is loading your behaviour. By claiming your baggage, you can unpack it and, therefore, lighten the load. Claiming your baggage doesn't mean it will suddenly disappear. However, it becomes lighter and more evenly distributed – with less influence on how you get through your day.

Claiming your baggage

Pritesh and Monique attended our private practice for couples therapy. They were busy, full-time workers who valued staying active and healthy. Although they got on well, they found themselves in regular conflict situations, especially when Pritesh brought up topics he wanted to discuss and action as a couple. Monique immediately became frustrated and irritable during these interactions. A recurring theme, for example, was when Pritesh brought up how he thought they would benefit from discussing and planning the upcoming week's dinners. Pritesh felt he was being proactive so they could share the load and maintain their health. But Monique would begin to squirm. She felt Pritesh was ordering her around. This made her feel anxious and pressured. She had a strong desire to avoid the topic altogether. Unclaimed baggage had burst open.

We believe all humans have lost or unclaimed baggage.

All humans accumulate negative stories of how they see themselves, others and the world. These stories become like an old worn out coat – a familiar item that seems to fit perfectly at the first signs of rain. However, this tattered cloak offers no protection from the downpour of life's difficulties. Instead, it becomes a hindrance, working against you, cloaking your thoughts, feelings and behaviours in the heavy fabric of unclaimed baggage.

Your baggage tends to live outside your conscious awareness. Similar to the way conflict personas can take over, your unclaimed baggage can burst open in any innocuous situation or interaction. You'll know when your baggage bursts open. You will feel it in your body, weighing you down. You'll have difficulty seeing anything other than your baggage scattered everywhere. Your baggage in these moments becomes the truth of your situation.

When your unclaimed baggage suddenly bursts open, it overshadows the present situation. This can have a serious and negative impact on your relationship. Rather than being responsive to the current context, your reactions are based on past experiences. You might be responding to your unclaimed baggage rather than the situation at hand.

Understanding how baggage forms

Your baggage tends to develop early in life, when your emotional needs were not fully met; however, it can continue to interfere with similar needs being fulfilled as adults. Baggage is similar to schemas in schema therapy or core beliefs in cognitive behavioural therapy (CBT). As discussed in chapter 4, schemas are enduring unhelpful patterns or themes developed during childhood that shape an individual's beliefs about themselves, others and the world. In CBT, core beliefs are deeply ingrained, fundamental assumptions and convictions that individuals hold about themselves, others and the world.

Your baggage is embodied. It produces a strong visceral experience. Similar to schemas and core beliefs, baggage is made up of your deeply held expectations, stories and beliefs about yourself and your relationships. But baggage is also a little different to schemas and core beliefs by being relationship focused. Baggage goes beyond beliefs about self. It's also different because you can develop baggage from previous relationships in adulthood, not just from childhood and adolescence. For example, you can have wounded love baggage, which specifically develops from an adult partner relationship. Until this relationship, you never saw signs of this wounded love baggage, but now you feel anxious and insecure in partner relationships. (See later in this chapter for an outline of all the different types of baggage.)

Your baggage is the layer beneath your conflict personas. Conflict personas are those parts of you that get triggered in conflict and try to protect you. But they only ever hide your true feelings underneath. As discussed in chapter 5, these are your inner vulnerable feelings, and your baggage is linked to these feelings.

Often your conflict personas are a reaction to your baggage bursting open. When your baggage arrives in this way, you may flip into a conflict persona. There is no set formula for which baggage causes what conflict persona. It is individually based and will depend on your particular experiences – for example, someone with a hypersensitivity to anger baggage may flip into their Conflict Avoider persona, whereas someone else with the same baggage might flip into their Angry Attacker persona.

Unpacking your baggage helps you unlock self-awareness. Understanding what is really happening allows you to have more choice in each situation you're struggling with.

As an example of this, let's return to Pritesh and Monique, who Shahn worked with.

Unclaimed baggage can keep busting open

In couples therapy, the conflict that developed when Pritesh wanted to discuss planning the week's dinners was unpacked to find Monique's feeling controlled baggage was bursting open.

Monique grew up with a controlling mother. She was demanding and critical of how Monique dressed, her appearance, how much she studied and who she hung out with. The list was endless. This left Monique feeling constrained and never good enough. Given she was a child, Monique had no choice but to begrudgingly submit to her mother's demands. But she was angry and resentful of them. Even as a child, Monique experienced a sense of injustice.

When Pritesh innocently attempted to talk and plan the week's dinners, Monique's body reverted back to childhood with her mum, and her unclaimed baggage burst open. The same feelings of constriction and resentment resurfaced. What Pritesh was asking her to do felt the same as her mother's unfair demands of her. Feelings of injustice culminated again deep inside. Her baggage had spilled out everywhere, making it impossible for Monique to determine what was reasonable in Pritesh's requests.

However, Pritesh wasn't anything like Monique's mum. If anything, he was the opposite; easygoing and supportive. He was asking for collaboration on their meals, without criticism or demands. This feeling controlled baggage in its unclaimed form was interfering in their relationship. Unless addressed, this dynamic would persist.

Unclaimed baggage causes harm. But, once claimed, its power is diminished. This is what Monique and Pritesh worked through. Once insight into her feeling controlled baggage was developed, Monique was able to learn strategies to tolerate her physiological arousal when Pritesh brought up topics of discussion. She learnt to articulate how she was feeling to Pritesh when the baggage was present. Pritesh was validating and accepting of Monique's feelings. He reassured her of his intention and expressed interest in her suggestions. They worked together to find a way through these challenging interactions.

Unclaimed baggage will hide beneath conflict topics, giving the impression you are arguing over something in particular. For Pritesh and Monique, this was the cooking of the dinners for the week. This can throw you into long and arduous conflict dances when the real culprit is baggage bursting open.

Working out why you might be ignoring your baggage

A common statement we hear from our clients is, 'I don't have any baggage. I had a great childhood.' However, even great childhoods tend to hold hurt. Some people have a lot of hurt and others have just a little. Maybe your baggage isn't as heavy as other people's. Making this assumption can lead you to unintentionally lose or ignore your own baggage. Ask yourself what is getting in the way of your claiming this baggage. Claiming baggage takes courage and vulnerability. And remember – baggage doesn't just stem from childhood. It can also grow from previous relationships. Ask yourself, 'What did I learn about myself in my previous relationships? How have my previous partners affected my expectations for relationships? Why did my previous relationships end? How was I left feeling?'

Perhaps you fear your partner will use your baggage against you. This is a tricky one. Having your vulnerabilities thrown back in your face hurts. But it is okay for your partner to suggest your baggage might have burst open. Don't avoid this. The way in which your baggage is pointed out and how it is addressed is what matters. If done gently and as an act of love, it becomes an opportunity for you both to take care of the open baggage.

Remember – baggage is experienced in one form or another by everyone. You are not weak for having baggage. But you are responsible for your own baggage. You must accept the existence of your baggage and your partner's baggage. Taking care of baggage is what matters most. Doing so takes strength. Shaming or blaming baggage is unhelpful. We provide strategies to help you take care of each other's baggage later in the chapter.

Types of baggage

In this section, we outline the different kinds of baggage. Read about each, and then claim those relevant to you. Many of us will have more than one type of baggage, so you can claim as many as needed. Avoidance is the most common barrier when claiming baggage. Baggage hits at your most vulnerable parts. Therefore, you will likely experience uncomfortable feelings and thoughts about yourself. Be assured that having lost or unclaimed baggage is not a weakness. It is an inevitability. Claimed baggage is empowering. You will have a clearer picture of why certain situations or interactions are so activating or painful.

Wounded love baggage

The wounded love baggage forms when your current or previous partner has been unfaithful and you are sensitive to interactions that can be interpreted as threatening the fidelity of the relationship. Common triggers include your partner seemingly flirting with another person, your partner not returning your calls, you seeing them having a private text conversation, or them not coming home at the expected time.

All of these actions could be perfectly innocent. However, when your wounded love baggage bursts open, you will feel high levels of anxiety, vulnerability, jealousy, insecurity and, at times, desperation.

For example, say your partner goes out for drinks after work. They are simply out having a fun time with friends. However, you feel sick to your stomach, convinced something is wrong. Unable to cope any longer with these feelings, you make an excuse to reach out to them. Or, worse, you pick a fight or demand to know who they are with. This baggage leads to reassurance seeking behaviours. Unfortunately, they will only offer temporary relief until the baggage is claimed and unpacked.

Criticism baggage

The criticism baggage is relevant to you if you are highly attuned to perceived criticism and tend to react in a strong defensive way. If you have criticism baggage, you have had a parent or previous partner who used to nag and criticise you often. Criticism may have been used in a toxic way to motivate you. The accumulation of criticism over time has left you highly attuned. Common triggers include your partner asking you to do something or commenting on something you have done, or your partner expressing what they need or would like from you. The point here is that your partner may have no intention to be critical.

An example may be you both come home and the house is a mess. Your partner groans at the state of the house. For them, they just feel tired and frustrated at the idea of doing house chores after a busy day at work. However, your criticism baggage bursts open and you feel attacked, worthless, misunderstood, not good enough and a sense of failure. You feel like your partner groaning is a direct criticism of your inability to keep the house tidy and you react defensively. This baggage keeps you bound and less flexible in the relationship, and blocks your ability to work as a team.

Abandonment baggage

The abandonment baggage refers to a sensitivity to any real or perceived abandonment from your partner. You believe your partner will leave the relationship. If you have abandonment baggage, you have experienced some form of abandonment in your life – from a parent or perhaps a previous partner who blindsided you and abruptly ended the relationship. Sometimes, the cause is not so obvious – for example, a divorce that meant you rarely saw a parent. You adjusted and you coped, but the abandonment baggage is real – although outside your conscious awareness.

Common abandonment baggage triggers include a felt sense your partner is pulling away, your partner choosing others over you, or your partner acting independently. When your abandonment baggage bursts open, you feel emotional, insecure, anxious, desperate and a sense of fragility.

When you have abandonment baggage, it can be triggered by even the slightest change of mood in the relationship. For example, say your partner is a bit grumpy. This sets off a deep, unsettled feeling of abandonment and you pursue them for reassurance. This reassurance seeking over time has the potential to cause major disharmony and power imbalances in the relationship, which perpetuates the abandonment baggage.

Neglect baggage

The neglect baggage is when you are particularly sensitive to your partner not looking after your needs. You feel your opinions, feelings and desires are overlooked and ignored in your relationship. If you have this baggage, you have been neglected in one form or another by a parent or previous partner. Sometimes the neglect is obvious and at other times it is more subtle. Your parents may have been preoccupied with their own life, or incapacitated through illness or drug addiction. Your basic needs were not taken care of, and you were not made to feel special or loved. Or perhaps your previous partner neglected you, putting work, social and personal needs before you. You were made to feel unimportant.

Common triggers of the neglect baggage include having other people or commitments prioritised over you and what you want, your partner forgetting something you have asked for, or your partner not considering you when making a decision concerning themselves. When your neglect baggage bursts open, you feel unloved, not prioritised, uncared for and lonely. As an example, you and your partner might go out to a social outing with a group of friends. Your partner spends a lot of time hanging out and talking to other people. You feel neglected. While for your partner, this might be as simple as catching up with friends, for you, you feel less valued by your partner. You believe your partner does not see you as important.

Failing incompetent baggage

The failing incompetent baggage refers to a chronic felt sense of inadequacy and failure within the relationship. You constantly question your own abilities, judgements and contributions to the relationship. No matter how hard you try, you feel you are always performing below what everyone else is around you. This self-doubt leads to reluctance to take initiative in your relationship. You feel incompetent as a person when your partner reacts negatively or does not approve of what you have done. When your partner succeeds, it invokes a sense of failure and incompetence within you. You compare yourself to others, particularly their successes and your comparative failings.

You will have failing incompetent baggage if you had a critical and over-functioning parent or previous partner. No matter what you did, it was never good enough for this parent or partner. They never celebrated your success and always took control of tasks and activities, leaving you feeling inadequate. In this dynamic, they diminished your power and self-belief.

Common triggers for failing incompetent baggage include other people's successes, failing to receive approval for an action you've made, receiving negative feedback or criticism, and perceiving disapproval or disappointment from your partner, even if it's not explicitly expressed. When your incompetence baggage bursts open, you feel inadequate, anxious, small, ineffective, hopeless, inept or silly. For example, your partner arrives home and tells you they have been given a promotion at work. Logically, you know you should – and want – to feel happy for them. However, you have a deep feeling of incompetence. Their success highlights and confirms an (untrue) belief that you are less adequate as a person.

Dependency baggage

Dependency baggage refers to a chronic lack of confidence and independence within the relationship. You seek validation and approval from others, particularly your partner, to feel worthy and secure. You struggle to trust your own judgement and rely heavily on external feedback to gauge your self-worth and decision-making. You struggle to embrace autonomy and avoid responsibilities in your relationship. You excessively rely on your partner, seeking their assistance with even simple tasks. You struggle to cope with challenges or stressors on your own. You feel overwhelmed and lost without your partner's support and may turn to them for comfort and guidance in even minor situations.

Dependency baggage occurs when you have had a controlling parent or partner in the past. Essentially, this parent or previous partner excessively controlled situations for you. They believed they knew best and dominated your decisions, leaving you dependent and unable to act with confidence. They have stunted your autonomy.

Common triggers of dependency baggage include having to make a decision on your own, having to take the lead or be in control, not receiving reassurance or approval for a decision you've made, facing challenges, facing uncertain or unfamiliar situations particularly in the absence of your partner, or feeling out of control or powerless in a situation. When your dependency baggage bursts open, you feel lost, anxious, unsure and uncertain. For example, say you want to buy a new product in an unfamiliar shopping mall. You really want the product but feel overwhelmed by the thought of driving to a location you have not been to before. You worry you won't be able to find parking and you don't want to deal with a shop assistant on your own. The anxiety of the task leads to avoidance, even though you want the product. You feel you can only complete the task if your partner goes with you.

Hypersensitivity to anger baggage

The hypersensitivity to anger baggage is a strong internal reaction to even the slightest sense of anger in your partner. You become preoccupied with their anger and react to this perception rather than any other part of the interaction. This baggage usually occurs when you have had a parent or previous partner who was prone to anger or rage. Their anger or rage left you in a highly anxious state, traumatised and feeling unsafe. You are now hypersensitive to the slightest bit of anger due to the associated fear.

Common triggers for this baggage include when your partner is frustrated, irritated or angry, either directly at you or about something unrelated to you. When your hypersensitivity to anger baggage bursts open, you experience high levels of anxiety and vulnerability. You feel overly responsible for your partner's emotions and reactions. An example may be you wake up feeling great. However, you then sense your partner is irritable, and your hypersensitivity to anger baggage is triggered. You feel completely unsettled and the feeling is intolerable. You have a deep sense of instability and a desire for your partner to neutralise any feelings of anger.

Entanglement baggage

The entanglement baggage is a belief you and your partner must do all things and make all decisions together. You feel responsible for how your partner is feeling, and your own emotions are entwined with theirs. Sometimes the entanglement might not be with your partner but with another family member or friend. When it involves a third person, it often causes triangulation in the relationship, with one party feeling on the outer. (Refer to chapter 6 for more on triangulation.) In this situation, this third person, often unwittingly, becomes the focus of attention, resulting in the partner relationship being destabilised.

You develop entanglement baggage when you have had an enmeshed relationship with a parent. The parent–child boundaries were blurred, erasing individuality and causing suffocation. The parent may overly rely on the child for support or control their every move, hindering the child's identity and independence.

Common triggers of entanglement baggage include actions of autonomy by self or other, such as you having to say no to your partner or your partner saying no to you, or one of you choosing independent activities, interests or friendships. When your entanglement baggage bursts open, you feel threatened or a sense of guilt, duty and obligation. You may also experience a sense of entitlement in the relationship and feel let down or rejected when your partner engages in their own autonomous behaviour. An example may be your partner's parents inviting them out for a birthday lunch during a work day when you cannot attend. You feel a deep sense of hurt because the plans were not made to include you. It feels very much like you are being left out even though, logically, you realise it is a nice moment for your partner and their parents.

Rejection baggage

The rejection baggage refers to a sensitivity to actions that bring about the feeling of rejection. This is felt as a complete rejection of you as a person, and can occur without your partner's intention. Your partner's actions of autonomy, for example, can be interpreted as a rejection of you. Rejection baggage can occur if you have had a parent or partner who has rejected you. You were made to feel second or left out of important events. Your parents or previous partner chose other people or activities over you on a regular basis.

Common rejection baggage triggers include your partner choosing to prioritise other people or activities over you, your partner not giving you their full attention, your partner speaking curtly or assertively to you, or your partner not returning your messages or calls promptly. When your rejection baggage bursts open, you feel hurt, small, rejected, unloved and unwanted. For example, whenever your partner wants some alone time or space to pursue their hobbies, you interpret this as rejection. Even though your partner reassures you whenever they seek personal time, the sensitivity to rejection baggage leaves you feeling hurt and unloved, straining the relationship.

Lack of discipline baggage

The lack of discipline baggage is when you were not taught effective discipline via healthy boundaries, guidance and responsibilities from your family of origin. You struggle to take action and complete tasks, even though it negatively affects your relationship. You find it difficult to tolerate any frustration in reaching your goals. This usually occurs when you had a parent who would rescue or over-function for you. They may have been compensating for something unpleasant occurring in the household, such as an angry parent or being a single parent. Either way, you have learned that completing tasks is difficult and leaning on low- or no-value activities (refer to chapter 6) is easier.

Common triggers of lack of discipline baggage include facing a hurdle when you are working towards a goal, doing mundane or boring tasks, or your partner asking you to do an unpleasant or boring task. When your lack of discipline baggage bursts open, you encounter resistance within yourself and feel irritated and bored. You experience an urge to run away or self-soothe with stimulating or pleasurable activities. For example, you promise your partner you are going to tidy the house. However, you find it difficult to start. You feel overwhelmed and trapped. You procrastinate to the point that the chores are not completed, which leads to significant disharmony in your relationship.

Perfectionist baggage

The perfectionist baggage refers to when you place great value on achievement and orderliness. You tend to have high internal standards and believe you must strive hard to reach these at whatever cost. These standards are projected onto your partner. You are sensitive to routines being broken, plans changed and disorderliness in the relationship. You find it difficult to tolerate change. You experience high levels of anxiety and frustration when things are not completed to your expectation or standard. You might have perfectionistic baggage for many reasons, including a parent or previous partner who had very high standards in a particular area. You have come to believe these standards are the norm and feel uncomfortable with anything below par. Sometimes the opposite is true. Your parents or previous partner were chaotic with limited standards. You developed the perfectionistic baggage because it allowed you to feel safe and make sense of the world.

Common perfectionist baggage triggers include your partner not doing what you have asked or expected, your partner running late, your partner completing a task not to your standard, or a cluttered or untidy home. When the perfectionist baggage bursts open, you feel irritated, frustrated, angry, disappointed, anxious or distressed. For example, when it is your turn to cook a meal, you put time, effort and thought into it. You also make sure the kitchen is cleaned and spotless by the time the meal is served. However, when it is your partner's turn to cook, they throw something together and the kitchen is left looking like a bomb site. You feel shocked, disappointed, let down and anxious at the state of the kitchen.

Mistreatment baggage

The mistreatment baggage is the expectation your partner will break your trust, cheat on you, or abuse or harm you in some way. Without any actual evidence, you believe the relationship is destined to fail, you will be taken advantage of, and you will face hurt and disappointment. You have mistreatment baggage if you were abused or deceived by a parent or previous partner – someone close to you who you should have been able to trust.

Common triggers of mistreatment baggage include your partner expressing differences of opinions or holding their ground, boundaries being set by your partner (interpreted as threats), teasing and joking by your partner, or competitive activities. When the mistreatment baggage bursts open, you feel threatened, put upon, hurt and angry. You experience an urge to attack first or get revenge later. For example, say your partner innocently teases you about the shape of the cookies you've just baked. Your mistreatment baggage bursts open, causing you to feel attacked and humiliated. You immediately become defensive, interpreting your partner's teasing as a form of mockery or contempt.

Feeling controlled baggage

The feeling controlled baggage is a sensitivity to any perceived control by your partner. This baggage is *not* about a controlling partner but rather the perception of being controlled. This baggage occurs when you have had a parent or past partner who was very controlling. You felt very stifled in the relationship and held resentment toward them because of their attempts to control you. These attempts left you want-ing to rebel against your parent or previous partner and break free from them.

Common feeling controlled baggage triggers include your partner asking something of you (from domestic duties to hearing how they are feeling), your partner enquiring about your activities and plans, or your partner talking about their needs in the relationship. When your feeling controlled baggage bursts open, you may feel anxious, constricted and restrained, and find yourself reacting in an angry or rebellious way. For example, perhaps your partner asks you in a direct way if you could start doing a new chore. The direct nature of their request triggers the feeling controlled baggage. Rather than having a discussion, you feel overwhelmed and a sense of being controlled, and the desire to lash out or rebel.

Ashamed baggage

The ashamed baggage refers to the embodied sense that you are inherently flawed and broken. When this baggage is around, you believe your authentic self, or the real you, is not enough and will inevitably be rejected by others as your flaws become apparent. You do not feel worthy of love or care. This occurs when a parent or previous partner constantly used unjustified shame against you. They may have blamed you for things beyond your control or maturity level. Rather than offering unconditional love and support, they used ridicule, injuring your self-worth.

Common triggers of ashamed baggage include any form of feedback or perceived criticism from your partner. Whether it's about your behaviour, appearance or choices, this perceived criticism can amplify feelings of being flawed or defective. Making mistakes or finding things challenging can also bring about this baggage. When your ashamed baggage bursts open, you feel ashamed, defective, worthless and inadequate. For example, say you are getting ready for a wedding when your partner gently suggests what you are wearing isn't formal enough for the occasion. This suggestion triggers feelings of inadequacy and unworthiness. You immediately feel ashamed and embarrassed, believing your partner is subtly implying that you are not presentable or attractive enough for the event.

Unpacking your baggage

Baggage sits outside of your conscious awareness. When it is unclaimed, it can burst open at any time, wreaking havoc in your relationship. You must unpack your baggage and get to know what's in there – so when it bursts open, you can circumvent conflict in your relationship. In this section, we show you how to do this.

When your baggage bursts open without conscious awareness, you will flip into conflict personas and you won't get what you need in your relationship. Knowledge is power. So you need to unpack the origins and consequences of your baggage. You can grow self-awareness by exploring your baggage, where it comes from and how it plays out in your relationship. Awareness of your baggage enables you to develop healthier coping strategies instead of relying on old potentially harmful ways of seeing the world and coping with pain. You can adopt more adaptive and constructive ways to deal with baggage bursts.

Unpacking the origins of your baggage

Unclaimed baggage can lead to projection, where you attribute your own unresolved issues onto others. Understanding the origins of your baggage helps prevent projecting your issues onto those around you, fostering healthier relationships and interactions. Your unclaimed baggage will be part of the reason you feel disconnected or in conflict with your partner. If you don't understand what is going on with your baggage, your conflict dance may continue and never change.

Meet Anna and David, a couple Helen was seeing at our Sydney practice.

Baggage keeps the conflict dance going

Anna has neglect baggage. She grew up in a family in which her younger sister had a chronic illness, and her parents' time, energy and care was funnelled into taking care of her. Anna was a naturally healthy, bright child and was generally quiet and compliant. After caring for her sister, Anna's parents had little left over for her. Anna learnt not to make a fuss and to push her own feelings aside. The unspoken message was clear to Anna: her sister's condition was paramount, and Anna's own feelings and needs were inconsequential by comparison.

David, on the other hand, has entanglement baggage. He grew up in a family with a domineering father and a passive mother. With an iron will and an unwavering sense of authority, David's father ruled the household with a firm hand, allowing little room for dissent or individuality. His mother, meanwhile, was a passive figure. She was resigned to her role in the family, yet would rely on David for emotional support and care. She would cry and complain to him about his father. David had to step into the role of emotional caretaker from a young age. He learnt to tiptoe around his father's volatile moods while offering solace and support to his mother. Caught between his parents' emotions, David struggled to carve out a space for himself to learn about his own feelings, needs and desires. He learnt to cut himself off from his own internal world.

Anna and David's baggage played out in their relationship. When Anna felt upset and sad about something, instead of speaking up, she passively expressed her emotions in the hope David would notice and take care of her. Anna had learnt her feelings weren't important. As a child, when her feelings were expressed overtly they were invalidated or diminished. Therefore, Anna felt it was safer to throw out hints of her mood state in the hope someone would notice.

David, having learnt to read and attune to his parents' moods, would pick up on Anna's passive emotions and immediately feel overwhelmed by them. He felt a responsibility to take on Anna's feelings and fix them. But when it was too much, his Cold Wall conflict persona would step in to protect him. He would shut off emotionally, leaving only an icy space between them. Anna would immediately experience the chill. Again her feelings were ignored. Her own Cold Wall emerged to avoid the pain of insignificance. A silent, icy war was waged.

Anna and David demonstrate that when baggage isn't claimed, it can become the source of conflict in any interaction or the relationship as a whole. Your unclaimed and unpacked baggage will continue to weigh down your relationship and cause damage to your couple bond.

Moving beyond blame

When unpacking baggage, a common thought is, *I don't want to blame my parents or past romantic relationships for all my problems.* This isn't a blame game. It's about understanding why you have this particular baggage. By understanding your baggage, you are taking on responsibility for it. You are not responsible for the creation of your baggage, but you are now responsible for what happens when it bursts open. Identifying where your baggage came from is the first step to breaking the legacies of past relationship traumas.

As you unpack your baggage, you may come to realise your parents or past partners have had some detrimental effects on you. This is challenging. It's uncomfortable to reflect on important relationships in this way. In the case of parents, most do the best they can with the resources at hand. It's often not a question of love. Sometimes, however, someone's best is not quite enough. When this happens, a need is not met and baggage has space to grow.

 **TIME FOR ACTION**

We've created a series of questions to help you unpack your baggage. First, go back to the list of baggage types and highlight those relevant to you. Then reflect on the following questions in relation to each of your baggage types. Share this information with your partner so they can understand your baggage too. Invite your partner to select, reflect and unpack their own baggage. Ask them to share this information with you. Listen carefully and be interested, non-judgemental and kind when hearing about your partner's baggage.

Consider the following:

- Everyone starts carrying little bags around from a young age. How do you think this baggage may have started to form in your family of origin? If not in your family of origin, what relationship do you think this baggage came from and why?

- Do you think this baggage and the feelings associated with it are related to your mother or father, a previous partner or someone else?

- Get to know your baggage by reflecting back to a time when you remember experiencing it. Spend some time here noticing what comes up, including images, thoughts and feelings. Now answer the following questions: What feelings did you experience? What and where in your body did you feel those feelings? What sorts of thoughts were going through your mind?

- How has the load of carrying this baggage affected you at different stages in your life?

- What sorts of situations and experiences have made this baggage heavier?

- At what time or circumstances in your life has the weight of this baggage felt unbearable?

- What makes this baggage feel lighter and better? And do these actions help you in the long term?

- How do you think this baggage presents itself today with your partner?

- Which conflict personas tend to show up when your baggage is not taken care of?

By answering these questions, you are getting to know your vulnerabilities and why the unclaimed baggage is such a sore spot for you. This information is priceless. Being able to identify the true cause of your pain – your unclaimed baggage bursting open, not your partner being an awful person – can change the game in relationships. You will learn how to take care of your baggage and your partner's baggage in the next section.

Exploring the origins of your baggage can feel uncomfortable, because you'll have to reflect on past hurts and relationships. Hang in there. Discomfort isn't the enemy. If hurt is surrounding a baggage, you are onto something. Always turn up to baggage with compassion and kindness. The knowledge you gain from understanding your baggage is worth the pain. Don't forget, everyone has baggage. You are not alone here.

Carrying each other's baggage

You need to take care of your own and your partner's baggage. Taking care of baggage helps heal the baggage wound and brings a secure attachment to the relationship. A secure attachment is a healthy and emotionally balanced bond between you and your partner. It is characterised by trust, a sense of safety, and the belief that both your needs will be consistently met.

Through the rest of this chapter, we outline ways to cope when your baggage bursts open and also how to help your partner when their baggage explodes.

Carrying your own baggage means learning ways to cope when your baggage arrives and bursts open. At these times, you only see the world from the perspective of your baggage. Carrying your own baggage means identifying the presence of your baggage, taking responsibility for your baggage, and willingly trying ways to be compassionate to yourself while setting a boundary with your baggage.

You don't need to carry your own baggage in silence or completely on your own. Carrying your own baggage may mean sharing with your partner that your baggage is here and how you are feeling. It might mean asking for help. We go into detail about different options later in this chapter.

Carrying your partner's baggage means finding ways you can support your partner with their baggage. Being more sensitive to your partner's baggage is part of carrying their baggage. By helping them carry their own baggage, the load will be lighter for both of you.

You are not responsible for your partner's baggage. You do not need to tiptoe around your partner's baggage. Walking on eggshells in any relationship is not helpful. Rather, when we talk about carrying your partner's baggage, we mean how you can be effective in response to the baggage outburst. You each have your baggage. It's going to burst open. Aim to turn up to it in a way that helps you both, and the relationship.

Benefits of sharing the load

You need to know how to respond when your baggage arrives and bursts open. Otherwise, it will keep blowing up your relationship, leaving pain and suffering. By attending to baggage – and sharing the load with your partner – you can enjoy a more harmonious relationship and even heal your baggage wounds.

Let's see this in action with Shahn and his couple Angela and Sophie.

Carrying baggage together to build attunement

Angela has hypersensitivity to anger baggage. This means she has a strong internal reaction to even the slightest bit of anger displayed by Sophie. An example of how this played out in their relationship was discussed in therapy. One evening Angela was at home feeling relaxed when Sophie came home from work. Sophie was frustrated by an incident at her work, and started venting to Angela as she arrived home. As she listened to Sophie, Angela became more and more anxious. She tried harder and harder to find ways to appease Sophie's anger. She took her coat. She offered her something to drink. She sat at the edge of her seat wringing her hands. She kept saying 'I'm sorry'.

Angela desperately wanted to reduce her own anxiety by appeasing Sophie's anger. Angela's Self-Sacrificing Partner Pleaser conflict persona was here.

Angela's previous relaxed, calm mind state was lost as she became consumed by Sophie's emotions. For Sophie, Angela's fussing and lack of attunement was frustrating, and she became annoyed with Angela. Sophie had a terrible thing happen at work and just wanted to vent and have Angela validate her. In this example, Angela's hypersensitivity baggage had burst open. This innocuous interaction between them started a conflict dance.

To carry her own baggage, Angela learned to identify when it was bursting open. She took some slow breaths and labelled the anxiety associated with this baggage. She reminded herself that Sophie was feeling her own feelings and they weren't directed at Angela. She told herself she isn't responsible for managing Sophie's anger, even if she'd learned to do so in previous relationships. Through this process, Angela learnt to carry her own baggage.

Sophie learnt to clearly inform Angela of her feelings including anger, reiterating that they were her experience and not about Angela. Sophie was also clear about what she needed from Angela and checked if that was okay. For example, 'I'm frustrated about my work. I'm not upset at you Angela. I just need some time to vent. Is that something you are up for?' In this way, Sophie was being sensitive to Angela's baggage. She was specific about what she needed and expressed the boundary between her feelings and Angela's feelings.

With these simple approaches of carrying Angela's baggage together, the couple were able to stop an interaction catapulting into a conflict dance. Angela began to heal her baggage wound. Angela learnt angry feelings aren't always dangerous and she doesn't have to submit and pander when anger is around. Sophie was able to help Angela heal this baggage wound. She did this by being more sensitive to how she expressed her anger and providing reassurance to Angela.

By carrying your baggage together, you will be better able to navigate tensions, heal baggage wounds and have more harmonious interactions.

You might be thinking, *I didn't cause my partner's baggage. Why should I take care of it?* You're right. You are not responsible for the existence of your partner's baggage. It most likely developed before you, in a previous relationship or in childhood. But, either way, your partner's baggage is playing out in your relationship. Your relationship has inherited the unclaimed baggage and it is now the relationship's responsibility to carry it.

We are not saying you are responsible for your partner's baggage. Each individual is responsible for their behaviours associated with their baggage. Your role as a partner is to care and support, but not take on responsibility for the baggage.

As an example of this, Sharon had wounded love baggage playing out in her relationship with Con. In previous relationships, she had been cheated on multiple times, leaving her devastated. When Con hung out or spoke to other women, her wounded love baggage would burst open and she would feel hurt, betrayed and insecure. She would flip into her Suspicious Detective conflict persona, becoming jealous and controlling of Con and causing problems in their relationship. To address this unclaimed baggage issue, Sharon needed to take responsibility for her Suspicious Detective behaviour because it was unfair on Con. He wasn't unfaithful to Sharon. On Con's side, although he hadn't cheated on Sharon, he still needed to be sensitive around her wounded love baggage. For Con, this would mean being transparent about who he was spending time with, reassuring Sharon he was committed to the relationship, and checking in with her when doing activities that she found particularly triggering.

Knowing when you shouldn't carry your partner's baggage

The exception to carrying your partner's baggage is when they are being aggressive or making demands of you to meet their baggage needs.

We love partners being open and assertive about when their baggage has arrived, and partners being sensitive to each other's baggage. But aggression and demands are not welcome when dealing with baggage. You might have worked out what you need from your partner so are tempted to become demanding. But this isn't the way to get your needs met. Instead, this keeps you locked in secondary conflict emotions and a conflict persona response. You are now in a conflict dance, pushing your partner into compliance, which is not effective.

If your partner is aggressively demanding you take care of their baggage, it's time to pull out the emotional mirror from chapter 5. You can adjust it to include the unclaimed baggage.

Let's revisit Con and Sharon. Con informed Sharon about a full-day workshop he'd just attended where all the participants were women except for Con – and the workshop had one more day left. Hearing this, Sharon's wounded love baggage burst open, followed by her Suspicious Detective. She became angry and demanding, insisting he not attend the workshop the following day. Con used the emotional mirror with Sharon by saying, 'Sharon, I know you are hurt and upset right now and I really want to understand better what's going on. But all I'm experiencing is your anger and control. I want to talk to you about this situation and come up with a way we can both be supported, but I can't when you're like this. Can we take a little break and then come back together when we are both more open to hearing how each other is feeling?' Here, Con is referring to their secondary conflict emotions and inner vulnerable feelings (discussed in chapter 5).

Self-help and partner help based on baggage type

When things are calm in your relationship, ask your partner to go through each of your baggage types together. Brainstorm ways you can help each other when each of your baggage bursts open. When doing this, consider what each of your emotional needs are and what might be helpful to meet those needs. The following sections provide examples of self-help and help for your partner when baggage bursts open. Don't be limited by these, because you know yourself and your partner best.

Wounded love baggage

Self-help:

- Sit with your difficult feelings and delay acting on them for an hour.
- Remind yourself that your partner is committed to you and the relationship.

Partner help:

- Don't be overly flirtatious other than with your partner.
- Be transparent about your friends and plans.
- Check in with your partner when you know they are having a difficult time with this baggage.

Criticism baggage

Self-help:

- Remind yourself your partner is not the critical person from your past and they are on your side.
- Pause before responding. When you do, express your inner vulnerable feelings.

Partner help:

- Be conscious of how you speak to your partner. Be kind and gentle, particularly if you are giving feedback or asking something of them.
- Start difficult conversations with 'I' statements.

Abandonment baggage

Self-help:

- Don't text or call your partner if the aim is to resolve anxiety. Awaiting a response can increase feelings of anxiety and abandonment. However, you can call or text to let them know in a direct way your abandonment baggage has burst open.

- Call or touch base with a supportive friend or family member instead of reaching out to your partner.

Partner help:

- Provide reassurance around the relationship and your commitment to them.

- Plan for communication in times of relationship stress and stick to it.

Neglect baggage

Self-help:

- Think about your own needs, values and interests. Acknowledge their importance and ensure you communicate clearly how you are feeling to your partner.

- Reflect on your relationship and how your partner does try to take care of some of your needs. Ask yourself, 'Am I feeling neglected right now in this moment, or is it representative of how I often feel in the relationship?'

Partner help:

- Be curious and interested in your partner and what they might want or need. Try to be validating of your partner's feelings.

- Make sure you have a good understanding of your partner's feelings and position on certain subjects and events. Prioritise making joint decisions.

Failing incompetent baggage

Self-help:

- Be kind to yourself and recognise that everyone has strengths and weaknesses.

- Remind yourself that it's okay to make mistakes and that failure is a natural part of the learning process.

- Identify and challenge any negative or self-critical thoughts that arise. Replace them with more balanced and realistic perspectives.

- Break tasks down into smaller, more manageable steps. Set realistic goals for yourself. Celebrate your progress along the way, even if it's small.

- Try out difficult or non-achievement-focused activities. Congratulate yourself for having the courage to try.

- Focus on trying and having a go rather than the desired outcome.

Partner help:

- Provide your partner with praise and recognition of their personal qualities that are not achievement based (for example, being caring, supportive or creative).

- Allow your partner to express their feelings and concerns without interrupting or judging them. Show empathy and validate their emotions, letting them know that it's okay to feel vulnerable.

- Reassure your partner that you love and accept them. Remind them of their strengths and accomplishments.

- Provide positive feedback about your partner's efforts and traits you love about them.

- Be patient, validate their feelings, and highlight gently to them you don't expect them to get everything right in the relationship.

Dependency baggage

Self-help:

- Choose to purposely not inform your partner of an accomplishment you have made, but instead give positive self-praise.

- Gradually increase autonomous activity and decision-making.

- Cultivate a sense of self-reliance and independence by focusing on your own strengths, interests and goals.

- Engage in activities that bring you joy and fulfilment outside of your relationships.

Partner help:

- Encourage and give positive feedback for your partner's autonomous activity and decision-making. Ensure you are not critical of this.

- Show an interest in your partner's own interests that are separate to yours. Support them to engage in activities based on their separate interests.

Hypersensitivity to anger baggage

Self-help:

- Sit with your discomfort and remind yourself you do not need to react or resolve your partner's emotion. Give them time to deal with their emotion.

- Remind yourself that your partner's emotion might not even be about you. Remind yourself that they are allowed to have their own feelings that are separate to you.

- Explain to your partner you feel activated by their anger and ask them if they are okay or if they would like to talk.

Partner help:

- Remember – your partner is sensitive to anger so try your best to communicate your inner vulnerable feelings.
- If you are feeling anger, remind your partner they don't need to fix your anger, you just might need some time to vent or cool down.

Entanglement baggage

Self-help:

- Remind yourself you are not responsible for everyone else's needs and feelings, especially when they have not been directly expressed to you. (For example, you don't need to make decisions based on what you 'think' other people want.) The opposite is also true – people are not responsible for your needs and cannot read your mind.
- Identify your own needs and feelings. Set boundaries based on your own needs while staying open to people's direct communication about their needs and feelings.

Partner help:

- Remember your partner has been entangled for a long time. Be kind, gentle and patient with their boundary setting.
- Be supportive and help them brainstorm what their own needs might be and possible related boundaries.

Rejection baggage

Self-help:

- If you are triggered, inform your partner you are experiencing feelings of rejection and open up a healthy dialogue around the concern.

- If you are triggered but think your reaction may be out of context, try to sit with the feeling instead of reacting. Rather, reach out to a supportive friend and tell them what is happening and how you are feeling.

- Remind yourself your partner has chosen you and the relationship above all else. When they express their own needs and desires, it doesn't mean they are rejecting you or the relationship.

Partner help:

- When saying no to your partner, be sure to add appropriate information around your decision and provide reassurance around the relationship.

- Make sure you inform your partner they are a priority and illustrate this through open dialogue, joint planning and making alternative plans.

Lack of discipline baggage

Self-help:

- Plan out your day the night before.

- Only commit to tasks you intend to do.

- Complete all 'must-do' tasks before engaging in any leisure activities, especially optional technology use such as social media and gaming.

- Remind yourself that to get anywhere in life you have to do uncomfortable or boring activities. Take a deep breath and take the first step to action the activity at hand.

- Remind yourself that when you face boring or uncomfortable tasks, you can only go in one direction – through them. If you avoid these tasks, they will not go away and will only bring more suffering later.

Partner help:

- Have an open discussion about your expectations and needs in the relationship. Be honest about how you feel when you have to over-function for your partner. Be kind and use 'I' statements in this discussion. Express your inner vulnerable feelings.

- Don't lead or take over for your partner. Rather, create room for them to step up. Have a brainstorming session about what they want to achieve and possible steps to help them get there. Agree to participate in such a meeting but inform them they need to schedule and lead it.

Perfectionist baggage

Self-help:

- Practise patience and delay reactions if you feel something is below your expectation or standard. Sit on it for a few hours, and then either let it go or talk to your partner about the issue from a calm and neutral perspective.

- If you think your partner's bar is too low, chances are yours is too high. Keeping to this standard will lead to perpetually feeling disappointed, hurt and frustrated. Try to imagine what a middle bar might look like between your and your partner's standards. Have a conversation with your partner about trying to meet in the middle.

- Remind yourself that your worth as a partner and a person isn't based on how well you perform. You are worthy just because you exist. Being perfect won't actually increase your sense of worth.

Partner help:

- If you think your partner's bar is too high, then yours might be too low. Try to imagine what a middle bar might look like on this topic and discuss a compromise with your partner.

- If you think your partner is upset because you cannot meet their expectations, try to be open about how you feel rather than getting involved in the content. For example, 'I feel anxious because I can't please you' or 'Right now I feel controlled by your standards and it blocks me from connecting with you'.

Mistreatment baggage

Self-help:

- Remind yourself your feelings may not always be accurate. Rather than suppressing your feelings, try to disclose them in a healthy manner.

- When triggered, ask yourself this question: 'How would I behave and feel if I did not believe the thoughts I am having around mistrust and mistreatment right now?'

Partner help:

- Be consistent and commit to honour what you say you will do.

- Relationships work best when you put your partner first. Remember to value your partner through your actions as an individual to build safety and security.

Feeling controlled baggage

Self-help:

- When triggered, indicate to your partner you are feeling controlled. Suggest multiple solutions around any circumstance rather than binary options.

- Remember – your partner is not trying to control you. Rather, they may just be trying to function effectively as a couple. Try to stay calm and ask for some time out to think before responding.

Partner help:

- Remember that autonomy is important to your partner. Try coming up with joint decisions rather than holding a fixed position.

- If you are concerned about a particular behaviour of your partner's, note down your inner vulnerable feelings as a result of the behaviour. Focus on your emotions in reaction to any given behaviour rather than focusing on the behaviour exclusively.

Ashamed baggage

Self-help:

- Encourage yourself with kindness and understanding. Treat yourself with the same compassion you would offer to a friend in a similar situation.

- Remind yourself that this baggage exists because people have shamed you in the past but your partner isn't one of these people. Your feelings are real but they might be a vestige from the past.

- Inform your partner that your ashamed baggage has burst open. Express your feelings of shame or unworthiness and tell them that you understand it wasn't their intention to invoke these feelings.

- Participate in activities that make you feel good about yourself and reinforce a positive self-image. This could include pursuing hobbies or interests you are interested in, accomplishing small goals, or engaging in acts of self-care.

- Remind yourself that it's okay to have flaws and make mistakes. Nobody is perfect, and it's okay to be imperfectly human. You are just like everyone else with strengths and vulnerabilities.

- Forgive yourself for past mistakes and perceived shortcomings. Holding onto guilt and self-blame only perpetuates feelings of shame and inadequacy.

Partner help:

- Be compassionate and non-judgemental with your partner when they express their feelings of inadequacy and shame. Allow them to express their feelings without trying to fix or dismiss them. Validate their emotions and let them know that you're there for them.

- Refrain from criticising or judging your partner, especially when they're feeling vulnerable.

- Acknowledge the impact of your partner's past experiences on their current struggles and offer validation for their emotions.

- Gently encourage your partner to treat themselves with kindness and understanding. Remind them that it's okay to be imperfect and that everyone experiences setbacks and challenges.

You may be questioning your partner's capacity to take care and be sensitive to your baggage. You may fear them using your baggage as evidence to prove they've been right all along and it has been your issue. This will lead to increased point-scoring.

These fears are why baggage claim is the seventh love link. By the time you reach baggage claim, you and your partner have connected on all the previous love links. You have built a sense of trust, care and bond with your partner. If you don't feel you have this yet, flag it with your partner. Take steps towards growth and connection in the previous six love links before tackling baggage claim.

Summing up

In this chapter, you have gone deep to identify your core vulnerabilities. You've discovered the lost or unclaimed baggage you've been carrying around for most of your life. You now understand why this baggage is a part of your life, and your compassion for yourself has grown.

You have learnt how your unclaimed baggage is adding to the relationship tension and how it contributes to conflict.

You have particular needs that must be considered in your relationship. Through claiming your baggage, you are now armed with strategies to care for yourself when it bursts open. You've also gained deeper insight into your partner's baggage, leading to heightened empathy toward them. You have learned ways to help your partner when their baggage bursts open.

Now you know all about your deepest vulnerabilities, those of your partner and how these play out in your relationship. You know how to take care of your baggage. Nothing is off limits in your relationship, which means you can reach a new height of emotional intimacy. In the next chapter, we dive into one of the hottest and most sensitive areas (pun intended) in relationships – sex and desire. Having learnt about your vulnerabilities and unhelpful coping responses, you are in a great place to address sex in a way that fosters acceptance and connectedness. It is time to smash through sexual blocks and unlock the secrets to desire and a sexually satisfying relationship.

Link eight
Sex and Desire

So you've made it to the sexy love link. You might be wondering if it is possible to have a fun, stimulating and passionate sex life in long-term relationships. Of course it is! Can you reignite the passion you once felt? Yes! Can you experience high erotic energy and tension with your partner? Yes! Can you recapture desire and flirtation? Yes! If you've never had a great sex life, can you turn it around? Yes! Yes! Yes!

Like other aspects of your relationship, sex and desire is dynamic and evolving, requiring investment and attention if you want it to thrive. Your sex life, good, bad or average, has an influence on your relationship. It's also true your relationship, good, bad or average, has an impact on your sex life.

A positive sexual connection will enhance and bring new depths to your relationship. You'll feel more satisfied and more connected, and have better health outcomes. It's worth noting, however, the path to a positive sex life is not the same for every couple. Sex can be a bridge for reconnection for some. For others, close emotional connection and stability is required to unlock sex and desire in their relationship. Either way, a strong emotional bond leads to a better sex life and a better sex life means you will have higher levels of emotional connection. When emotional and sexual intimacy are going well, it acts as a positive feedback loop for the relationship.

If you have an amazing sex life already, fantastic. You will develop insights and strategies in this chapter to keep it strong over time. If you're struggling and you and your partner are ready to work on sex and desire, jump straight in while you concurrently continue to strengthen the other love links. If you don't yet feel ready to tackle sex and desire, you need to focus on strengthening the other seven love links first. When you make good progress with these, the Sex and Desire love link will feel like a natural progression.

This chapter is an invitation to embark on a journey of self-discovery and mutual exploration as sexual partners. The eighth love link is about increasing sex and desire in your relationship. We run through reigniting the flames of desire and breaking unhelpful dynamics and myths that can stifle your sex life. We shine a light on your sexual connection and its evolution throughout your relationship, and explore the interplay of emotions and sexual intimacy. We also examine how attraction, communication and relationship connection form a foundation for a fulfilling and lasting sexual connection.

We suggest you ask your partner to join you in this chapter while you unravel the mysteries of desire and draft a road map to a passionate, fulfilling and enduring sexual relationship. We cover why it's important to talk about sex, and help you develop insight and strategies to smash through roadblocks to intimacy. We explore the key elements to increasing sexual intimacy, attraction and sexual desire. You will come to understand why couples who have more Magic Moments in their relationship also have more magic in the bedroom. And we delve into different categories of sexual activity to give you a platform for discussion, review and exploration.

Uncovering what sex means to you and your partner

What sex means and how it operates is different for every couple. It is also different for each individual within the couple. Sex is part of your evolving relationship. How important it is and what it looks like is dependent on the negotiation of the two people – you and your partner – in the relationship. A healthy sex life can look like anything as long as it is within the boundaries of the relationship. It's important not to compare what other couples might be doing or find normal. Rather, stay present with your partner and within the bounds of what you both are in agreement about.

This chapter is not a treatment for sexual dysfunction. If your relationship is suffering from a sexual disorder, sex could be difficult due to arousal issues, pain or other concerns. While you might benefit from continuing to read on, we recommend you seek professional help from a medical doctor or sex therapist.

Sex is the interplay between emotional intimacy and physical connection. While there is a physical nature to sex, it may or may not be intercourse. Desire is a yearning for physical and emotional intimacy with your partner. Sex and desire are influenced by many factors, including biology, social and cultural norms, your personal beliefs about sex, and the interpersonal relationship dynamics between you and your partner. How you feel about sex is also influenced by your experiences in past relationships, family of origin and culture. What sex entails is varied and different from one couple to the next. In this chapter, we don't give you specific rules or ideas around what sex should be. Rather, we guide you on a mutual journey of sexual intimacy defined by you and your partner.

Perhaps you're thinking, *Our relationship is okay and sex is not that important*. You must look at your sex life even if it's just for selfish health benefits. A healthy sex life provides physical, emotional and relational benefits, as highlighted by clinical psychologist Professor Stuart Brody. In his 2010 study Brody shows that sex assists stress reduction, and can also have a positive effect on migraines and reduce pain. Sex improves cardiovascular health and reduces health risks and mortality rates in general. It is also good for your mental health. Amazingly, Brody's research indicates all of the psychological and health benefits achieved from sexual intercourse with your partner are not replicated by masturbation. So it is pretty conclusive – a sexy relationship is great for your health!

Sex leads to higher levels of emotional satisfaction. When you have regular sex in your relationship, you experience heightened levels of desire for sex and your partner. You also experience an increased sense of being desired, so it is a double positive for your relationship and self-esteem. Studies by Anik Debrot and colleagues found a healthy sex life leads to higher satisfaction and enhanced emotional wellbeing within the relationship. The researchers also found couples who have regular sex also report more fun in their relationship. And through analysing national health data, researchers Kathryn Gangon and Erik Larson concluded a regular sex life is highly associated with lower levels of depression for women and men.

Sex unlocks and maintains deeper bonds. Sex is vulnerable, intimate and differentiates the couple relationship from other important relationships. It also leads to relationship stability where both partners can feel desired and have their needs met. A strong sex life leads to a stronger relationship with more oxytocin, the love and desire hormone. A healthy sex life also adds to a secure attachment, deepening bonds and trust between partners. Sex can be a secret and sacred journey between partners. It is an expression of love, a safe non-verbal way to feel and give love to one another – simply, it's 'making love'.

If you don't have a satisfying sex life with your partner, you are losing out on more than just a good time. In the Sex and Desire love link, we navigate the complexities of desire, addressing the nuanced interplay of individual needs and shared experiences. We show you the keys to unlocking a vibrant and satisfying sexual connection with your partner.

Let's talk about sex

For some, talking about sex is easy. For others, it's difficult. Your individual beliefs, family attitudes, cultural background and religious influences all play a part in how comfortable you are to talk about sex. When it comes to relationships, talking about wants, desires and sexual connection is more the exception than the norm. Talking about sex can feel awkward and embarrassing. It can also feel risky, bringing up fears of being shamed or making a partner feel insecure. However, talking about sex is an essential step to making changes in the bedroom – and talking once is not enough. Desires, preferences and sexual connection all change over time. It's not the length of a relationship that kills sex. Rather, it is a lack of attention, priority and evolution.

Talking about sex sheds light on each other's preferences, interests, concerns or insecurities as they evolve throughout the relationship. Without this transparency, one or both partners might be in the dark when it comes to understanding their own or their partner's sexual desires or needs. While talking about sex might be awkward for some couples, for others it's an aphrodisiac. Talking about sex can feel naughty and spark memories or fantasies, leading to heightened sexual desire.

How you feel when talking about sex is influenced by many factors – for example, your family of origin. If sex was discussed without judgement or shame during your childhood, chances are you feel comfortable talking about sex. However, if shame was associated with sex, whether directly spoken about or not, discussing the topic might be uncomfortable. Do you talk freely with your partner about your sex life? If the answer is no, you are not alone. Many couples struggle to raise the topic.

Considering the risks of not talking about sex

Not discussing your sex life can backfire on you. As an example, let's look at Sara and Peter, who Helen saw for couples therapy.

Lack of discussion can lead to disharmony

Just as it can be challenging to talk about sex within the relationship, couples are often reluctant to talk about sex in therapy. When I inquired about Sara and Peter's sex life, Peter made it clear he believed their sex life was satisfactory. He exclaimed, 'We don't need to talk about sex. It doesn't happen often but we are both on the same page.' Sara's face remained blank, neither confirming nor denying Peter's statement. When I probed further, Sara said, 'Yeah, it's fine, no problems there.'

I sensed Sara might have a different perspective to Peter, so suggested they revisit the issue after looking at other important aspects of the relationship requiring attention. I also made a note to return to the topic of sex in their next session.

A couple of weeks later, at their next session, Sara and Peter presented in crisis. Peter had discovered Sara was on Ashley Madison, the dating website for people who are married and want to cheat on their partners. Peter was in shock. He thought they were both content and happy with their limited sex life. He had a lower sex drive and had been comfortable thinking Sara was in the same place. His whole world was turned upside down.

Sara confessed she hadn't been happy with their sex life for a long time. Despite this, they also hadn't discussed sex for a long time. Peter hadn't wanted to talk about sex and avoided doing so, happy with its decline. Sara had tried to raise the issue many years ago. She gave up when Peter said, 'We just have sex a lot less. It's normal in long-term relationships.' This was no excuse or rationale for Sara to go outside the relationship for sex. However, it demonstrates how avoidance led to an inauthentic connection.

Peter and Sara did not come to couples therapy for their sex life. Nor were they complaining about it. Despite this, a hidden truth was lurking. They had discord in their sexual relationship, and the lack of attention and discussion was causing disharmony in their relationship. For a thriving relationship you must look at your sex life and talk about it, even if you think it's going well. Otherwise, you might be missing something. Saying you are too busy or tired to talk about sex are just excuses. What you are really saying is, 'I am not prioritising our sex life.'

In the case of Peter and Sara, not talking about sex led to infidelity. However, many other consequences are possible, even with faithful partners – including increased resentment, disconnection, parallel partner dynamics (refer to chapter 6), not to mention missing out on all the positive effects.

General rules for talking about sex

Talking to your partner about sex is liberating and is a key to having better sex. When you are open, non-judgmental and comfortable talking about sex, you can break down barriers and overcome feelings of awkwardness. The more you practise talking about sex, the easier it gets and the more fun it can be. If you are experiencing any anxiety or awkwardness in the bedroom, talking about sex is a good first exposure step. It is the safest place to start. It might be tempting to avoid the topic, but how can your sex life improve if you can't comfortably talk about it?

As you get started, make sure you keep the following rules in mind when you talk about sex with your partner:

- *What people like in the bedroom is not a reflection of their personality, values or morals:* For example, if you're into submission in the bedroom, this is not a reflection of your personality. It does not suggest you'd like people to walk all over you in real life. This rule is important because when you accept it, you are free to explore desires without judgement of your whole self.

- *You have to be non-judgmental:* This means no punishments, cold shoulders, rejection, shame or laughing at your partner's preferences, interests, desires or concerns. You don't have to share their desires or agree to participate in them, but there must be no shaming. If you have the urge to be critical, something about the desire is activating an insecurity within you. Shaming your partner means their desire is buried and your relationship is less authentic. Your partner's desires or preferences do not have to become part of your sex life, so you don't need to fear them.

- *Stay open-minded and curious:* This allows for better communication and encourages open communication in the future. By embracing an open mind and staying curious, both you and your partner can be safely honest and transparent. In turn, this results in a more authentic relationship.

- *It's okay for your partner to like or dislike different things to you:* This is very common. It's okay to have deal breakers and for some desires to remain as fantasies. Remember – you can talk about desires without committing to anything. Try to stay open and curious and even discuss compromises. Shahn saw a couple with one partner wanting a threesome. However, the other partner was not interested, stating it went beyond the boundaries of their relationship. They decided to come up with a compromise of watching pornography together. While not a threesome, it was a new activity they hadn't done and was enough of a deviation from the norm to satisfy both partners.

- *Your partner's preferences are not a reflection on you:* If you have strong emotional reactions to your partner's preferences, try to sit with the feeling and examine the vulnerabilities arising for you, rather than becoming critical of your partner. You'll feel more connected and have a better sex life when you become comfortable talking about sex and discussing emotions that come up. When you feel comfortable and safe talking to your partner about sex, it will increase your emotional and erotic connection.

If you talk about sex and you're both on the same page, then you don't need to change anything. This suggests you are both happy with your sex life. We would just recommend you check in with each other every once in a while to stay connected. It can be difficult to start the conversation, but it's well worth it.

We also have some exceptions to talking about sex. Don't bring up your sex life (or lack thereof) when you're in conflict. Bringing up sex in conflict leads to negative associations with sex and drives a deeper wedge between you. Stress and sex do not mix – and stress and anxiety is a sex killer. (See the section 'Navigating intimacy roadblocks', later in the chapter, for more on this.) If sex is on your mind during a conflict, delay the conversation to a time when you're both feeling more open and willing.

Tips for getting started

You might be thinking, *It's uncomfortable to talk about sex. Both my partner and I are awkward when we try.* This is not uncommon. Talking about sex with your partner can be awkward and uncomfortable. Just because it isn't comfortable, however, doesn't mean it isn't worthwhile. If you're struggling, use the skills you've learned in the previous seven love links. Start by doing a feeling the story exercise (refer to chapter 4) on how difficult it is to talk about sex. Sometimes, anticipatory anxiety is getting in the way and, once you start the discussion, it gets easier.

If you're still wondering where to start, including how to bring sex up with your partner and what to actually talk about, don't worry – we've got you covered. The following list includes a sample of questions from the Let's Talk About Sex exercise in our My Love Your Love app. (Access the full list if you and your partner are after some extra homework!)

You can begin exploring by both answering the following questions:

- Would you prefer a slow build up to sex? For example, maybe just hugging and some kissing and slowly working into sexual acts, or is it your preference to get straight to it?

- How often is your ideal amount to have sex?

- What times and when do you feel most like *not* having sex?

- Do you ever worry about giving me non-sexual affection because you feel I may want to initiate sex as a result?

- Do you find me more or less sexually attractive when I am independent, self-sufficient and less available?

- If I don't feel like sex, what is the preferred way I could let you down?

- What is your favourite sexual act/position?

- Are you satisfied with our sex life?

- Describe the most passionate love-making sex you remember having with me (when and where if you can remember).

- Are you more connected to yourself when we are having sex or more concerned about my experience?

- What would you like more of during sex?

- What do you like to happen after sex?

 **TIME FOR ACTION**

Find a time to sit down with your partner and ask each other the preceding questions. Then add any more questions that come to mind. You don't have to answer them all in one sitting. Go slow and explore the answers with curiosity. Before you commence, review the rules provided earlier in this chapter for talking about sex. Make sure you both agree to stick to them before starting.

If this task seems difficult, you might be self-conscious, shy, feel exposed or anxious your partner won't be supportive. Start by discussing your vulnerabilities with your partner rather than talking about sex. This might sound like, 'Hey, I'd like to talk about our sex life, but it feels really hard', 'I want to talk about our sex life, but I feel shy' or, 'I'd like to talk about sex, but I'm worried you might judge me'.

Discuss the dynamic and the vulnerability between you and your partner first. If you feel supported, move on to talking about sex. Take it slow and communicate vulnerability if it comes up during the conversation. Openness and flexibility is one of the principles of all eight love links. You have learnt many new skills to use to stay connected as a team. You might be surprised by your partner's response. Such conversations are an opportunity to receive or give support.

If you fear judgement, ask yourself, 'Is this my fear or has my partner indicated they might shame me on this topic?' Internalised fears can still be very anxiety-provoking. Reflect on your vulnerability and emotion. Try to name it. Perhaps baggage (discussed in the previous chapter) has been activated. For example, has your criticism baggage popped up? Or is it your ashamed baggage? We encourage you to discuss the activation with your partner so they have an opportunity to carry this baggage with you. Having a positive conversation will help you process your feelings. You will feel more settled. It will also enhance your relationship because you are gaining evidence that suggests it's better to discuss your feelings than to suppress them. However, if you think your partner will shame you, you are either in a conflict cycle or a toxic relationship. Revisit the Conflict Compass love link (chapter 5) and address this dynamic with your partner before moving forward with sex and desire.

Navigating intimacy roadblocks

Beyond not talking about sex, two types of roadblocks can affect your sex life. The first is the toxic sex dynamics and the other is sexual myths.

Toxic sex dynamics

Toxic sex dynamics (TSDs) are negative holding patterns in your relationship that interfere in your sexual connection. TSDs become negative feedback loops, making sex more stressful and less frequent. We outline the different types of TSDs here.

The pursuer–distancer TSD

When the pursuer–distancer sex dynamic is in play, two partners are at odds. One partner feels they need sexual intimacy to feel emotional closeness and the other needs emotional closeness to want to have sex. Conflict follows this perfect storm of frustration, feeling uncared for and misunderstood, and sex avoidance within the relationship.

For partner one, sex allows them to feel connected in the relationship. They experience growing resentment and disconnection during a lack of sex. Partner two needs emotional closeness to unlock arousal and desire. They feel repelled by the idea of sex during emotional disconnect. Partner one pursues partner two for sex and thereby connection. This leads to inevitable conflict because the meaning of sex for each is in opposition.

Partner two becomes wary of any physical contact. They worry any touch might give a false signal they are up for sex. So they start avoiding all intimacy and physical affection, including non-sexual intimacy such as holding hands or having a hug. On the other hand, when non-sexual physical touch does occur, partner one falsely interprets the sexual activity doors are open. This leads to conflict. Partner one feels further rejection and partner two feels more misunderstood and uncared for. The more partner one pursues sex, the more partner two will distance.

When this occurs on repeat, both partners tend to disconnect, stifling both the emotional and sexual aspects of their relationship.

If you find yourself in this dynamic, you must understand that the emotional bond and sexual connection is different for you and your partner. While you might need sex to feel a deeper connection, they may need emotional connection and safety to want to have sex. When this dynamic is in play, you must break the cycle. If you keep pursuing your partner, they will keep distancing. And if you keep distancing, they will keep pursuing. Imagine one person continuing to step towards the other while the other person continues to step away. To break the cycle, the pursuer needs to step back in the opposite direction, allowing space for the distancer to step forward.

If you need emotional closeness to have sex, being sexually intimate during conflict can be challenging. The pursuer must be patient and work on the emotional bond. The distancer must commit to being open to engage in a sexual connection.

If you are in this TSD you need to take sex off the table for a couple of weeks to a month. This is to allow you to work on your emotional connection. During this time, you are not allowed to have sex. However, it is important to introduce non-sexual physical touch to re-establish affection. For a few months following this period, if either person wants sex, they need to ask directly. Be clear and open when you want to have sex. You may think this will kill spontaneity, but initiations for sex must be verbal. This allows physical affection to flourish and not be interpreted as a bid for sex. This ensures a continued connection and offers a buffer from this TSD.

When it comes to the pursuer–distancer TSD, the aim is to have a strong emotional connection and a regular sex life. When this is achieved, you have broken the TSD and created a positive feedback loop, satisfying both partners. Just remember – you and your partner might be opposites. Just as you feel you might need sex for emotional closeness, your partner might need emotional closeness for sex.

Working together and understanding this can help bring your relationship back into balance.

The parent–child TSD

In this TSD, partner one is over-functioning in the relationship and partner two is under-functioning. Partner one feels like the parent in the relationship and partner two feels they are treated like a child. Both don't find the other attractive. Having to be the parent in a relationship is boring and frustrating, while the child in the relationship feels pursued and criticised. This TSD also leads to rebellion by the 'child' who feels controlled and a loss of respect from the 'parent' who's tired of carrying the load.

The solution here is balancing out the non-sexual power in the relationship. Partner two, who's under-functioning, needs to increase their responsibilities and reliability, and the change needs to be consistent so partner one can stop over-functioning. Partner one needs to reduce their over-functioning to allow space for the under-functioning partner to step forward and do more. The aim is to bring more equity and a sense of partnership back into the relationship. It's worth noting, both parties must discuss their expectations and standards. Often a mismatch of standards and expectations also exists within this TSD. If you identify with this TSD, review the couple domains outlined in chapter 2 and the two truths exercise provided in chapter 5. This will help you to reflect on your own standards and expectations and come to a decision together on the standards and expectations for your relationship.

The anxiety/stress mind versus the sexy mind TSD

Have you ever felt sexual arousal while doing your taxes? Or sexual desire when swamped with work pressure? We are guessing the answer is no (unless taxes are your thing). Why? Because humans don't naturally feel horny when under stress and pressure. We're not biologically wired to have sex when in a stressed state. When in a stressed state, your body sees survival as more important than procreating. Let's say you are being attacked by a rival village. Is that a good time to drop your pants and have sex? No, you will be defenceless. You need to survive to have sex another day! Sex and stress do not mix.

Couples get into trouble when they associate sex with stress, anxiety or pressure. Good sex is exciting, tactile, passionate and pleasurable. Stress, anxiety and pressure do not equal good sex.

What mind state are you and your partner in when having sex? You can be in your sexy mind or you can be in your anxiety/stress mind. But you can't be in both at the same time. When you are both in sexy mind states, you can't be in this TSD. If you or your partner is in your anxiety or stress mind while engaging in sexual activity, it's going to affect your experience. It can lead to sexual disconnection, frustrations, and problems with performance and arousal. Remember – this is a normal reaction to feeling stressed or anxious because you are not biologically wired to have sex in this state. If the anxiety/stress mind state continues to occur while trying to have sex, you will start to form negative associations, leading to avoidance for one or both partners.

When in anxiety/stress mind, it's normal for sexual arousal to cease. This means worrying about performance during sex will only lead to a self-fulfilling prophecy – the issue you are most worried about will happen. The more you worry about how aroused you are, the less likely you will become aroused.

When you're in your sexy mind, you're excited and horny. You're feeling a sense of connection and stimulation. You're present in the moment. You're focused on tactile experiences.

When you're in your anxiety/stress mind, you're not in your sexy mind. You are not present with the experience. You're in your head. You might be worried about performance or life stressors. A common mistake people make in this situation is to think their way out – for example, through distracting themselves or 'trying harder'. Partners of people stuck in anxiety/stress mind often make the mistake of being critical or frustrated instead of supportive, which increases the anxiety and stress of the other partner.

If your relationship is suffering from this TSD, you must talk about it. To break this TSD, the person in their anxiety/stress mind needs unconditional support. The aim is to extinguish the association of anxiety, pressure and stress with sex.

Take the following steps:

1. Take the pressure off climaxing.

2. Talk about how you both like to lead into sex. Sometimes a slower start helps – for example, lying together, having a hug, a massage and taking some time to get mindful in the moment can help activate the sexy mind state.

3. Agree to take breaks. If a partner identifies they are in their anxiety/stress mind and not their sexy mind, take a break. Move way from sexual touch for a while and only resume if you feel relaxed.

4. Try to be as present as possible with tactile sensation when engaging in sex. Out of your mind and into your body is the way back into the sexy mind.

5. It's okay if sex doesn't work. Stop making completion and climax the be all and end all. You will have sex many more times. If you can commit to being okay with not climaxing, you will remove a lot of pressure.

6. Have a plan B. If it's important for one partner to climax, have an option you can both be supportive of. Whether it's manual masturbation or using a vibrator, a plan B can reduce frustration and minimise pressure.

The too busy TSD

In this world of schedules, commitments, chores, work and family, it's easy to avoid making time for sexual connection. Avoidance can be by one or both partners. If one partner is too busy, too often in this dynamic, the other joins in by giving up on sex.

When you make time for sex, you tend to have more sex because you experience positive pay-offs. If you're in a rut, remember the old saying 'use it or lose it'. The solution is simple and practical. It's about making time for sexy time. Only couples having sex can have hot sex.

You might be thinking, *Sex should be spontaneous; it should come naturally.* If you have a busy schedule, children, pets or work commitments, you might be waiting a long time for spontaneity. The problem with not planning sex is you will fall out of the habit of having sex. Sex is a high-value activity so it's okay if it takes planning to fit into your life.

Scheduled sex doesn't have to be boring and monotonous. You can flirt and talk about sex coming up in your scheduled spot. You can talk about different things you want to experience together. Make it a sacred time. It all comes down to your attitude.

The 'other' TSD

When we talk about the 'other' TSD, we're talking about another person or object getting between the sexual connection of the couple. In the case of another person, it could be an emotional or physical affair. Or, it could be far less sinister, such as one partner always spending time with friends at the expense of the relationship, or a parent sleeping in one of the children's bedrooms. With regards to objects, it could be one person prioritising drinking over the relationship. Or one person might be using too much porn, impacting their physical sexual connection with their partner.

With this TSD, a triangulation is causing the problem. Triangulations and how to break them are covered in chapter 6, so use the strategies provided there to tackle the triangulation, thereby overcoming this TSD.

Sexual myths

Sexual myths (SMs) are the second category of roadblocks to a thriving sexual connection. SMs are false beliefs and attitudes that influence a couple's sex life. They're unquestioned, implicit ideas, and can contribute to unrealistic expectations and unnecessary pressure. If entrenched, SMs can lead to dissatisfaction or issues in the bedroom. It's important to identify the myth you hold and work in opposition to it. We've outlined some SMs, and how to oppose them, here. Keep in mind many SMs exist and this list is by no means exhaustive.

Spontaneity is key SM

This is the belief sex should always be spontaneous and unplanned. Holding this myth, however, can lead to no sex. With busy lives, it is easy for sex to slip off the priority list. This myth disregards the importance of communication and intentionality in a healthy and active sex life. Solution: schedule sex into your life. In the My Love Your Love app, we have created an exercise where you discuss and schedule sex called Making Time for Sexy Time.

Penetrative sex is the only real sex SM

This is the misconception that sex is only valid if it involves penetrative intercourse. Such a myth neglects the diversity of sexuality and intimate activities while adding pressure to perform penetrative sex, potentially leading to performance issues both in men and women. It neglects other forms of sexual pleasure that can be equally or more sexually satisfying. Solution: spend more time on non-penetrative sex. See foreplay as sex, rather than something that happens before sex. Try a no-penetration sex challenge and focus on touching only!

Orgasms are requisite for satisfaction SM

This myth perpetuates the idea that every sexual encounter must lead to orgasm for both partners to consider it successful or satisfying. Holding onto this myth will lead to frustrations and even resentments. Orgasms are great, but they can be elusive, particularly if you are stressed, depressed or stuck in your thoughts. Performance pressure is real when it comes to arousal and orgasm. The more pressure you put on yourself to be aroused or to orgasm, the more elusive that arousal and orgasm will be. People are different in their capacity to orgasm, so by holding onto this myth you will be unknowingly adding pressure to yourself or your partner, which will inevitably result in the opposite effect. Solution: when having sex, focus on the process rather than the end result. Spend more time in foreplay and be okay with ending sex if you are no longer feeling the desire.

Desire declines in long-term relationships SM

This myth assumes desire diminishes as individuals age in long-term relationships. Holding this assumption will inevitably result in your sexual connection being neglected. Age may be one factor that influences sexual desire, but there are also many others, including changes to physical health, mental health, relationship dynamics and attitudes around sex. Holding such a myth discounts the need to invest in your sexual connection no matter what life stage you are in. It also overlooks the potential for fulfilling and enjoyable sex lives at any life stage. Solution: prioritise your sex life. Talk about sex on a regular basis. Reignite passion and desire. We provide more details on enhancing attraction as you progress through this chapter.

No communication is needed SM

This myth assumes partners should know each other's desires and preferences without the need for open and honest communication. This can result in unsatisfying sexual encounters and avoidance of sex. Everyone is different and will have different preferences when it comes to arousal and sex. You're unlikely to have the same preferences as each other or previous partners. Solution: talk to your partner about what you like and don't like. You can get started by asking each other the questions included in the section 'Tips for getting started', earlier in this chapter.

More is always better SM

This is the misconception that the *quantity* of sexual encounters is proportional to the *quality* of a relationship. It prioritises the quantity over the quality of sexual encounters, ignoring the importance of emotional connection and intimacy. Solution: take the focus away from how much sex you are having and focus on the quality of the sex you are having. Schedule time to sexually connect when you won't be interrupted or rushed.

Sex should be perfect every time SM

This myth is about believing every sexual encounter should be flawless and without any challenges or awkward moments. Holding such a view will inevitably lead to disappointments and frustrations. Sex can be exposing and messy. You may encounter awkward positions, sensations and sounds. Arousal varies day to day, and can be influenced by current health and how present you are. So it's impossible for each sexual encounter to be flawless. Solution: try to see every sexual encounter as an opportunity to be with your partner. Focus on the intention and connection rather than a set of outcomes.

Effortless and natural SM

This is the notion that good sex should happen naturally and effortlessly without any need for learning, practise or effort. Sex is something we get better at with practice and exploration, so holding the myth that it should be effortless and natural not only results in disappointing sex but also doesn't allow you to explore the potential of your sexual connection. Solution: discuss with your partner what kind of sex you both would like for this particular sexual encounter. Be open to new experiences and give encouraging feedback throughout.

Men always want sex/women don't SM

This myth involves stereotypical assumptions about gender and sexuality, perpetuating the idea men are always ready for sex, while women are not as interested. This myth adds unnecessary pressure on men to sexually perform at any given time, while diminishing women's desires as secondary to men's. Solution: discuss when each of you prefers sex and take turns at initiating sex.

Women who want and enjoy sex are sluts SM

This myth perpetuates the idea of sex as a conquest for men and shameful for women. If you are a man and hold this belief, you are suppressing your partner's sexuality. If you are a woman holding this belief, you are experiencing 'unjustified shame' and suppressing your sexual identity. While unjustified shame feels the same as shame, it is unjustified. You are not shameful for enjoying or wanting sex with your partner. Someone or culture has unfairly given you ashamed baggage.

Solution: both partners need to discuss and understand the origin and functions of this myth. For example, the SM allows the man to feel in control and avoid any feelings of insecurity by supressing their partner's expression of desire. In this case, the male partner would benefit from looking at the conflict personas Suspicious Detective or Superior One-Upper from chapter 5 and consider what baggage is beneath. For the woman, an aspect from her formative years may have overtly or subtly implied that being sexual was dirty or shameful. Go back to chapter 7 and read about claiming ashamed baggage. If this SM is present in your relationship, seek couples therapy to further process this and allow for a safe space for supported sexual exploration within the relationship.

Breaking through TSDs and SMs

If your sex life has been blocked by TSDs or SMs, you're missing out on the wonderful benefits of a healthy sex life throughout the lifespan of your relationship. As an example of this, let's look at Roslyn and Jonathan, who Shahn was seeing.

Breaking down walls with understanding

Roslyn and Jonathan were in a pursuer–distancer dynamic. Jonathan felt he needed sexual connection to feel close and intimate. While he enjoyed sex, it was also a way to bridge any distance between them. Roslyn, on the other hand, needed emotional closeness and a positive connection to consider the idea of having sex. Without this, she did not feel like or want to think about sex.

After a conflict, Jonathon made advances for sex that Roslyn rejected. At the time, Jonathon felt abandoned in the relationship. He communicated frustration and wanted closeness. Rosalyn felt invalidated and uncared for. She couldn't understand how Jonathon could ask for sex while they were fighting. The more Jonathan pursued Roslyn, the more Roslyn rejected his advances. Jonathan was left feeling rejected, frustrated and unsatisfied in the relationship. Roslyn was left feeling baffled and confused as to why Jonathan didn't understand she did not want to have sex while they were in conflict.

They became disconnected. Both felt resentful. They were in a stand-off and had stopped being a team. They'd lost their friendship. By the time Roslyn and Jonathan came to therapy, they had ceased meaningful conversation. This dynamic had spun out of control.

Once the pursuer–distancer TSD was explained, their walls began to come down. Their inner vulnerable feelings were discussed and they explored how the TSD was destroying their relationship. They developed insight into the TSD and understood they had opposing wants and needs when it came to emotions and sex.

In therapy, Roslyn and Jonathan decided to take sex off the table for two weeks. Even if they were having a great time, they were not allowed to have sex. They were encouraged to have as much non-sexual touch as possible in this period – including hugging, holding hands, things they used to do in better times.

Over the course of the two weeks, I advised Jonathan and Roslyn to practise feeling the story three to four times each week. They were also completing deep connections activities such as 'getting to know more of you' and coming up with a joint value and goal to work toward. They had a newfound respect for each other's position. They worked hard to get close and, after two weeks, they were able to talk about having sex again.

To ensure the dynamic was further broken, Roslyn was the only person to initiate sex over the following four weeks. This allowed Roslyn to feel safe. If Jonathan approached her with any physical affection, she had no need to reject it, which made her feel closer to him. Roslyn understood that Jonathan was genuinely working toward emotional closeness so she worked hard to be open and encouraging.

Before long, they were back having a fulfilling sex life. Both were aware of the potential to slip back into the TSD. When in conflicts in the future, they made time to do feeling the story (refer to chapter 4), and explore secondary conflict emotions and inner vulnerable feelings to repair (chapter 5).

 **TIME FOR ACTION**

TSDs and SMs get in the way of a good sex life. Without a solution, you're stuck in a negative cycle. Go back through the TSDs and sexual myths covered here and see if any apply to your relationship. If they don't, great. Keep moving forward. If they do, discuss it with your partner. Insight is the first step to change. Now look at the suggested solutions provided for the TSDs and SMs and see if you can break the cycle. For example, if you find you are suffering from the 'spontaneity is key' myth, get together and schedule time for sex. Start by setting the bar low in terms of frequency. Pick a day and time when you're both more likely to want to have sex with minimal distractions. Don't pick the end of the night if one or both of

> you are always exhausted by that time! Ask each other for a
> preferred time for having and not having sex and see if you can
> reach a compromise. Remember – it doesn't have to be boring
> just because it's scheduled. Make it fun by talking about it
> before it occurs.

In the following section, we outline some exciting ways to increase erotic desire you can implement for your scheduled sexy time.

Unlocking the secrets to sexual connection

To be good lovers, you must understand sexual attraction goes beyond physical attraction and the act of sex. Many factors influence how much you desire and are desired by your partner. Sexual tension and sexual energy have many potential charging sources, and these can be divided into two main categories. The first is related to the overall 'relationship connection', while the second category is concerned with what we call 'erotic charging dynamics'.

Couples who have a better relationship connection have a healthier sex life. This is something we see evidenced in our practice on a regular basis. As couples work through our therapy program, their sex life improves as a by-product. It is no coincidence that when couples feel better connected, are kinder, more playful, have less conflict and have more fun, they also have more sex.

Erotic charging dynamics (ECDs) are far less obvious than the positive interactions associated with relationship connections. Unlike overt displays of affection, ECDs often operate beneath the surface of our awareness, yet they have a profound effect on sexual attraction between partners. The origins of ECDs are complex, and are influenced by personality, family beliefs, culture, interpersonal attachment and past experience. It is important not to get caught up on the why.

Rather, identify and understand what ECDs are charging for your relationship and utilise them.

Here are some common ECDs:

- *Seeing your partner as independent and self-sufficient:* For example, seeing them get dressed up, going out to a work meeting or a social occasion and displaying autonomy can be arousing. Your partner becomes more valuable in your eyes. They are going out into the world looking nice without you. They are confident and looking forward to interacting with other people. This dynamic allows you a glimpse of how you saw your partner when you were dating. It sparks attraction and unconsciously makes your partner attachment unsettled/exciting. Therefore, you seek to conquer the attachment again. It increases your sexual desire to feel physically connected to your partner.

- *Being naughty together and going out of your comfort zone together:* Being naughty together can be stimulating and exciting. You are also creating a shared private and personal experience with your partner. Being naughty is going out of your comfort zone together and doing something taboo, which is often associated with increasing sexual erotic energy. What is considered 'naughty' is different for every couple. For some, it could be ditching work together for a secret rendezvous. For others, it might be sexual exploration in uncharted territories.

- *Seeing your partner desired by others or thinking they might be desired by others:* This can be erotically charging – and can happen in reverse also. Feeling desired by others in front of your partner can be erotically charging. This ECD creates vulnerability, attraction and desire in your sexual connection. While it might create some vulnerability in the attachment, it can supercharge the desire for sexual connection, bringing stability to the attachment. For example, let's say you're at a party with friends and you see somebody talking with your partner with great interest and perhaps even a little flirtation. This observation might be enough to create some sexually charged energy within you. A more exaggerated version of this is encouraging your partner to flirt with other people in front of you when you're out – with agreed boundaries, of course.

- *Creating mystery and doing the opposite of being mundane and predictable:* When one partner becomes mysterious or withholds some information, it can create sexual energy. We're not talking about being disrespectful or hiding things in your relationship. We're talking about creating a bit of mystery and moving away from the usual. For example, you could create an exciting date and keep your partner in the dark about it.

- *Creating novelty:* This can also be a good way to supercharge sexual energy in the relationship. The excitement of doing something new often leads to better sexual connection. This is one of the reasons couples have more sex when travelling to new destinations and experiencing different cultures.

- *Trying sexual adventure and exploration:* Sitting down with your partner and talking about different ways you might like to have sex or about erotic realms you'd like to explore can charge erotic energy. Even the discussion alone can supercharge erotic energy. Perhaps you'd like to try a sex toy or new positions. Erotic energy exists in the discussion, the anticipation and during the act. The exploration *and* the adventure increase the desire and experience.

- *Using your imagination:* Sexual chemistry also occurs in the imagination. Esther Perel, a famous psychotherapist who works with couples and is an expert on sexual desire, explains that your next orgasm starts moments after having sex. What she means is the sexual tension between partners is ongoing, moving through cycles. Sexual attraction is held as much in the anticipation of sex, as in the act. Keeping your sexual imagination in mind and being aware of this tension can fuel sexual energy between you and your partner. This might involve recalling a positive sexual memory or giving a flirty look or touch.

Focus on connection – and friendship – first

While ECDs can be a great way to inject erotic energy into your love life, ECDs alone will not lead to a positive sex life. We have found couples who have a great relationship connection are able to tap into ECDs. Passion, love, friendship and affection are key to feeling safe and secure in your relationship. When you feel safe, loved and secure in your relationship, you can play into ECDs. When the relationship connection is not stable, ECDs can lead to problematic issues in the relationship. For instance, instead of generating attraction you might generate insecurity, or instead of inducing excitement you might create resentment or further disconnect.

We've mentioned world-renowned researchers and clinical psychologists Dr John and Dr Julie Gottman a few times in this book, and their work is also relevant here. Co-founders of the Gottman Institute, they are arguably the most famous couples therapists in the world having studied more than 40,000 couples and authored countless books and articles. They combined their own research with data provided by a survey of nearly 100,000 respondents (published in *The Normal Bar*, by Chrisanna Northrup, Pepper Schwartz and James Witte) to conclude the following: couples who 'turn toward one another with love and affection to connect emotionally and physically' have a healthy sex life. In other words, couples who have good and regular sex are also good friends. They prioritise each other and create time for sex. They care for each other. They surprise each other. They know what turns each other on and off. They're physically affectionate. They play together and they're romantic. Couples who show warmth, affection and love towards one another have much better, more regular sex.

Because your emotional relationship and sex life are connected, every interaction, positive attitude and affection towards your partner has an influence on your sex life. For example, a hello and goodbye hug, a goodnight kiss, and listening with warmth are all undercurrents of your sex life. Just think of the Magic Moments and Deep Connections love links (covered in chapters 3 and 6). Regular sex over the course of your relationship is less about how good sex is in the bedroom and more about how good your relationship is. Being great friends and then tapping into ECDs is going to lead to a healthy sex life.

When you have a positive relationship connection, ECDs will sexually charge your relationship. They're in play whether you are aware of them or not. They take sex out of the realm of simply being physical, which means along with relationship connection you can work on your sexual connection any time.

As an example of this, let's look at Sarah and Rodd, who Helen was seeing.

Build your erotic energy and sexual chemistry

Sarah and Rodd explained they'd experienced a lack of desire and sexual connection in their relationship. When going through the ECDs, Sarah identified she felt erotically stirred when she saw her husband getting dressed up and going out without her. He seemed somewhat unfamiliar again, attractive and a little bit unattainable. She was left in her comfort clothes at home with her movie and glass of wine while he was dressed up, well-groomed and smelling beautifully. Her level of attraction increased whenever this occurred. This situation didn't necessarily lead to sex. However, it charged the erotic desire in the relationship, which increased warmth and interest in one another.

Prior to commencing therapy, Rodd had not gone out on his own for some time. It was post-pandemic and he was in a pattern of staying home and not socialising. As soon as he heard Sarah's ECD, however, he suddenly had extra motivation to go out and start seeing his friends again. He immediately felt better. He enjoyed reconnecting with his friends and experienced higher levels of self-esteem. It also created some much needed distance in the relationship, tapping into increased desire through more autonomy. Further, Sarah experienced erotic energy each time Rodd got ready to go out without her. It built sexual chemistry back into their relationship and, before long, they were back into the habit of regular sex.

Getting playful

You might be thinking, *Things are good in our relationship sexually.* Great! We're not here to convince you otherwise. If this is the case, you don't need to change anything. Just be sure to remember the theory behind a sexual connection and agree to check in with each other occasionally.

If you feel like your relationship is a bit stale, we invite you to explore some exercises we've created that aim to increase eroticism. These activities tap into attraction dynamics to enhance sexual connection. All of these games assume mutual consent that can be withdrawn at any point.

The first fun game you can play is Who's the Boss? This is a game exploring your and your partner's willingness to take charge in the bedroom and ask for what you want. You take turns at being the boss in the bedroom, with one partner leading the direction of the sexual experience. You then switch roles next time you have sex together. This game is about mutual pleasure and exploration, not about exerting control or pressure. The other partner's role is to be receptive and responsive, actively participating in the exploration. It's all about lowering inhibitions, letting go of control or taking control. This can lead to a change in sexual power dynamics and also encourage exploration.

Another brilliant and fun game we've created is the Traffic Lights game. In this game, each partner is privately presented with a list of erotic sexual activities they may be interested to participate in. You and your partner can each then choose green for 'Yes, I'm totally up for this', orange for 'I'm not sure, but I'm not ruling it out' and red for 'No way, this is not something I'm interested in' (hence the use of Traffic Lights for the game's name). You can access this game via our My Love Your Love app, and the beauty of playing the game in the app is that when one partner chooses red, the item disappears. It doesn't show in the joint list of options, so no-one ever has to know the other may have chosen green or orange with that particular activity.

After you've gone through the list and made your selections privately, you and your partner can compare your green and orange lists. We suggest you start with the green list and work your way through all the things you both said you'd be interested in doing when you weren't face to face. Then start exploring all the sexual activities in the orange category. If accessing this game via the app, you're provided with a lengthy list of options, and your green and orange choices are collated for you. The anticipation of discussing and potentially doing these options builds as much tension and excitement as the acts themselves.

Another fun game facilitated in the app is one we call Stranger Date. You choose this activity in the app if you know you're able to go out on a date together within the next 10 days. This game helps you increase the mystery and excitement in the relationship – and is guaranteed to get you both giggling and having some fun. When doing Stranger Date via the app, you choose from a vast range of pre-set characters (or you can make up your own). You then text each other in character leading up to your date. If you don't have the app you can play this game by choosing a character from one of your favourite movies or TV shows. The idea is to try to embody their personality and what they might find sexually charging. If you missed the Tinder tidal wave, Stranger Date is a way to recapture the fun parts of the dating game without going outside of your relationship. When you are ready for your date, meet at a new location. Spend some time apart for at least a couple of hours before. You should also wear new outfits or even a wig if you like. It's all about having fun, being naughty and going out of your comfort zone. It helps increase mystery, novelty, adventure and exploration, and fuels sexual chemistry and imagination.

Balancing your sex life

It can be helpful to think about sex in three different categories:

1. *Highly connected, passionate sex:* This sex is about being present with your partner in the moment, and being in tune and in comfort. It is softer, but can be euphoric with a sense of love making with your partner. It facilitates a strong physical and emotional bond between partners.

2. *Everyday vanilla sex:* While this sex is not highly passionate or stimulating, it is still nice. It keeps sexual connection alive and regular.

3. *Highly stimulating sex:* This sex is more adventurous and risqué. It is in the realms of naughty and spicy, focused on acts or styles of sex rather than the partner connection. This facilitates a sense of exploration and shared pleasure with a focus on feeling sexually charged together and letting go of inhibition.

None of these categories is more important than the other. However, if you're heavy in one category, putting more energy into another category could invigorate your sex life. Also, if you are putting too much emphasis on one category, it could lead to disconnection if it is not your partner's preference. Two partners having different preferences in the preceding three categories is not unusual. For example, one partner might desire highly stimulating sex while the other prefers softer and more passionate sex. Ideally, you can join each other in the categories you like. It is okay to have a different preference if both partners are getting their needs met. However, if one partner pushes sex in one category all the time, the sexual connection will be unbalanced. The other partner will feel dissatisfied, which can lead to sex avoidance.

It's good to be aware of these three categories. If your sex life feels a bit boring and stuck in one category, shifting to one of the other categories can reignite it. Then, moving back to the other category at a later time can charge excitement. Even if your relationship operates on highly connected, passionate sex or highly stimulated sex, introducing everyday vanilla sex can be worthwhile. The rationale here is that the former two categories can take more energy. Having the third option of everyday vanilla sex means you might be open to sex more often. This also makes the other two categories more pleasurable when they occur. Communication is key here. You will need to stay open to the three categories but also be able to come over and compromise (using the two truths skill from chapter 5).

If you and your partner are content having sex in one category, great – there is no urgency to change. However, if sex is stuck in one category and is the preference of one partner at the expense of the other, there is a high probability it will lead to sex avoidance.

Roy and Zahira, who Shahn was seeing at our rooms in Sydney, provide an example here.

Experimenting with all three categories of sex

Roy was into watching porn and having sex at the same time with Zahira. Together, they would act out what was happening in the porn. Zahira did not mind this because she knew it excited Roy. However, this was not her preferred method of sex. Over time, it became a habit and the only way they had sex. For Zahira, sex became less desirable. Roy, who desired this style of sex, felt frustrated by the decline in their sex life.

Through therapy, they were able to develop open discussion about their preferences. Zahira missed slower, more present-minded sex that started with cuddles and kisses. We discussed the three categories of sex, and both Roy and Zahira were able to see they had different needs and interpretations of sex, with neither being more important than the other.

While Roy did not enjoy highly connected, passionate sex as much as highly stimulated sex, he began to understand Zahira had not been getting her sexual needs met for a long time. Further, mindfulness-based touch interventions to help Roy commit more to highly connected, passionate sex were discussed and initiated. This involved Roy letting go of the visual experience of sex and honing in on the tactile experience, while holding loving thoughts of his partner.

Zahira and Roy also agreed to an experiment of having sex spread across the three categories for two months in rotating order. While you might be thinking this sounds too prescribed, Zahira and Roy reported it took the pressure off their sex life and also built sexual tension and excitement. They reported having sex more often and higher levels of satisfaction.

Sex does not have to be one way. While you and your partner can easily get into a sex routine that follows the same pattern every time, having a mix of passionate, stimulating and vanilla sex is healthy. You might be thinking, *I like one type of sex. I shouldn't have to do anything else I'm not comfortable with.* We agree – you shouldn't do anything you are uncomfortable with. An essential part of a healthy sexual connection is consent so all parties can feel safe during sex. If you start something but then don't want to continue, consent can be removed at any time.

We do encourage you to explore a little and stay open to what your partner is interested in. Getting out of your comfort zone can be rewarding as long as you have safety, respect and boundaries within your relationship. If you feel uncomfortable about any of the three categories discussed, it can be helpful to consider whether any myths are getting in the way. Is any baggage bursting open? Talking to your partner about your concerns will be helpful.

 **TIME FOR ACTION**

Review the three categories of sex and reflect on your relationship. Do you have sex in just one of the categories? If so, discuss with your partner about expanding your sex life into the other two categories. It's okay if you're both happy to stay in one category, as long as you talk about it and it stays on the table.

Perhaps you're thinking, *Our sex is habitual. I am willing to move into a different category but my partner is not.* Explore together the pros and cons of shifting to a new category. Discuss any vulnerabilities either of you experience even when just talking about changing. Then if you choose to try one of the other categories, set the bar low and take the pressure off the end result. It's better to start with a lower bar than to go for some grand sex act. Taking the pressure off the outcome of sex, such as climax, allows you to explore in a present way.

Summing up

Congratulations! You've now learned the secrets to a healthy and exciting sex life. Sex and desire play an important role in your evolving relationship, and sex has benefits for your emotional, physical and relationship health. Toxic sex dynamics (TSDs) and sexual myths (SMs) could be preventing you from accessing all of the benefits of sex across your relationship lifespan. Even if your sex life is good or okay, you can use certain strategies to ensure continued regular sex or to supercharge erotic energy when needed.

If you don't feel great about your sex life, it's time to start talking about it! It is not just the pleasure and excitement of sex you are missing out on. You're missing out on a longer life with better mental and physical health. Ask your partner if they would be willing to read this chapter, and then discuss each section as a guide to assess your sex life. Together, make a plan for creating exciting change! If you would like a practical guide without having to involve a third person such as a couples or sex therapist, download the My Love Your Love app and get started on the Sex and Desire module.

The secret to a thriving relationship is continued investment in all of the eight love links. Each love link is important and can become a positive or negative feedback loop influencing each other. The Sex and Desire love link is no different. For example, if you do the Feeling the Story and Magic Moments love links well, the Sex and Desire love link will come easier for you and your partner. And if you do Sex and Desire, well you will be more motivated to use strategies from the Conflict Compass and Baggage Claim love links when your relationship needs some help.

You've almost reached the end of *The 8 Love Links*. However, this is just the beginning of your eight love links journey. You now have the secrets to unlocking all of the benefits to long-term relationships. You can reflect on any of the eight love links at any point in your relationship to bring lasting positive change to your relationship.

Stick with us. Before we go, we've got a few more words of wisdom to pass on.

Final words

Congratulations on completing *The 8 Love Links*! You have delved into all eight love links, gaining insight into how each link intertwines to craft a resilient tapestry of connection in your relationship.

Each link holds its own significance, dedicated to a specific theme crucial for fostering a healthy relationship. However, neglecting or failing to address any of the love links will weaken the tapestry of your relationship, because each love link intentionally connects to those preceding and following it. In fact, each love link is mutually influencing. Creating positive cycles and feedback loops in one link feeds positivity into other links, reinforcing your relationship. The eight love links are curated to establish a secure and intimate connection between you and your partner.

The eight love links will help two people in a relationship get on well and have fun together. This is an amazing opportunity to set your relationship up to propel your life in the direction you desire. Your relationship can be a springboard for everything to come. It should be improving your life, not making it worse – and if it's not, you must do something about it. The eight love links will allow you to tap into your authentic self. After all, you have finite time on the planet.

Take responsibility for enjoying it. Embrace and accept the gift, limit suffering, and live and thrive as the person you want to be with the person you love.

Imagine waking up each morning to the warmth of shared affection and the promise of a day filled with genuine connection. In this newfound reality, communication with your partner flows, unburdened by the weight of misunderstandings. The air is charged with a sense of intimacy, as if each word spoken deepens the bond between you. Conversations are no longer hurdles but bridges, connecting you on a profound level.

The eight love links guide your actions, and lead you into a relationship where understanding becomes second nature. You navigate disagreements with grace. Conflict evolves from sources of tension into opportunities for growth. Your partnership is no longer a journey navigated alone; it's a shared adventure where mutual support is the cornerstone.

As you move through the day, the positive energy from your relationship radiates into other aspects of your life. The resilience and self-growth developed within your relationship empowers you to confront external challenges with newfound strength. Even when you stumble and make mistakes in life, you can forgive yourself and grow from it, and your partner is there by your side with compassion and acceptance.

You return home at the end of the day knowing home is a safe place where you can be yourself and be cherished for it.

Embracing the eight love links doesn't just improve your relationship; it elevates your entire existence. Every day you have an opportunity to deepen your connection to your partner and to yourself. You foster a life where love and self-expansion are not just a part of it, but the very essence that colours each moment.

You must learn to master all eight love links. Even as you learn, you will see immediate improvements. You need to take full responsibility for your role in your relationship, as every interaction contributes to the shared experience between you and your partner.

To navigate differences, you need to create a safe haven in your relationship and to protect and nurture that haven at all costs.

Remember – the small moments between you and your partner collectively shape the overall feel of your relationship. Choose positive action to generate a stable and mindful relationship. You must validate and attune to your partner's experience.

Approach conflict with curiosity to find the meaning and cycle of the conflict rather than just trying to find a solution. Invest in your relationship via shared values and goals. Take a close look at your deep vulnerabilities and learn to understand them. Make room for those of your partner and work together to care for one another. Don't neglect your sex life – embrace it. Commit to maintaining your sexual connection even when times are tough.

The biggest risk to your relationship is the avoidance of issues. You stay silent when you are upset. You delay and defer talking to your partner until the 'time is right'. Your tendency to avoid arises from the fear of causing discomfort to your partner or the apprehension of facing tension. Ceasing this pattern of avoidance is imperative. Be the one to take the first step.

As psychologists, couples therapists and partners, we live and breathe our goal to foster as many happy and healthy relationships as we can. We love working with couples and seeing their relationships get stronger and more meaningful. That's why we've written this book and created the My Love Your Love couples app. Now you've read this book, you have the framework, rationale and tools to create a thriving relationship. Go one step further. Get the app. It's the companion to this book, and makes the whole process fun and easy. The app will prompt you to act, and guide you to improve your relationship on a daily basis.

And, of course, if you need further guidance, we provide couples therapy. If your journey gets stuck, please don't hesitate to contact us at our clinic, via our My Love Your Love email (hello@myloveyourlove.com) or on Instagram (@myloveyourloveapp) or on Tik Tok (@myloveyourloveapp).

For anyone willing to do the work, our wish is that your relationship is a source of comfort, growth and happiness.

It's our mission to see relationships bloom and flourish. Let's put an end to the misery and pain, and start spreading love and connection.

Join us.

About the authors

Shahn and Helen have over 34 years of combined experience as clinical psychologists. Together, they founded Drummoyne Psychology – a successful private psychological practice in Sydney – where they have helped hundreds of couples improve their relationships.

Shahn and Helen have worked with people with complex mental health disorders in various settings and circumstances. They have worked extensively with thousands of individuals, both in private practice and as part of multidisciplinary teams in community mental health and hospital settings. This has allowed them to gain a comprehensive understanding of human psychology, family dynamics and interpersonal relationships.

Helen is a certified Schema Therapist and Shahn has delivered training programs on personality disorders and has been an Accredited Person under the Mental Health Act. Shahn and Helen have provided training for other psychologists and are Board Approved clinical supervisors for psychologists.

Their expertise and insights have gained widespread recognition, leading to features in numerous online and print articles, as well as appearances on radio, podcasts and television. Their ability to communicate complex psychological concepts in a relatable and accessible manner has made them sought-after experts in the field of relationships and mental health.

Shahn and Helen are dynamic individuals with a multifaceted approach to life. They have dedicated their careers to fostering healthy relationships and promoting mental wellbeing.

Their journey together extends beyond their professional collaboration, spanning over a decade marked by the complexities of being a blended family, navigating the challenges of founding a successful private practice, and pioneering Australia's first couples coaching app.

Shahn and Helen aim to inspire and empower individuals to cultivate fulfilling relationships, prioritise mental wellbeing, and embrace life's adventures.

Further reading and references

Ainsworth, M. D. S. (1969). 'Object relations, dependency, and attachment: A theoretical review of the infant-mother relationship', *Child Development*, 40(4), 969–1025. https://doi.org/10.2307/1127008

Aron, A., Lewandowski, G., Branand, B., Mashek, D., & Aron, E. (2022). 'Self-expansion motivation and inclusion of others in self: An updated review', *Journal of Social and Personal Relationships*, 39(12), 026540752211106. https://doi.org/10.1177/02654075221110630

Bowlby, J. (1958). 'The nature of the child's tie to his mother', *The International Journal of Psychoanalysis*, 39, 350–373.

Bowlby, J. (1969). *Attachment and loss*. Pimlico.

Brody, S. (2010). 'The relative health benefits of different sexual activities', *The Journal of Sexual Medicine*, 7(4_Part_1), 1336–1361.

Buettner, D. (2012). *The blue zones: 9 lessons for living longer from the people who've lived the longest*. National Geographic.

Coulter, K., & Malouff, J. M. (2013). 'Effects of an intervention designed to enhance romantic relationship excitement: A randomized-control trial', *Couple and Family Psychology: Research and Practice*, 2(1), 34–44. https://doi.org/10.1037/a0031719

Debrot, A., Meuwly, N., Muise, A., Impett, E. A., & Schoebi, D. (2017). 'More than just sex', *Personality and Social Psychology Bulletin*, 43(3), 287–299. https://doi.org/10.1177/0146167216684124

Ganong, K., & Larson, E. (2011). 'Intimacy and belonging: The association between sexual activity and depression among older adults', *Society and Mental Health*, 1(3), 153–172. https://doi.org/10.1177/2156869311431612

Gilbert, R. M. (2004). *The eight concepts of Bowen theory*.

Gottman, J. (2002). *The seven principles for making marriage work*. Harmony.

Gottman, J. M. (2008). 'Gottman method couple therapy', *Clinical Handbook of Couple Therapy*, 4(8), 138–164.

Gottman, J. M., & Gottman, J. S. (2015). 'Gottman couple therapy', in Gurman, A. S., Lebow, J. L., & Snyder, D. K. (eds), *Clinical handbook of couple therapy*, The Guilford Press, pp. 129–157.

Gottman, J., & Gottman, J. (2017). 'The natural principles of love', *Journal of Family Theory & Review*, 9(1), 7–26. https://doi.org/10.1111/jftr.12182

Graham, J. M., & Harf, M. R. (2014). 'Self-expansion and flow: The roles of challenge, skill, affect, and activation', *Personal Relationships*, 22(1), 45–64. https://doi.org/10.1111/pere.12062

Hambach, A., Evers, S., Summ, O., Husstedt, I. W., & Frese, A. (2013). 'The impact of sexual activity on idiopathic headaches: An observational study', *Cephalalgia*, 33(6), 384–389. https://doi.org/10.1177/0333102413476374

Hammond, W. (2010). *Principles of strength-based practice*. Resilience Initiatives, 12(2), 1–7.

Hari, J. (2022). *Stolen focus*. Bloomsbury Publishing Ltd.

Kashdan, T. B., Blalock, D. V., Young, K. C., Machell, K. A., Monfort, S. S., McKnight, P. E., & Ferssizidis, P. (2018). 'Personality strengths in romantic relationships: Measuring perceptions of benefits and costs and their impact on personal and relational well-being', *Psychological Assessment*, 30(2), 241–258. https://doi.org/10.1037/pas0000464

Khalil, S. (2023, February 14). 'Racy act couples do on holiday', *News; news.com.au — Australia's leading news site.* https://www.news.com.au/travel/travel-updates/travel-stories/aussies-are-having-more-adventurous-sex-on-holiday/news-story/16601c89944c010756df43714e863894

Lamb, M. E. (1978). 'Patterns of attachment: A psychological study of the strange situation', Mary D. Salter Ainsworth, Mary C. Blehar, Everett Waters, and Sally Wall. Hillsdale, N.J., Erlbaum, 1978 [distributor, Halsted (Wiley), New York]. *Infant Mental Health Journal*, 1(1), 68–70. https://doi.org/10.1002/1097-0355(198021)1:1%3C68::aid-imhj2280010110%3E3.0.co;2-3

Linehan, M. M. (1997). 'Validation and psychotherapy', in Bohart, A. C., & Greenberg, L. S. (eds), *Empathy reconsidered: New directions in psychotherapy*, American Psychological Association, pp. 353–392.

Mattingly, B. A., & Lewandowski, G. W. (2014). 'Broadening horizons: Self-expansion in relational and non-relational contexts', *Social and Personality Psychology Compass*, 8(1), 30–40. https://doi.org/10.1111/spc3.12080

Maybee, J. E. (2020). 'Hegel's dialectics', in Zalta, E. N. (ed.), *The Stanford encyclopedia of philosophy* (Winter 2020 Edition), https://plato.stanford.edu/archives/win2020/entries/hegel-dialectics

Muise, A., Harasymchuk, C., Day, L. C., Bacev-Giles, C., Gere, J., & Impett, E. A. (2019). 'Broadening your horizons: Self-expanding activities promote desire and satisfaction in established romantic relationships', *Journal of Personality and Social Psychology*, 116(2), 237–258. https://doi.org/10.1037/pspi0000148

Newport, C. (2019). *Digital minimalism: On living better with less technology*. Penguin Random House.

Northrup, C., Schwartz, P., & Witte, J. (2014). *The normal bar: The surprising secrets of happy couples and what they reveal about creating a new normal in your relationship*. Harmony.

Perel, E. (2006). *Mating in captivity: Reconciling the erotic + the domestic*. HarperCollins.

Rabstejnek, C. V. (2012). *Family systems & Murray Bowen theory*. Posted Articles (January 2009), 4, 1–10.

Richardson, D. (1999). *Family ties that bind: A self-help guide to change through family of origin therapy*. Self-Counsel; Northam.

Rosenberg, R. (2019). *The human magnet syndrome: The codependent narcissist trap*. Morgan James Publishing.

Seehausen, M., Kazzer, P., Bajbouj, M., & Prehn, K. (2012). 'Effects of empathic paraphrasing – extrinsic emotion regulation in social conflict', *Frontiers in Psychology*, 3(482). https://doi.org/10.3389/fpsyg.2012.00482

Siegel, D. J. (2010). *Mindsight*. Bantam.

Tal Ben-Shahar. (2008). *Happier*. McGraw-Hill.

The Gottman Institute. (2015, September 22). *The Gottman Institute*. https://www.gottman.com/

Weiner, L. (2017). *Sensate focus in sex therapy: An illustrated manual*. Routledge.

Yalom, I. D. (2008). *Staring at the sun: Overcoming the terror of death*. Jossey-Bass.

Young, J. E., Klosko, J. S., & Weishaar, M. E. (2003). *Schema therapy: A practitioner's guide*. Guilford.